Invoking Animal Magic

A Guide for the Pagan Priestess

Invoking Animal Magic

A Guide for the Pagan Priestess

Hearth Moon Rising

MOON BOOKS

Winchester, UK
Washington, USA

First published by Moon Books, 2013
Moon Books is an imprint of John Hunt Publishing Ltd., Laurel House, Station Approach,
Alresford, Hants, SO24 9JH, UK
office1@jhpbooks.net
www.johnhuntpublishing.com
www.moon-books.net

For distributor details and how to order please visit the 'Ordering' section on our website.

ISBN: 978 1 78099 929 6

A CIP catalogue record for this book is available from the British Library.

Design: Stuart Davies

Printed and bound by CPI Group (UK) Ltd, Croydon, CR0 4YY

CONTENTS

This book is dedicated to
The great goddess Diana
Lady of the Mountain
Keeper of the Forest
Mistress of the Beasts

Acknowledgments

I am grateful to my coven mates Susan Nimue and Jamie Lantz for encouraging me to write this book and encouraging me to continue when the process became rough. I would like to thank Martha Allen for volunteering to copyedit the manuscript and Rebecca Petersen of Draconus Arcanum for providing feedback. My village librarian, Karen Glass, tracked down and obtained the often obscure reference books needed by a writer on this subject. Including pictures would not have been possible without the people at Wikimedia Commons. The high quality meditation audio available for download is the work of producer Stan Oliva. Harp accompaniment is by Martha Gallagher. Wendy Hall and others at Adirondack Wildlife Refuge provided access to wild animals I would not have been able to observe closely in other settings. Lastly I would like to thank my first teacher in the Craft, Zsuzsanna Budpadest, for starting me on this journey.

Also visit
www.invokinganimalmagic.com
for more information about working with animal magic.

Chapter 1

Creatures of the Underworld

An immortal serpent guarded them ... with one hundred heads which spoke with voices of various types.
—Apollodorus, *The Library of Greek Mythology*[1]

Snake Dreams

I came to be soothed by the ssssssss of snakes circling around my bed. The sound comforted me like the distant train of my childhood, traveling with me to the land of sleep. There is nothing more hypnotic than a snake, and the sound of slithering snake bodies transported me to another place.

I was living in a mud house not much larger than an office cubicle. It was underground, with a dirt platform along one side for a bed. A small table, a stool and a wood stove rounded out the furniture. The windows were eye level, with old pieces of tarp that could be closed against the rain. Mice, snakes, stray cats and other animals came and left at will. There was a nest of scorpions under the mattress where I slept. I loved this house because I felt like I was outdoors all the time, even when I was inside.

The three snakes I lived with were very respectful. They slithered everywhere in the house, but stayed to the edge of the mattress, buttressing the walls. I was glad for the distance. While pet snakes can be sensual and even erotic as they slide over your body, through your hair and under your clothes, I really didn't want wild snakes in my sleeping bag with me, especially since one of the snakes was a rattler.

The idea of living with a rattlesnake did not appeal to me at first. The king snake and the gopher snake were right enough, but I worried that I would step on the diamondback in the dark or roll over her in my sleep. When she first appeared, I went to visit a neighbor who had a snake catcher.

A snake catcher is a long piece of PVC pipe with a rope through it. The rope is looped like a noose at one end. Snakes like to poke their heads through things and will usually slip into the noose. When the snake slips her head through, the rope is quickly tightened, pulling her upper body against the end of the pipe. The pipe is a little more than nine feet long, since nine feet is the outside striking distance of a large rattler. You can catch a rattlesnake with this homemade contraption without getting close enough to be bitten (at least in theory).

Nine feet turned out to be too long a snake catcher for my house. Even though the snake was resting at the windowsill, there still was not enough room to maneuver the pipe. "Tap him on the head," my neighbor told me, watching from outside.

Hitting a rattlesnake that is eye level and three feet away with a PVC pipe may sound like a stupid thing to do, and in fact it is, but I'm the sister of the boy who jumped off the bridge. I tapped the snake on the head, and she pulled her neck back in surprise.

"Hit him again," said my neighbor. I obliged, and the snake again had this bemused reaction. "Hit him again," said my neighbor. The third time I tapped the snake on her head, she turned and slithered away. That is how I came into possession of the power of the snake: by looking into her eyes and tapping her head three times with my magic wand.

The snake lives much of her life underground—hibernating in winter, escaping the hottest part of the day in summer. Soil is the final resting place of the body and the place where plant life germinates. The snake is surrounded by the continual process of death and rebirth. Several times a year, she sheds an old skin and reveals a new one in symbolic rebirth. The shell left behind is her way of telling us, "I know the mysteries of life; I know the mysteries of death."

The very first snake we can call Proserpina, since the name of this goddess means First Snake. Worship of this Roman goddess eventually merged with rites of the Greek Persephone, but one Proserpina rite that remained uniquely Roman was the Century Game. As the name implies, this rite was enacted once in a century, every 110 years to be exact, considered the ideal span of a human life. The rite consisted of three days and nights of ceremony and athletic games. The rarity of the event did not diminish its importance, because the sibyls had prophesied that Rome could survive only through continued propitiation to Proserpina at each mark of a human lifespan.

An athletic dedication to the snake goddess is evocative of Crete, where the snake goddess was supreme and athletics were an integral part of religious life. The writing of the Minoan civilization of Crete has never been deciphered, but the archeological record shows a plethora of female and animal images, including images of snakes, in temples, mountain sanctuaries and household shrines. The most charming images are small figurines showing a priestess or goddess clasping snakes in either hand. Sometimes the figure has snake arm bracelets, or even snake arms, and snakes coiled around her body or in her hair. Are these poisonous snakes? It is hard to tell, even from a color photograph, whether a snake is venomous, but there are no snakes on Crete today that are dangerous to people. Perhaps in peaceful Crete all the snakes were friendly.

Feminine figure holds snakes in her hands while a panther rests on her head. Crete, seventeenth century BCE. Photo Chris73/Wikimedia Commons.

It's easy to imagine snakes moving freely through the Minoan temples, guarding the grain that was stored there. Living snakes might have been as ubiquitous as artistic ones, welcome in mountain sanctuaries and household shrines. Minoan deities were probably identical to early Greek ones, although we do not know this for sure. One clue comes from a Minoan cup that is believed to represent a scene from the myth of Persephone and Demeter.

In this myth, Persephone is painting flowers as the earth opens unexpectedly and the underworld death god Hades appears, abducting the young maiden. Persephone's distraught mother, the grain goddess Demeter, searches everywhere, and in anger and grief withholds her attention from the grain, threatening the whole of humankind with famine. To avert disaster, the god Zeus demands that Hades release Persephone, but unfortunately since the young goddess has eaten pomegranate seeds while in the underworld she must remain there. A compromise is reached whereby Persephone is reunited with her mother, but returns to her now-husband Hades four months of every year. During this time, Demeter mourns her separation from her daughter and the earth is fallow.

As goddess of the world of the dead, Persephone is associated with creatures which live underground or in caves, especially snakes and bats. Persephone's rites, known as the Eleusinian Mysteries, were the most popular in the Mediterranean world. What occurred during enactment of the Mysteries is not completely known, but the ceremonies revolved around three important symbols: the pomegranate, the grain and the snake.

These three symbols reflect across time and space to the island of Malta, where an earlier funerary cult can be traced to the sixth millennium. Sometime during their three thousand year tenure in the western Mediterranean, the people of Malta began using snake, grain and pomegranate in ritual to their goddess, who may or may not have had a resemblance to Persephone. The early Maltese erected huge statues to this goddess and engaged in religious ceremony focused on ancestor worship. They buried their dead in small oval cells—first in caves, later in human-made subterranean structures.Like many Neolithic peoples, they used red ochre in their rites. Underground rooms adjoining the burial cells were used for ceremonies that involved trance or sleep. Spirals adorn the entrance and altars of later temples, and querns (primitive devices for grinding grain) are part of the sacred imagery. The ceiling of a room in the largest underground temple is painted with fruit that looks like pomegranate. Originally native to Iran and Afghanistan, the pomegranate would have been a perfect symbol for this culture: its tiny red seeds are arranged in cells within fleshy cavernous dividers. The pomegranate room has an adjoining pit of unknown function that is called "the snake pit." Many believe the two statuettes of sleeping women found in this room represent a trance ritual involving snakes or snake venom.

Spirals and snakes carved into a mammoth tooth bead. Siberia, 13,0000 BCE.

An animal that is venomous has divinatory powers, whether or not the venom induces trance. Snakes were an integral catalyst for prophesy transmitted through the Delphi temple complex in Greece. This sanctuary was originally dedicated to the goddess

Gaia before being usurped by Apollo. Here the oracular priestess (the "Pythia" or "serpent woman") sat on a stool above a vaporous crack. A chemical pouring through the crack helped induce an altered state, from which the priestess made her pronouncements. The role of the snake is less understood but was apparently important. Some believe the snake brought messages through dream incubation. Delphi was called the navel of the world, and this was symbolized by a hollow conical meteorite at the site—the Omphalos—that was once guarded by the snake Python.

Copy of the Delphi Omphalos made during the Greco-Roman period. Photo (adapted) Yukatan/Wikimedia Commons.

An animal that is venomous has the power to heal as well as harm, so snakes are healing allies. In the hospitals of the Greek god Asclepius, snakes crawled freely while the patients slept. Their dreams (the dreams of the patients, not the snakes) would be interpreted by doctors in making prescriptions. Ascelpius' symbol, a snake entwined around a staff, is still used in medical contexts.

The Greek goddess of health, Hygeia, is portrayed with a snake wrapped around a bowl or chalice. Hygeia's snake imbibes and neutralizes poison, and Hygeia is considered the goddess of preventive medicine.

Hermes is another Greek god with a snake symbol and a reputation as a healer. His caduceus—twin snakes wrapped around the winged staff—is an amalgam of symbols he stole from other gods (he's the god of theft), but his birth on the mountain of Kyllene, which has other snake associations, might indicate an early affinity with snakes. Hermes obtained his

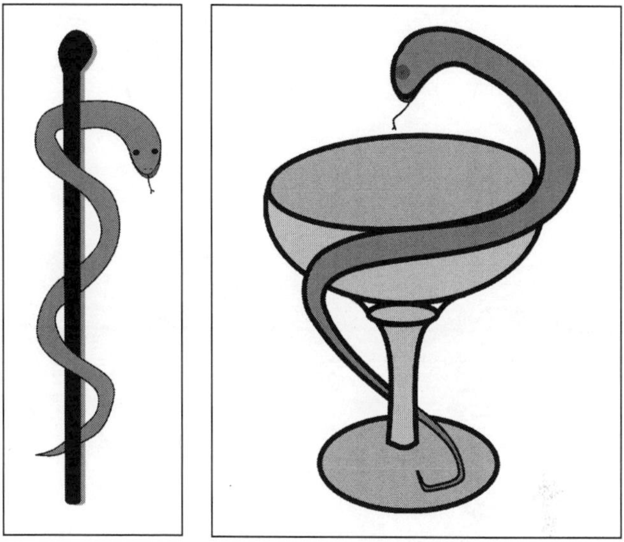

Left: Rod of Asclepius. Right: Symbol of Hygieia: cup and snake.

powers as Father of Alchemy from the snake.

Caduceus.

The Oscan goddess Anagtia, of the region now known as Abruzzo, Italy, is a snake goddess whose priestesses were legendary for their knowledge of healing craft. They were famous for their skill in charming snakes. Anagtia's main temple was on a large lake that has since been drained, close to the village of Cucullo, the home today of the annual *Serpari Feste.* This festival celebrates the eleventh century San Domenico, who is reputed to have cleared the land of a snake invasion. His statue is draped with large snakes and paraded with marching band through the village for devotees and tourists, many of whom also carry snakes. San Domenico heals snakebite, rabies and toothache. The snakes are caught by men who inherit the honor, and the snakes are fed milk as they await their meeting with the good saint. In the centuries preceding the Christian conversion, a statue of Apollo was draped with snakes for this ceremony, Apollo being credited with having "tamed" the region's snakes.

The snake has a habit of coiling during rest, which may be the inspiration for certain kinds of labyrinths. A lost labyrinth on Crete was described by the Greeks as a dancing ground, and speculation is that a snake dance was performed there. One simple walking labyrinth is a double spiral, meandering inward to a central point, then turning outward to the starting place. This symbolizes an individual's journey to the core self, where she experiences rebirth. The witch's spiral dance involves this principle.

The Cretan labyrinth appears on many Greek coins from the third and fourth centuries BCE.

Serpents in spiral. Detail from Dromiskin Cross, County Louth, Ireland. Drawing Henry S. Crawford.

Spiraling snake motifs on Irish crosses are intriguing, considering Christianity's condemnation of the snake and the fact that the snake apparently never made her way back to Ireland after the last ice age. Spiral themes pre-date the Irish Celts at places like Newgrange, which dates to 3200 BCE. Newgrange is oriented to the winter solstice and has spirals in its passageway.

Snake imagery can be found at the Neolithic site at Avebury, believed to have been the center of Britain's early religious practices. A historian who chronicled the short-sighted destruction of the site for commercial reasons wrote that the inner megaliths formed a meandering serpent. Megalithic constructions in other places in Britain and Ireland are often oriented to the sun.

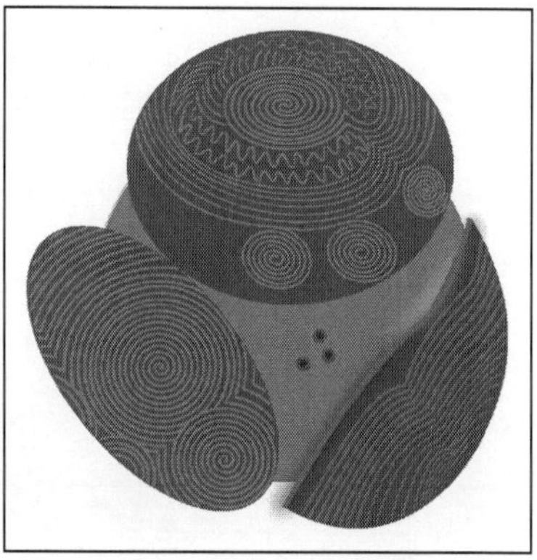

Carved ball. Spirals, stripes and wavy lines are associated with snakes in prehistoric art. Aberdeenshire, Scotland 2500 BCE.

In Scotland, the ruins of a Bronze Age serpent mound stretches along a ridge for over three hundred feet. The twenty foot mound is constructed of stone with earth on top. According to a nineteenth century account, a circle of stones once stood at the head of the serpent, enclosing an altar. The mound provides an expansive view of the mountain range of the crone goddess Caillech Bhear, probably not a coincidence. Unfortunately, astronomical data has not been gathered for the site, which has suffered from vandalism and development.

A look at snail and other spiral imagery in Celtic ornament suggests that spirals don't always symbolize snakes. In fact, the snake may symbolize the spiral rather than the spiral symbolizing the snake. Certainly this is the case in modern witchcraft, where anything with a spiral may find itself in the brew. In magic the spiral represents the accumulation and release of psychic energy. Ordered, intensifying energy moves inward in a spiral, while climactic, destabilizing energy moves outward in a spiral. The force of this energy can be felt in a whirlwind or a

Spirals are not always about snakes. Octopus spiral stamped in gold disk, Mycenaean Crete.

draining pool. The snake moving into a coil represents the gathering of energy. The snake resting in a coil represents potential energy. The snake striking from a coiled position represents the release of energy.

While the snake can represent energy in a generic sense, often the snake is used to represent energy that is specifically sexual. The snake arouses sexual feelings in humans through scale to skin contact. The shape of the snake is phallic, and the snake's movement through the earth's tunnels is analogous to intercourse. In the symbolic Ouroboros, where the snake is pictured as a circle with mouth swallowing tail, the mouth is female and the tail male. This illustrates the cycle of regeneration.

The androgyny of the snake might appear to be solely a human projection based on the sexuality of women and men. Male garter snakes, however, are known to occasionally mimic behaviors normally peculiar to females. So linked is the snake with sexuality in our minds that scientists puzzled for years over the reproductive motive for this. Eventually the true motivation became apparent: the male snakes were cold, and wanted a cuddle.

The complementary nature of the snake is not always sexual: she cradles polarities of many kinds. The snake likes to bask in the sun, soaking up and storing warm energy, yet she also moves underneath the cool earth. During cool weather she is diurnal, while in the hottest months she is nocturnal. The snake can be a catalyst in spells of attraction, drawing on the workings of polarity.

Attraction spells are often about money, and snakes have a lot of spare change. Creatures living below the earth are believed to amass riches because the earth harbors valuable metals and stones. The egg-bearing snake coiled around her brood seems to be guarding treasure, since precious stones are often round or elliptical. Legend has it that like the venomous toad the snake has a gem in her head.

Many occult stores sell a "snake oil" for making money (making money for the spellcaster, that is, not just for the store). Such oils capitalize on the association of snakes with wealth and don't have (or shouldn't have) fatty liquids from actual snakes. The snake oil elixirs of Wild West fame have their origins in China, where actual snake oil is still used to treat arthritis and similar ailments. Fat from a common Chinese water snake is high in an anti-inflammatory acid known as EPA, which is the active ingredient in the Evening Primrose oil that many women take to regulate their menses. Chinese immigrants introduced snake oil to the American West, and the substance quickly developed a reputation as a panacea for all kinds of ailments, much like Evening Primrose today. The problem was that American snakes, which have much lower amounts of EPA, were soon used in widely touted but often ineffective snake oil concoctions, making the term "snake oil" synonymous with medical fraud.

A few "snake oil" salesmen apparently made their way through Britain in the seventeenth century, selling a supposed snake product called an "adder bead." Travelers of the time marveled at the ubiquity of the beads in rural communities, and at the attestations of their miraculous cures. The bead was worn as a charm to bring prosperity, protect against evil and heal a host of ailments, especially snakebite. In reality a plain glass bead, it was reputed to be produced by a gaggle of adders (a type of poisonous snake) drooling until a hardened crystal ring formed from their saliva. There are fantastical historical references to a similarly produced magical "druid's egg" going back to Roman times, although once upon a time not everybody had one. The adder bead sounds similar in function to the "holey stone" still used in witchcraft. The holey stone is a small water-smoothed stone with a natural perforation, tied with red yarn and used as an amulet.

Common European Adder. Photo Highlandtiercel/Wikimedia Commons.

Spindle whorls were once used in folk medicine the same as adder beads and were called "adder stones." The whorl, a flat perforated carved stone, was dipped in special water, an incantation was spoken and sick livestock would drink the water. As late as the 1800s, adder stones were still being used in Scotland to heal both humans and livestock from snakebite and other ailments, especially "elf-shot," sharp stitching pains thought to be caused by the invisible arrows of elves.

The spindle is a powerful magical tool because it is transformative, changing raw material into a finished thread that spirals around a core. The spindle whorl must have been a very personal object, because it was often buried with its owner. Spinning and weaving deities are almost always sun, spider or snake goddesses, so it is not surprising a spindle part would be named for the snake.

The beauty of the snake's markings has been the inspiration for many types of handicraft. Snake imagery is common in Neolithic pottery. The rattlesnake design is one of the most popular patterns in American quilts. The snake's pattern of beauty makes her a special friend of women. As women we create beauty, enjoy being surrounded by beauty and try to make ourselves look beautiful, but we often do not appreciate the magical power of beauty. Beauty is an attractive force that helps us elicit cooperation from our magical allies.

Minoan urn with snake-like geometric features: wavy lines, bands, stripes. 1500 BCE Photo (adapted) Marie-Lan Nguyen/Wikimedia Commons.

The snake can be a metaphoric umbilical cord linked with motherhood or nourishment. On a pictorial stone found on the island of Gotland, off the coast of Sweden, a female figure in birth position holds a giant snake in each hand, with three large twining serpents above her. Snake and breast imagery is a near universal theme in pre-historic art. Sometimes the breast of a goddess figurine is marked with spirals.

Sometimes a snake wraps around the breasts of the woman or goddess figure. Sometimes a woman, bird-woman or snake-woman nurses a snake.

Snake imagery is often found around Neolithic hearth shrines. Non-poisonous snakes became welcome in households after people began storing grain, since snakes hunt rodents. Some people still honor the snake in their home. The goddess Aspelenie is the Lithuanian goddess of the hearth, and her special animal is a little ringed snake which lives behind the stove.

Picture stone showing female figure in birth position holding snakes. Gotland, Sweden. Sixth century CE. Photo Berig/Wikimedia Commons.

Perhaps because she enjoys warm places, most people associate the snake with fire, but she is also linked with water. Appalachian rain charms utilize black snakes, and Ozark lore says rattlers and copperheads become agitated before a storm. The Nordic ocean goddess Ran is depicted with a snake, probably the world serpent Jormungand, who was tossed into the sea long ago by the god Odin. Jormungand grew until his serpent body wrapped the earth and he could hold his tail in his mouth, and in this way he holds the world together.

The motion of the snake is a large part of her fascination. She moves quickly and easily over land, without legs. She molds to tree limbs, bodies or whatever she glides around, contorting her body in a wide variety of postures. She can move up, down, straight ahead and over water. Moving freely between worlds, it is not surprising that she conveys messages from the ancestors and the gods.

The snake speaks her words silently, with her tongue licking the air. Cryptic communication is associated with special, hidden and important knowledge. In the Old Testament book of Genesis, the snake understands the wisdom of the "tree of the knowledge of good and evil." Adam and Even have been warned not to eat its fruit, or they will die. The fruit tastes good and it's not poisonous, the snake tells Eve, and the young couple have to agree. After they are not killed by eating from the tree, God gets mad and kicks them out of paradise for disobeying him. The somewhat illogical lesson usually drawn from this story is that woman needs the moral guidance of man, so she doesn't listen to an evil serpent. If this really is the back story, it's laid out pretty weak. Taking it prima facie, all the story says is that God lies, God punishes when his lies are exposed, snakes have the real scoop, and women understand snake-speak better than men. Another explanation is that vestiges of a snake worshipping tradition are mixed with a later patriarchal perspective, confusing the story line.

Snakes are repeatedly associated with trees in Near Eastern and European mythology. The association may be for good or evil, but where there is a sacred tree, there is also a snake. In Sumerian mythology, Inanna sobs when the "serpent who could not be charmed" makes a home in the roots of her *huluppa* tree. This tree of unknown species Inanna has plucked from the Euphrates and planted along its banks. She is tending the tree to become her throne, which is symbolic of government and implies civilization. The snake and other inhabitants of the tree belong to the wilderness and must be driven out of the tree so it can be carved as Inanna's throne. The hero Gilgamesh, who becomes king of Inanna's city, banishes the serpent and other residents of the tree to the wild places. This will not be Gilgamesh's last tangle with the snake. In another myth, the snake steals the herb of eternal life that Gilgamesh has acquired, thus depriving Gilgamesh of immortality.

A serpent curls in the roots of the Nordic world tree Yggdrasil, nibbling at the root system. The dragon-serpent Nydhogg and his allies keep the copious roots in check, just as the magical deer prune the foliage. Nydhogg assists the earth in the process of decay and rebirth.

All over the world, wherever there are snakes, nature worshiping people have listened to the snake. Hosting more venomous snake species than anywhere on earth, Australia would be expected to have a rich snake mythology. In the belief of many aboriginal tribes, the first ancestors were snake people who took movement and form as the present world began. The moving snakes disturbed the earth, creating rocks, mountains, valleys and other geological features. The creative power of the snake is personified by the androgynous Wagyal, who lays her eggs upon a hill overlooking her sacred river, once inspiring women to give birth in this place as well.

Ancient Egyptians accorded so much respect to the snake that the hieroglyph for goddess is a cobra. Snakes were revered for their relation to the great serpent, the first form to emerge from the primordial waters. The hieroglyph for the Lower Kingdom was the cobra goddess Wadjet, and the cobra rested on the crown of the pharaoh. One cobra goddess is never enough, and people outside the higher echelons of government had the goddesses Renutet and Mertseger. Prevention of snakebite was an ongoing concern in ancient Egypt, addressed through propitiation to cobra deities and spells to control malicious snakes. Despite coordinated efforts to reduce snakebite, dying from an accidental cobra bite was enough of an honor for the state to pick up the tab for the funeral.

India is another place where snakebite is an ever present concern, with thousands dying yearly despite anti-venom for all of the deadly species. The Hindu snake goddess Manasa is worshiped as the "remover of poison," providing protection from snakebite and infectious diseases. Manasa bestows fertility and assists in childbirth. She is worshiped along with other snake deities on Nag Panchami, a special holiday just for snakes. On this holy day, women offer silver jewelry and milk to living cobras. They also fast and visit their mothers.

India may have the biggest snake holiday, but the largest snake monument in the world is Serpent Mound in southwestern Ohio. It was constructed at the beginning of the last millennium by settled farming people referred to as the "Fort Ancient Culture," who assimilated with other tribes after Native populations were decimated by Eurasian diseases. Serpent Mound is a stylistic but unmistakable replica of an uncoiling snake. The serpent complex winds for a quarter mile and averages three feet in height, shallow at the tail. A large oval sits just beyond the snake's head. The oval may be an egg, the sun, remnants of a ceremonial platform or all three. The head is oriented to the summer solstice sunset and various undulations are oriented to sun points at the winter solstice and the equinoxes. There is no rattle. Serpent Mound is not a burial mound, and appears to have been constructed for ceremonial purposes. The most striking feature of the Mound is not its impressive size, but the gracefulness of its flow, which seems inspired by the snake herself.

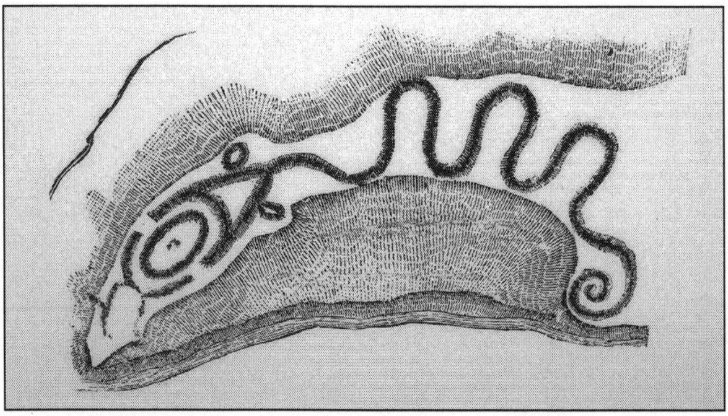

Serpent Mound. From the book *The Prehistoric World of Vanished Races* by E.A. Allen.

Nowhere is the beauty of the snake more apparent than in designs incorporated in south-western and Mexican Native weaving, embroidery and beadwork. Snake designs are woven into baskets by the Tohono O'odham, for whom the snake is a protector of water sources. Stylized snake symbols are incorporated in Hopi pottery. The Hopi perform a ceremonial snake dance in August to Avanyu, the feathered sky snake who brings thunder and rain. While an association of snakes with rain occurs worldwide, the rattle of the indigenous Sidewinder sounds particularly like the hard desert downpour striking the caliche.

The Huichol Indians of the Sierra Madre in west-central Mexico incorporate snakes in beaded objects, yarn paintings and embroidered pouches. The snake symbolizes rain, agricultural prosperity, good health and long life. She serves as an intermediary between gods and humans.

Also in central Mexico is the serpentine legacy of the Aztec civilization. The feathered snake god Quetzalcoatl, who gifted humans with the arts and sciences, is the most recognizable of the Aztec gods. His mother the creator goddess Coatlicue wears a snake skirt and has two snakes replacing her severed head. The snake is a complex Aztec symbol, incorporated by a number of deities. The snake is mother, father and child; earth, sun and moon; wind, thunder and rain; knowledge, creation and time.

And so the snake speaks—in silence, in movement, in pattern, in the hard rattle of her tail. Listen to what she says and become imbued with her knowledge. It holds a greater power than you can dream of.

The Hag and the Serpent

Few stories of the goddesses of Ireland, Scotland and England have remained. One goddess that appears repeatedly in legend is an old crone known as Cailleach Bhear, Cally Berry, Black Annis and many other names. The word Cailleach means "old hag." The hag in this story is Carravogue, who takes the form of a young maid or an old hag as she chooses. Legend says Carravogue now slumbers, but will someday rise again.

Once she was a spritely Lass who brought the joy of spring, but now she was Cailleach, she was old. As she hobbled to church that sunny morning, she spied berries, sweet berries that in her childhood she loved. The Cailleach picked the berries greedily and let the red juice dribble down her beard. Suddenly she was not Cailleach, she was Serpent.

The spritely Lass who was a Cailleach and now a snake was monstrously huge. The people leaving church called St. Patrick, for he was near, and St. Patrick flung holy water on her.

Such a thoughtful gesture, because snakes need water. Where there had been drops of holy water on her skin, now there were lakes. The spritely Lass who was a Cailleach and then a Serpent was now a Lake.

When she rises from that body of water, what form will she take? Will she be a serpent? A young girl? An old hag? We wait and wonder and think of her, when the berries are ripe along the banks.

The Transformation of the Seer

Tiresias is one of the greatest of Greek seers, appearing frequently in myth to impart some cryptic wisdom to the plot. In this story he stumbles upon the snake goddess Athena naked in her bath. This is an analogy for discovery of a secret women's cult.

Writhing snakes fringe the dress of Athena. Upper portion of bronze statue. Fifth century BCE.

The goddess Athena guards her mysteries diligently. The Gorgon on her shield and her snake-fringed shawl provide fair warning to men who desire the wisdom she shares only with a cherished priestess. The Theban Tiresias, neither priestess nor priest, had a desire for knowledge that could not be quenched, and he would not obey the signs or would not see them. His own mother a priestess of Athena, he should have known better. One day in the forest he gazed upon Athena while she bathed, and there was no evading punishment: the goddess blinded him immediately. Oh, how his mother pleaded with the goddess, but there was no undoing what was already done.

Athena is known for her mercy, however, and she allowed herself to be softened. Pulling a serpent from her breastplate, she directed her snake to lick the ears of Tiresias. The snake poked a forked tongue into the ears of the young man, so that he could understand the language of birds. Athena also gave Tiresias a staff of cornel wood, a dense tree that sinks in water, famous for its divinatory power.

With his staff as a guide, Tiresias wandered the countryside, noticing everything and missing nothing. It was on the mountain of Kyllene that he again stumbled upon an important mystery: two snakes copulating at a fork in the trail. Tiresias used his staff as a spear and killed the female snake.

Why did he do this? Some say to stop the coupling between the snakes, for seeing snakes in the sexual act is known to make men fey. Yet Tiresias could not see in the literal sense, so perhaps he was immune. Some say he killed the snake to avoid becoming effeminate, a known consequence of approaching mating snakes. Others say Tiresias struck the female snake because with powers of foresight he knew what would happen. You see, killing the female snake did not make Tiresias womanly; it made him a woman.

As a woman, Tiresias could apply to the temple to become a priestess. Tiresias became a famous temple prostitute and bore several children. Her daughters Manto and Daphne would also become celebrated seers.

The temple career of Tiresias only lasted seven years. She was walking down the road with her staff one day, when she reached a fork in the road where two snakes coupled. She struck and killed the male snake with her staff, and Tiresias was again a man.

Sometime later, Tiresias was called to settle an argument between the god Zeus and the goddess Hera. They wanted to know who enjoyed the sexual act more, man or woman. Tiresias replied without hesitation that the pleasure of the woman was nine times more.

This was not the answer Hera was looking for, so she blinded Tiresias. But Tiresias was already blind! you say. Still, that's what Hera did. Zeus compensated Tiresias for being blinded a second time by giving him divinatory powers. Perhaps these, too, were redundant, because by this time Tiresias had acquired tremendous powers of prophesy. Zeus also gave Tiresias a lifespan seven times that of a normal human. This is how Tiresias could be called on for wisdom through almost a millennium of history.

Snake Review

Magical Qualities:
sheds skin, venomous, hibernates, lives under and aboveground, rattles, moves in an undulating pattern, rests in a spiral

Magical Applications:
healing (of all kinds, but especially detoxification, rejuvenation, reversing impotence, pain management), divination, increasing wealth, rain making, attraction of all kinds

Other Associations:
death and rebirth, preventive medicine, sexuality, beauty, the underworld, water, the spiral, androgyny, sensuality, textiles, wisdom, immortality, motherhood, nurturance, breast milk, fire, the hearth

Approaching Animal Magic

The priestesses at Delphi had scribes to record their wisdom; you're going to have to write things down yourself. I recommend a pencil with a good eraser. What you write is perfect, but you might want to refine it later. You might find a highlighter useful for marking odd bits in this text that grab you, and post-it flags invaluable for marking pages you return to regularly.

Once you begin doing the activities, spells and meditations in this book, you may want a separate notebook for recording your experiences. For doing the meditations, you will need a space where you will not be abruptly interrupted, for instance by pets or small children. For some of the meditations you need an audio player or a friend with a drum.

The word "magic" in the title is used in two senses, referring to spellcasting and to the feeling that comes with direct connection to the divine. Not all Pagans perform spells, but there is information here that is useful for many purposes. Those looking for ideas to bring to Pagan worship will be particularly interested in the mythology presented here. There are twenty-six sacred stories of varying lengths, many of which can be adapted to mystery plays.

This book is written from a Western Pagan perspective, with some cross-cultural material included to deepen understanding within this framework. The word "pagan" comes from a Latin word meaning "country dweller," the earlier Christians being urban dwellers. Christians at one time referred to all polytheistic, nature worshiping people as "pagan," but in recent years aboriginal peoples of Africa, Australia and the Americas have objected to the word, seeing it as pejorative. I use the words "pagan" and "witch" to refer exclusively to shamanic paths of European legacy. These words do have a negative connotation; however, they are the words we have.

When choosing animals to include, I have tried to make

things, if not balanced, then at least representative. In these pages you will find creatures of the earth, water and sky; creatures who hibernate and migrate; creatures of the snow and the desert; creatures domestic and wild. This is not, however, a catalog of magical animals. That would be either a very long book or a very cursory one. The intention is to improve your ability to work magic with any animal, even animals not discussed here.

This guide is designed to help you get a better "feel" for the subject. You don't need to consciously sort and categorize the information because it's not presented in a format that lends itself to that. Nor do you need to memorize things; there's too much material. Instead of memorizing, categorizing and referencing, you will need to concentrate on experiencing, understanding and imagining. Experience the stories and myths. Think about what it means to hibernate, to migrate, to live in a cave, to live underground—from the animal's point of view and from your own. Get a feel for the folklore that evolved around various animals. Use the questions and activities to integrate the information with your own perspective and experience.

You do not need to answer every question or do every activity in order. If you can't respond now, or don't feel like it, just skip the question or activity—or flag it and go back to it later. If you are a person who does not like to write things down, read over the questions and think about them. Most of the questions are geared to both neophyte and adept; a few assume a bit of a knowledge base. If you don't understand a question, go back to it another time. The answer key is at the center of the world, and there are no "right" answers to the questions.

Most of the spells are self-explanatory, but it you are unfamiliar with a few of the terms (such as "casting a circle"), you can skip the spell or consult one of the many introductory books on witchcraft, such as *The Simple Sabbat: A Family Friendly Approach to the Eight Pagan Holidays*, by M. Flora Peterson or *A Ceremony for Every Occasion:The Pagan Wheel of the Year and Rites of*

Passage by Siusaidh Ceanadach. One caveat about most beginning magic books is that they explicitly state or unintentionally give the impression that you must work with a male partner and invoke both a god and a goddess in your magic. This is incorrect. While you need a goddess for balance if you work extensively with a male deity, the converse is not true. The Mother Goddess gives birth to the male and is complete and whole within herself. Woman is also complete within herself and does not need a male counterpart. There are all-female covens worshiping only goddesses that have been around for decades and have produced some very powerful priestesses. Invoke male deities and worship in mixed sex rituals, or not, as you prefer.

The spells will require simple items which you may or may not already have, but these should be easy and inexpensive to acquire. If you have trouble getting an item, just skip the spell. Some of these spells will not pertain to your situation anyway.

Where there are inherent dangers in an activity—which is seldom—they are spelled out clearly. Use your judgment regarding whether you are ready for an activity. Naturally, you are undertaking this exploration at your own risk: if you get eaten by a tiger or something equally bad happens, that's your hard luck.

It's not a requirement, but I recommend you find a friend to go through the guidebook at the same time. You will want someone to compare notes and share experiences with, someone who understands what you're talking about. If you normally work solitary, consider touching base with another priestess and being solitary together.

In the appendix are glossaries you may find helpful while completing this guidebook. Take a minute to familiarize yourself with what's there in case you need to refer to it. You may also find useful information at the book's website, www.invokinganimalmagic.com.

In the next section we will study the bat, an animal associated with birth and rebirth, which will take us into a reflection on the prototypical animal birth goddesses.

The following section will take us back to Apollo, as we investigate the healing significance of the mouse. This will provide a starting place for defining the magical beast.

Next, we will explore the idiosyncratic nature of the bear, a favorite of many, and practice some animal meditation. The incisive owl will lead us into a discussion on interpreting information arising in meditation.

Examining the potent magic of the toad will stir up a lot, but we will particularly concern ourselves with questions about power. How comfortable are you with your power?

The clever spider weaves magic of all kinds, and we will use her as a jumping off place for uncovering the nature of deception. What makes a magical practice authentic?

The hare is a bewildering creature, which makes her a perfect guide for shapeshifting. We will continue our shapeshifting investigation through a study of the dog and the werewolf.

Animal magic is the most logical of sciences, yet it requires a sound knowledge base and an intuitive feel for the subject that can only be gained experientially. To invoke animal magic in an effective way, we must do more than memorize things or look them up in a book: we must explore the language of the animal herself. We must become sibyls.

Such a Deal

A sibyl is a female seer. Sibyls in early Greece, Rome and Anatolia were connected with the deity of the temple where they served. In late classical times, as Apollo expanded his patronage, sibyls became automatically associated with Apollo as god of prophecy. The Apollonian influence can be seen in the distillation of sibylline offices to nine and later ten official ones. Still, sibylline prophecies retained a decidedly cryptic flavor, reflecting their feminine roots. Sibyls served the public and the state less by predicting the future (though they did some of that) than by prescribing rituals tailored to particular problems.

The following legend recounts how The Sibylline Books, *the most important Roman sacred text, originated in the sixth century BCE. The* Books *were housed in the Temple of Jupiter in Rome, the temple most closely associated with Roman government, and were consulted in times of crisis, such as invasion or plague. The* Books *were destroyed when the Temple burned in the first century BCE. Scribes were sent throughout the Empire to gather new fragments, which were compiled into another text. This compilation was deliberately burned during the reign of the Christian Emperor Flavius Honorius Augustus in the year CE 405.*

While many theories have been proposed to explain the collapse of the Roman Empire, from debauchery to endless expansion to ecological degradation, the Romans themselves attributed it to the destruction of the sibylline text and the consequent abandonment of the rituals it prescribed. So important was this text that various Christian and Jewish writings were compiled into a completely new document called The Sibylline Oracles, *to prophesy after-the-fact the coming of Christ and lend credibility to the emerging vision of Christianity. While most of this text did not become incorporated in the Bible, sibyls continued to be portrayed positively in Christian art and liturgy through the Renaissance, as purported endorsers of the new religion.*

They were acquired in the last years of the Roman kingship, during the reign of the Etruscan King Lucius Tarquinius Superbus. The king was receiving subjects in the garden outside his palace when a woman of foreign appearance stood before him, simply yet oddly dressed, with wrinkled skin and thick unplaited gray hair curling down her back.

"How may I be of service to you, Mother?" inquired Tarquinius.

"Great King, I have no favor to ask of you," the woman replied, "but I have come to offer you my own assistance."

"I do not know of any aid I require of you," rejoined the king, "but if there is a need of which I am unaware, I am grateful for your offer." This is the polite way their conversation began.

The woman opened her cloak, revealing that she carried many sheaves of papers in her arms. "I have here nine books of valuable prophesy," said the crone. "In these pages are the ceremonial responses to all the great problems of your country, those you are aware of and those that will arise in the future. Here can be found the formulas for responding to threats of invasion, plagues, meteors, droughts, civil conflicts. By consulting these oracles, your country will be assured the favors of the gods and their everlasting protection."

"How much payment for a safe nation favored with the everlasting protection of the gods?" asked the king dryly, with the weary air of a man who realizes he is about to be bilked.

"For you—only three times three hundred pieces of gold," she replied.

The king sputtered. "Name a reasonable price, woman, or we will discuss this no further."

Without a word, the crone walked over to a small brazier, removed a few of the coals, and burned three of her books. Her eyes flared like the fire as she turned back to the king. "Now, I have six books of prophesy to sell you," she said.

"And what do you ask for the six?" the king asked in a hard tone.

"The same amount," the crone replied. "Nine hundred in gold."

"Are you in your second childhood, hag?" the king exclaimed. "Go to the kitchen and you will be given a meal, then you must be on your way!"

The woman walked back to the brazier and burned three more of her books.

"I scarcely dare ask," remarked the king, "but how much are those remaining three?"

"Nine hundred," said the crone stubbornly. By this time the small group in the garden was laughing uncontrollably.

A functionary intervened. "Mother, you are trying the king's patience and you are not going to make a sale. Come to the kitchen with me, while you still have three books left to peddle."

Tarquinius himself was becoming amused at the absurdity of the situation. "Wait," he said laughing. "Since this is a question of our nation's security, let us bring the augurs here and dispose of the matter properly."

The augurs were priests trained in the language of birds. The species, the flight pattern, the numbers, the noises, the direction of movement—all of these were studied to determine the nature of a situation. The augurs observed the birds surrounding the crone and the king and the garden. From the birds they divined the worth of the divination offered by the crone. Finally they said, "Mighty king, this is a happy day for you and for Rome. You are being offered a rare and useful legacy. Pay the sibyl her price, for the worth of these books is beyond measure."

Because the books had been so dearly bought, Tarquinius placed them in the great temple he built for Jupiter. Only a few priests were trained in the study and interpretation of the texts, which were written in Greek. For almost a thousand years, these priests would consult the books and advise the government in times of greatest peril.

And the woman who brought the books? As soon as her treasure was loaded on her donkey cart she departed, never to be seen again.

Musings on a Multi-Patterned Scale

1) One of the core skills of wilderness survival involves the spiral. If you believe you've strayed from the path, the strategy is to move in an outward spiral until you discover it again. The logic of this approach is obvious; a bit more experiential is the quieting effect of spiral motion on the mind.

Study the double spiral diagram below for a moment and then trace inward along the path with your pencil until you reach the

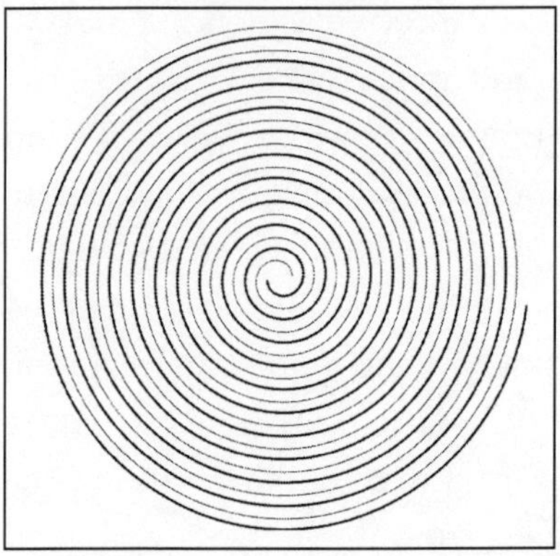

center. With your pencil still touching the center, close your eyes for a conscious breath or a moment of contemplation. Open your eyes and continue drawing the path as it moves outward. You have just "walked" the labyrinth.

Remember the difference between a maze and a labyrinth: in a maze you get lost; in a labyrinth you find yourself.

2) Only a gullible person would believe a glass bead is crystallized snake slobber, but this does not mean adder beads had no power. The charm's potency may have come from the string tied through the bead, representing the Ouroboros. You can make a snake amulet with a piece of red yarn and a button. Choose a button with a serpentine theme such as a spiral. The button should be bronze or gold colored.

Take a piece of colorfast red yarn, ribbon or embroidery thread and loop it through your "adder button." Leave the string big enough to get over your head before you tie and clip it. Go outside and hold the amulet to the sun as you pray to the snake goddess to empower it. To continue charging the bead, place it in a sunny window for several days. You can store the bead in a red cloth, but take it out occasionally and charge it again. This is a sun amulet, so it would be appropriate to wear during a solstice or equinox ritual.

To use your snake amulet for healing, you need shadow water. Rainwater collected overnight is good, but don't let the sun shine on it. Clean water filtered from a shaded pool which gets no sunlight is fine. Potable well water is acceptable. Keep the water in a dark place. It will not keep well, so use it within a day or two.

When you are ready for your healing ritual, pour the water in a glass. Put the snake amulet around your neck and invoke the snake goddess. Ask her for the healing you require. Take the amulet off and dip it three times in the water. The person or animal to be healed should drink a swallow right away. The remainder is poured on the ground as an offering. If this is not practical, pour the water in a potted plant.

For this ritual you need:
Red colorfast yarn
Chalice or glass
Shadow water
Button with snake theme

3) The rattlesnake is indigenous to the Americas, so there is no European rattlesnake mythology or magic. What would the rattle of the snake signify in Euro-pagan magic?

4) A rattle is a useful tool that is easy to make. Take a small plastic container about three inches in diameter and fill it with a teaspoon of *red* lentils. Replace the cover. Voila! Shaking this rattle approximates a rattlesnake warning;

swirling the rattle approximates the sound of a snake sliding over dirt.

5) Here is a short ritual to invoke Proserpina. Fill a glass three quarters full with pomegranate juice. Place the glass in front of you on a small plate or set it on your altar. Be careful, this can cause a wicked stain. It is preferable to sit on the floor, but if this is uncomfortable, at least make sure your feet are touching the floor. Take your rattle and swirl to simulate snake slithering. When you sense the time is right, begin whispering Proserpina's name softly. It's pronounced pro-SER-pin-nah. Continue for a few minutes. After invoking Proserpina, state your petition. Thank her for coming and say "blessed be." The pomegranate juice is poured on the ground later, if practical.

For this ritual you need:
Chalice or glass
Plate to put under glass
Pomegranate juice
Rattle

6) Write your initial impressions about the magical qualities of animals who
   a. Live underground
   b. Live in the water
   c. Live in a cave
   d. Can fly
   e. Live in the desert
   f. Walk in the snow
   g. Hibernate
   h. Migrate
   Add to these ideas as you continue the book.

Chapter 2

Creatures of the Womb

> Then Hermes of Cyllene summoned the ghosts of the suitors, and in his hand he held the fair golden wand with which he seals men's eyes in sleep or wakes them just as he pleases; with this he roused the ghosts and led them, while they followed whining and gibbering behind him. As bats fly squealing in the hollow of some great cave, when one of them has fallen out of the cluster in which they hang, even so did the ghosts whine and squeal as Hermes the healer of sorrow led them down into the dark abode of death.
>
> —*The Odyssey*[2]

Bat Savvy

In the summer dusk the bats would pour out of the factory chimneys, thousands circling the high towers. An individual bat's flight is erratic, but as a group these factory bats formed a spiral: thicker in the center, thinner around the edges. I used to sit in the yard of my childhood home and track their shadowy silhouettes as they hovered above the garden. A stray would occasionally flutter close by. Once, our cat Bootsie caught one. We took the bat away from her and brought the poor thing in the house to show our mother. She hit the ceiling.

Bats are connected with witches for good reason. Their night activity, their curious flight pattern, their solid group affiliation, their winter hibernation, their penchant for resting upside down and, especially, their hidden life in caves make them a potent magical force. The cave represents the womb of the goddess, where creatures originate and return. Bats spend their days, and their winters, absorbing the creative energy of the Goddess, then bring that energy into the outer world.

Halloween postcard from 1909. The writing at the bottom is a spell to banish witches.

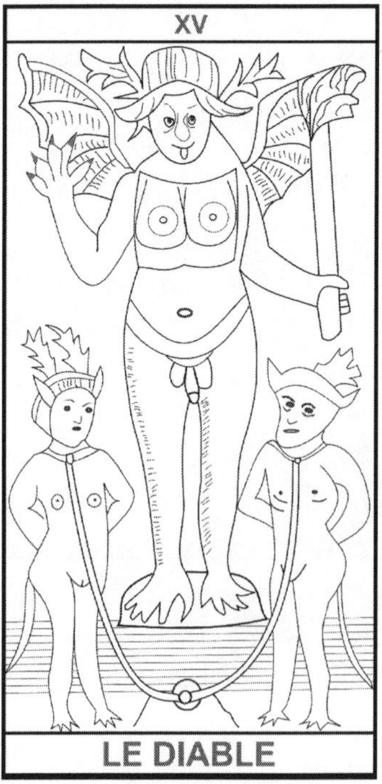

The tarot of Marseilles shows the devil with bat wings. France, circa 1700.

As messengers from the hidden realms, bats carry associations with danger. A bat in the house is said to portend death or other misfortune. Bats supposedly get tangled in women's hair. A few hundred years ago, stories about bats biting people to suck their blood began to circulate. Bats are said to belong to the devil, and the devil is often drawn with bat wings. Hollywood has exploited bat fears with an unrelenting stream of horror movies that date back to the silent era.

For people too rational to succumb to these superstitions, bats have become the focal point for fears around disease. There is little truth behind these fears, as bat guano is no more dangerous than other animal feces, and bats are no more likely to be rabid than any other animal. Most cases of rabies transmission do come from bats, but that's only because humans and bats have fairly frequent interaction. Despite being the villain of too many B movies, bats have decided they like living with us.

Most bats live in colonies; some are solitary. Colony bats have been observed bringing food to feeble adults. We know that their high pitched squeaking (humans can't hear most of their notes) is partly for communication, as other bats change behavior in response to these sounds. Group affiliation is an animal power used to promote familial and organizational strength. In this context it is interesting that the bat is sometimes pictured on heraldry for both clans and cities.

Most bats eat insects, some eat fruit and a few eat smaller animals or fish. The Long Nose Bat eats saguaro and agave nectar and is an important pollinator. Vampire bats in Central and South America suck small amounts of blood from sleeping livestock. Blood (usually menstrual blood) is used in spellcasting, so the vampire bat's feeding habits would link her with womb magic.

Coat of arms for German town of Fiefbergen.

The Little Brown Bat, found throughout North America, is an example of a common bat. She has an eight-inch wingspan and weighs about half an ounce. She eats half that weight in flying insects, which she hunts near water or around street lights. She is not photo-phobic and is active at night to harvest more insects and avoid avian predators. She can mate any time of the year, storing the sperm in her body until fertilization is convenient. She gives birth to one or sometimes two babies in the spring, nesting with other females in a large nursing colony. The babies look like adults in about four weeks. The males live in separate smaller colonies by their second summer. Summer colonies can be buildings or caves, but are often trees with dense foliage. During the winter, Little Brown Bats migrate up to a hundred miles to larger caves and mine shafts, where perhaps a quarter million will hibernate for the season. Migration is significant in magic because it is tied to pilgrimage, adventure and alternate perspectives.

The term "blind as a bat" is not strictly correct, since bats do have limited vision, but obviously they are not dependent on sight to navigate a dim cave. Blindness is associated with internal vision, and it was once believed that bats used psychic powers to fly at night. Even knowing they use echolocation to get a sense of their surroundings does not make their perception less mysterious. What would it feel like to map the environment with your ears?

Little Brown Bat.

The German word for bat is *fledermaus*, "flying mouse," and the archaic English words flittermouse and reremouse also emphasize the mouse connection. The bat gets her connection with shapeshifting from her rodent-like appearance combined with her ability to fly. In medieval times witches were believed to shapeshift into bats on their way to coven meetings. In Finnish folklore any sleeper can take the form of a bat to travel through the night during sleep.

Bats are associated with androgyny, again because of their one-time classification as a bird and mouse hybrid. Probably the ancients did not know that male bats engage in homosexual activity during hibernation. Bats are sexy creatures; both males and females are promiscuous. The interesting sex life of bats has been hidden until recently, although the vampire entertainment cult has a titillating element to it. In any case, bats are good symbols for magic utilizing sexual energy.

Bat from bestiary of Anne Walshe, circa 1400. Note the mousy character of this bat. Photo courtesy of the Royal Library, Copenhagen.

Where the afterlife is conceptualized as underground, bats are believed to travel back and forth between the lands of living and dead. This may be how the bat and the Christian Devil got merged. Mesoamerican archeology is rich with funerary bat objects. While witches regard bats in a positive light and Christians equate them with evil, Mesoamerican Indians have a more nuanced view of these creatures. They are sometimes protectors and other times fearful in their own right.

While some medieval bats look like mice, others have a dragon-like appearance. Photo from Church of St. Orso choir stall. Italy, fifteenth century. Photo Laurom/Wikimedia Commons.

The Chinese pick up on the winged rodent idea by giving bats the appellation "flying rats," which is meant as a compliment. The Chinese also have a bat superstition with hair—this time that touching a bat will make a person's hair fall out. The concept of five bats together is a popular art theme, as bats symbolize the "five blessings": old age, wealth, health, love of virtue and a natural death. What is there to add to that?

The War Between Beasts and Birds

Uncertain whether to classify her as a mouse or a bird, some ancient people considered the bat deceitful. In the following Aesop fable, the bat plays a trickster role.

It must be said that the war was started by the fox, which killed and ate a goose. The eagle retaliated by killing a hare and the owl by killing a mouse. At first the bat sided with the birds, which appeared to be stronger, declaring "I'm a bird." As the battle turned in favor of the beasts, the bat declared, "I'm a beast." When the birds and beasts finally made peace, they both turned on the bat for her lack of allegiance. Forever after she has been forced to hide herself during the day, coming forth only at night.

Rebellion of the Minyades

This Greek myth involving bats begins in the home of King Minyas, mythical ancestor of the Argonauts.

The day of an important festival to Dionysus arrived, and all the people in the kingdom gathered in the city square to celebrate. Or rather, almost all the people. The daughters of Minyas, the Minyades, refused to attend. They stayed home instead to weave and tell stories and riddles.

Dionysus was not pleased. He retaliated by tormenting the naughty girls, changing himself into a lion, a bull and a panther as he chased them over the countryside. In their frightened state the women sacrificed one of their own children, killing and eating him, which earned them the wrath of the maids of Dionysus, the Maenads.

Eventually Dionysus changed the women into bats to save them from the Maenads. Homebodies that they are, the Minyades now congregate near human habitations, building their nests in houses wherever possible.

Bat Review

Magical Qualities:
cave dwelling, nocturnal, group affiliated, rest upside down, promiscuous, bisexual (males), maternal, regulate family size, hibernating, vocal, exceptional hearing, migrating, erratic flight, attracted to human dwellings, may feed on blood

Magical Applications:
creativity, transformation, dreaming, shapeshifting, psychic ability, conception, birth control

Other Associations:
birth, death, ancestors, same-sex fraternities, pilgrimage, insight, deception, androgyny

The Animal Mother-Goddess

Early religious art was predominantly animal. The cave paintings of Spain and southern France are mostly of animals and animal symbols, like the chevron, egg, crescent, vesica piscis, and spiral. Even obvious goddess figures often have an animal theme, such as the horn that the "Venus of Laussel" holds in her right hand or the feline creatures crouching beside the "Seated Woman of Catal Huyuk." As the Stone Age progressed, goddess imagery became more pronounced, yet goddess/animal combinations were still common. With the development of writing, goddesses were associated in picture, inscription or verse with specific animals. Some of these goddesses were linked with many animals, or even given the title Mistress of Animals.

Venus of Laussel rock carving from Dordogne, France. 23,000 BCE.

One of the oldest animal mistresses on record is the Sumerian goddess Ninhursaga, addressed by worshipers of her day as Lady of the Animals, Queen of the Mountain, Lady of the Vulva, Midwife of the Gods, Mother of All Children and Lady of the Stony Ground. Her worship began in southeastern Asia Minor by at least 3500 BCE and spread throughout Mesopotamia. Ninhursaga is mother of both animals and people, which is not a contradiction when you consider humans a part of the animal family. Her place of residence is the rugged mountain steppes, an acknowledgement of the wild origins of humans.

Along with her symbolic omega (Ω), which bears a stylistic resemblance to the womb, Ninhursaga is typically depicted with horned headdress, a bow and some type of animal, especially a lion cub or doe. We could call her the Goddess of Bow and Doe. Sometimes Ninhursaga is pictured with a trilogy of cow, bull and calf, a popular motif throughout the region. More obscurely, Ninhursaga is the mother of a dying and resurrecting ass-god of the western deserts. Many of Ninhursaga's attributes are associated with goddesses we remember today: the Akkadian Ishtar, the Anatolian Cybele, the Greek Artemis, the Roman Diana.

Seated Woman of Catal Huyuk. Turkey, 6,000 BCE. Photo (adapted) Roweromaniak/Wikimedia Commons.

Ishtar is the popular name of the fertility goddess originating in Mesopotamia. She became bridged with the goddess Inanna of the older Sumerian kingdom and was worshiped elsewhere under the name Astarte, which means womb. Ishtar controls the fertility of all things, including people, animals and plants. She has a multitude of lovers, but the bull and vegetation god Dumuzi is her most celebrated consort. She calls him her honey-man, her sweet shepherd, the one her womb loves best. She eventually kills her mates, as her would-be lover Gilgamesh complains bitterly when repelling her advances. Ishtar initiates life, so she must also take it.

Though spells are addressed to Ishtar for protection in pregnancy and childbirth, she is not strictly speaking considered a mother goddess. Rather, she rules the sexual force that allows life to perpetuate itself. Nor is she a goddess of the wilderness: she is credited with bringing the many gifts of civilization to her city of Uruk—gifts like writing, building, irrigation, religious ceremony and medicine.

Ishtar surrounded by birds, fish and turtle. Larsa, early second millennium, BCE. Photo Marie-Lan Nguyen/Wikimedia Commons.

Although she rules fecundity on earth, Ishtar bears the title Queen of Heaven. Ancient Mediterranean peoples did not see heaven and earth as disconnected spheres, since the movement of celestial bodies affects life on earth. Ishtar is identified with Venus, the biggest star of the morning and evening skies, or with the beautiful multicolored Sirius, known even in ancient times to be a twin star.

Ishtar is most commonly pictured with a lion, but she is also associated with cattle, sheep, bees, spiders, owls, snakes and scorpions. She wears a horned or crescent headdress and has large wings. Often she carries a weapon. Her symbols are the eight-pointed star, the omega and the reed bundle. Ishtar is a benevolent, generous goddess, whose sweetness is compared to honey.

Ishtar's temple complex in Uruk housed priestesses who participated in sacred sexual rites with men. The king was

This owl-lady, once thought to be Lillith, is now believed to represent Ishtar. Sumerian bas-relief, 2000 BCE. Photo Aiwok/Wikimedia Commons.

the earthly husband of Ishtar and nominal head of her priesthood, but both women and men served in her temple in many capacities. Homosexual cross-dressing priests performed special dances at some of her ceremonies. While initiated priests and priestesses performed the obligatory rituals to the gods, temples in Mesopotamia were open to members of the public who wished to show obeisance. Animals were extended the same courtesy, and birds, bats and cats could be found in the main chamber with the statue of the deity.

Animal deities were once worshiped in caves, and the Anatolian goddess whose cult eventually dominated Rome has a name that translates as "cave." We know her as Cybele. The Greeks put her birthplace on Mount Ida east of Troy, but she is associated with other mountains as well, including another Mount Ida on Crete. Her titles are Mother of the Mountain, Great Mother of the Gods, Nourishing Lady, Most Holy Lady and Queen of the Wild Beasts.

Cybele flanked by lions. First century BCE.

Cybele is usually portrayed with a pair of lions seated beside her or pulling her chariot. She is associated with bees, and the Greeks referred to her priestesses as Melissae, or bee nymphs. The bees link Cybele with a special pine tree that bees love to swarm. This pine thrives in the low to mid elevations in Asia Minor and produces a sticky sap that aphids feed on. The aphids in turn sweat sweet nectar that attracts the bees. The honey produced from the pine nectar is still prized for its flavor, but in ancient times it was valued for its medicinal qualities. The love of the bee for this pine is the source of the myth of Cybele and her honey-man, Attis.

Attis is the grandson of Cybele, who conceived his father when the god Zeus tried unsuccessfully to rape her. He ejaculated on the ground when he could not enter the goddess' vagina, but since she is also the stony soil of the mountain, she conceived anyway. The son of Cybele became an almond tree, and a river nymph conceived Attis when she ate an almond from that tree. Attis was abandoned by his mother and raised by a billy goat. Cybele fell in love with Attis when he matured, and at first he returned her love. Eventually, however, his eye wandered to another, and Cybele attacked him in fury, until he tore off his genitals in despair, bleeding to death under a pine. With much sorrow, Cybele wrapped the body of Attis in wool and took his body and the pine tree to the mouth of her cave, where she planted both.

Cybele's maddening attack on Attis is obviously bee-like, but his self-castration has other parallels in the life of the bee, as the sexual organs of the drone are torn when he completes his copulation with the queen. Attis the drone dies and is reborn as an evergreen tree, which the bees dote upon.

The cult of Cybele is most remembered for the self-castration of her cross-dressing priests. On the final day of her festival, new male initiates would dance themselves into a frenzy and cut off their testicles, throwing them as an offering to the base of her statue. The hyper-masculine Romans, who had concerns about maintaining population growth, were horrified by the practice. It is possible that the convention originated as a means of maintaining social equality. Castration of priests, like celibacy of priestesses and sacrifice of kings, has the function of discouraging accumulation of power along parental lines. In the political context of Rome, the tradition of eunuch priests met heavy opposition and was eventually discontinued.

Cybele got to Rome not through dispersion of her cult, but through an amazing set of circumstances. The Empire was facing a series of military setbacks, and in the face of this uncertainty the land was plagued by "showers of stones." *The Sibylline Books* were consulted, and they recommended that Cybele's image be brought from Asia Minor and installed in Rome. Cybele's image was a meteorite, no longer extant, the very stone Zeus attempted to rape. The stone arrived in April 204 BCE. Annual week-long spring rites to Cybele commemorated the arrival of the stone and the death and rebirth of Attis. Men wishing to be reborn during the ceremony who wanted to keep their balls could stand underneath a sacrificed bull or ram to be bathed in the symbolic blood of Attis.

Some say the famous shrine of Artemis at Ephesus was once dedicated to Cybele. Statues of Artemis originating there do have symbols associated with the Mother of the Mountain. These symbols include flowers, sheaves of grain, the cylindrical crown, and clusters of fruit, in addition to the mélange of animals such as lions, goats, bulls and bees. Worship of a goddess at Ephesus predates the first Greek settlement, so Artemis was not the first goddess worshiped at this place—nor would she be the last. Her temple site would be rededicated to Diana and then to the Virgin Mary before its eventual destruction by Christian hands.

Artemis of Ephesus. First century Roman copy. Photo Pedro Lassouras/Wikimedia Commons.

Statues of Artemis of Ephesus from the Greco-Roman era depict a serene goddess with rows of animals and plants covering most of her body. Around the neck of one statue are the emblems of the zodiac, which would make Artemis of Ephesus a queen of heaven as well as earth. The multiple pendulous appendages resembling breasts on her upper front torso are meant to emphasize her all-giving nature.

In Greece the classical Artemis is more circumscribed than Ephesian Artemis, Cybele or Ishtar. Part of this has to do with the Greek penchant for distinguishing the roles and boundaries of their deities. Thus, the goddess Hera is assigned marriage, Demeter agricultural fertility, Aphrodite love and sexuality, Athena civic activity and defense, Hestia family stability, Persephone and Hades the underworld, and Artemis the wilderness and midwifery. Within her sphere, Artemis is contracted further. She is mistress of the animals but not their mother. She shuns marriage and all sexual contact with gods and men. She has no children. Of course this makes no sense. How can she be ruler of the wilderness and be infertile?

A tale about Artemis from the third century BCE gives a glimpse of the vastness behind the chastened goddess. She is a child on the knee of papa Zeus, who as head of the pantheon is dividing the world and assigning the deities their realms. Artemis asks for eternal virginity, more names than Apollo, bow and arrows, the title Bringer of Light, a short comfortable tunic coming down to her knees, sixty ocean nymphs all nine years old, twenty river nymphs to tend her hounds, all the mountains in the world, and one unspecified city, she doesn't care which. Zeus responds that she is too modest. He will give her thirty cities and a legion of temples, shrines and groves. He will make her guardian of highways and harbors, in addition to everything else she asks for.

Let's examine the nine requests of Artemis individually. Her virginity is not something Zeus, a late arriving deity, could have bestowed on the goddess, but it is one of her key aspects. It has nothing to do with chastity in the way the word is used today: Artemis is virgin in the sense of being inviolate. She protects her virgin forest from being altered by logging or farming, yet the forest is still fruitful and may even be visited and loved by men. She protects her virgin priestesses from rape or enslavement, yet she allows them to love and be loved.

In the Greek city states, the stronger the cult of Artemis, the higher the status of women. In some of the loosely banded tribes outside the cities, the rule of Artemis—or a goddess the Greeks identified with Artemis—was supreme, and women enjoyed rights denied to more urbanized women. They could marry or divorce at will and retained ownership of their possessions in marriage. Children belonged to the mother's family, not the father's. Women were allowed military roles and fought alongside their husbands or in all-female groups. Patriarchal Greeks were repelled and fascinated by these tribes and perpetuated some of the first urban myths about them. The women sawed off one breast to better hold the bow. The bones of boy children were broken so they would grow up weak enough to be bossed by women. They practiced human sacrifice so enthusiastically it's a wonder there were any men left to boss.

The second thing Artemis requests is more names than her twin brother Apollo. This request alludes to the enthusiastic rivalry between the cults of Artemis and Apollo, which temple administrators of both sects tapped for gifts and labor. The many names of Artemis support the claim that Artemis is a greater deity than Apollo.

The bow represents a significant power. With this weapon Artemis takes life—plant, animal and human. As mistress of life on earth, it is her privilege to decide when the time has come for a mortal to meet Persephone in the underworld. The story goes that upon receiving the bow, she first kills two trees, then a wild beast, then a whole city of people. City dwellers lived in fear of Artemis' plagues. She was propitiated with both human and animal sacrifices—possibly more than any Greek deity. The dances of young girls at Artemis festivals, designed to charm the

Goddess, had a serious message behind them: *See what sweet girls we have, Artemis! Don't send a plague on our city.* Countless myths attest to the deadly wrath of Artemis against deities, kings, families and cities. The bow and arrows are also used to defend the righteous, as Artemis fiercely protects women against rape, forced marriage and infanticide.

Artemis requests the title Bringer of Light. This refers to her role as midwife at the birth of her twin brother, the God of Light. One myth of their origin says that their mother gave birth to Artemis easily and without pain, but that she needed Artemis' help with the longer and more difficult birth of Apollo. Again, the followers of Artemis emphasized her earlier birth as proof of her superiority over Apollo.

Artemis' fifth request, the short tunic, is an old fashioned style of clothing long favored by female warriors. It represents the freedom of the Goddess to move however she pleases and go wherever she wants.

Zeus grants Artemis sixty ocean nymphs, which tells us Artemis' sphere extends to the ocean, where she rules the sea creatures. Artemis and other animal mistresses are frequently shown with fish. An urn from the Greek coast shows the Mistress of Animals with a large fish on her dress. The nymphs are nine years old to symbolize their perfection, nine being the number of moons for human gestation.

Artemis asks for twenty river nymphs, and she is often depicted in Renaissance painting cavorting with these female attendants. One of the most endearing characteristics of Artemis is the favor she shows the female sex. Her devotees are not exclusively female—the hero Theseus was her most celebrated follower—but she prefers the company of women. Artemis is not asking for nymphs so she can pose for a titillating bathing scene by the riverbank, however. The river nymphs are requested to care for the dogs. Since dogs are emblematic of death and the underworld, Artemis is claiming authority at the rivers which separate the living and the dead.

Artemis asks for all the mountains in the world, emphasizing that the wild and remote places belong to her. This would mean that pantheons which reside on mountaintops, such as the Olympian one, do so at her pleasure.

When asking for a single city, Artemis mentions that she prefers the mountains and only goes to town to aid women in childbirth, a duty imposed by the Fates. Midwifery seems an odd function to bestow on a childless goddess who doesn't like being around people, and so this is explained in the story by referring to the painless childbearing of Artemis' own mother.

Zeus gives Artemis more than she asks for, which is significant. The nine items requested in the story represent areas of influence Artemis claims before regional domination of the later Greeks. At this time a multitude of cities, temples and shrines become re-dedicated to Artemis, and she takes on many functions and titles of other goddesses.

Notice Artemis does not ask for the moon, at least not literally. While she was worshiped at the full moon in early antiquity, she does not become Moon Goddess until sometime after this tale, possibly as late as Greco-Roman times.

Artemis is mistress of all creatures, but some animals are particularly favored by her. The deer is most often mentioned, and the bear ranks a close second; dogs, of course, and wolves. Quail are the birds she most favors. Other animals include hares, lions, pigs, goats, toads, fish and cats. There is a myth where Artemis and the other Olympians, on the lam from the monster Typhon, flee to Egypt disguised as animals. Hermes is an Ibis, Zeus a ram, Hera a cow, Apollo a crow, Aphrodite a fish, Dionysus a goat and Artemis a cat. This story is basically giving Egyptian equivalents of the Greek gods, so the Greeks evidently saw parallels between Artemis and the cat goddess Bast.

The goddess Diana, who subsumed Artemis in Greco-Roman times, is sometimes portrayed as a black cat. Originally a local goddess of Lake Nemi, Diana's a tough lady to sort out, because her history is complex. It's easy to assume when a goddess is worshiped at a lake, mountaintop or grove that she's a goddess of that particular waterhole, mountain or forest, but in forested regions these are also places that give worshipers an uninhibited view of the sky. Encyclopedia Britannica says Diana's name is related to Latin words for sky and daylight. Others have translated her name as Queen of Heaven, Queen of Light, Holy Mother, or simply Goddess. It's difficult to understand how Diana was first perceived, because the earliest Latin tribes had a rather abstract concept of their deities and did not produce statues or develop mythology. At any rate, their perception changed with Etruscan influence and then with more direct contact with Greek culture.

Artemis with quail on ivory votive offering from her temple in Sparta. Sixth century BCE. Photo Marsyas/Wikimedia Commons.

The oldest known temple to Diana was built outside Rome in 540 BCE by the heroic King Servius Tullius. Servius was inspired by stories of the collective efforts of Greeks on the coast of Anatolia in rebuilding the ravaged temple to Artemis of Ephesus. He believed a similar project would unite the Latin tribes, and Diana was presumably chosen as a parallel goddess to Artemis. The statue of Diana inside the Roman temple was a replica of the statue of Artemis at Ephesus. Diana immediately absorbed the symbolism and legends of Artemis, although her structure of worship remained more Roman. Servius had been born a slave, and the temple was designated as a refuge for slaves. During the Roman occupation, the Temple of Artemis in Ephesus (renamed the Temple of Diana) also became a slave refuge.

With few exceptions, Roman conquest resulted in local deities being renamed Apollo, Faunus, Mercury, Venus, Minerva or—especially—Diana. These gods grew in complexity as the boundaries of the Empire expanded. The Romans, like the Greeks, viewed deities with superficial similarities as manifestations of their own gods. The outcome of this view was that aspects of many local deities disappeared, even before the imposition of Christian theology.

Christian leaders saw Diana as a persistent challenge. This is first documented in the Bible in Acts 19, when Diana's worshipers at Ephesus chant her name for two hours to drown out speeches of Paul and his supporters. After becoming the official religion of the Empire, the Church initially responded to the intransigence of Diana's worshipers in the time-honored way of changing her name to Mary, appropriating festival dates and erecting a church at the site of former temples or groves. This strategy does not appear to have been entirely successful, at least from their point of view. Edicts of bishops and Church councils from the fourth to the fourteenth century continued to condemn the worship of Diana and equate it with demon worship. Women were particularly mentioned as the misguided followers of demonic Diana. The

Diana with stag. Second century. Photo Eric Gaba/Wikimedia Commons.

biggest mistake Christian leaders made in trying to destroy the Pagan cults was failing to incorporate women into their priesthood. Since even in patriarchal Pagan cultures priestesses held vital roles, it's hard to see how resistance could not have persisted.

Writings of Inquisitors attest to the tenaciousness of Dianic worship. Italy is most often mentioned as the site of Dianic covens but the worship of "Diana" (the Roman name for the local goddess) continued across Europe. Nor was Dianic worship confined to clandestine meetings of pocket Pagan rebels. A group of English friars were chastised in the fourteenth century for keeping a woodland shrine to Diana. Erasmus (who died in CE 1536) wrote in disgust about a ceremony involving a stag in St. Paul's Cathedral in London, and likened the worshipers to "the mad votaries of Diana."

The intensification of witch persecutions and the reaction of Protestants against paganism in Christian worship meant that Diana eventually had to leave church. This does not appear to

Diana Reclining by Lucas Cranach, sixteenth century. Note the quail and cave in the background.

have dampened the enthusiasm of artists and poets for the old gods, however, and Diana features prominently in Renaissance art. Queen Elizabeth I, though she furthered the Protestant goal of removing Pagan elements from Christian churches, enjoyed comparisons with the virgin goddess and capitalized on Diana's popularity to mute criticism of her decision not to wed. Diana reached an apogee of favor during the Romantic movement of the nineteenth century, when nature's virtues were an aesthetic and political ideal.

In modern covens, Diana is often referred to as "The Lady" and worshiped at the full moon, with or without her horned consort. Of course, "Our Lady" is an appellation for the Madonna, which is Italian for "my lady," and "that lady" is a title which children have bestowed on me, but "The Lady" of the witches is usually Diana.

There are European animal mistresses who were not eclipsed by Diana, such as the Lithuanian Medeine, the Scandinavian Freya, the Russian Baba Yaga, the Finnish Mielikki, the Latvian Laima or the Scottish Cailleach Bhear. Being northern goddesses, they do not have a written mythology that predates Christianity. We will, however, catch glimpses of them as we examine more of the folklore surrounding magical beasts.

The Lord of the Flute

The Mother of Animals often plays in tandem with her male consort, who is her son, lover and priest.

Attis was not the only devotee of Cybele. There was Marsyas, who played the stag horn flute so beautifully that all the beasts in the forest were charmed. Hawk would suspend chase of the mouse and wolf would cease stalking the deer in order to hear the sweet notes of his flute. Marsyas won such acclaim that stories reached the ears of Apollo, who of course was jealous.

The god of music challenged the woods' musician to a contest—Marsyas on the flute and Apollo at the lyre. The match would take place on Mount Helicon, with the nine Muses as judge. Marsyas foolishly agreed.

The Muses are known to be partial to Apollo, but the performance of Marsyas must have been spellbinding, because they declined to choose a victor. At this point Apollo turned his lyre upside down and sang as he plucked his notes. No flutist can sing as he plays, or blow notes out the back end of his flute, so Apollo was declared the winner. Marsyas had been tricked.

Apollo chose to flay his worthy opponent and nail his skin to a pine tree. Evidently he was risking no chance of a rematch. Yet the animals did not turn their allegiance to Apollo, but cried and cried for the loss of Marsyas. The tears of the grieving animals formed a river that was named for the great musician. This river now plays the most beautiful of songs, all of them sung in memory of the gentle consort.

Musing in a Dark Cave

1) Most tarot decks continue the devil-and-bat symbolism for the #15 card. Do you think this symbolism should be continued? How would the meaning of this card change if the bat was retained, but not the Devil?
2) Do you think the association of bats with craziness makes sense?
3) What deity might the Minyades have been choosing over Dionysus by their decision to stay home and weave?
4) If you're able to consciously direct your dreams, try dreaming you're a bat and record your experiences here.
5) Which animal mother do you feel most strongly drawn to?
6) The city of Artemis referred to in the Zeus myth is Ephesus, home of her famous temple. Ephesus is now in ruins. Does Artemis have any cities today? Which modern cities would you associate with her?
7) Diana is considered a minor Roman deity, so why would Romans rename so many goddesses Diana in their northern territories?
8) Some say that witches perceive Diana erroneously, that originally she was not a moon goddess or a triple goddess and so should not be worshiped as such. Do you agree?

Draw lines showing which symbols or titles of Ninhursaga are associated with more familiar goddesses.

Lady of the Animals	
Lady of the Stony Ground	Cybele
Midwife	
Deer	
Lion	Diana
Bow	
Lady of Heaven	
Queen of the Mountain	Ishtar
Horned headdress	
Cow or bull	
Giver of fertility	Artemis
Great Mother	
Grantor of Kingship	

Chapter 3

Creatures of the Soil

> And when *Diana* saw that the light was so beautiful, the light which was her other half, her brother Lucifer, she yearned for it with exceeding great desire. Wishing to receive the light again into her darkness, to swallow it up in rapture, in delight, she trembled with desire. This desire was the Dawn.
>
> But Lucifer, the light, fled from her, and would not yield to her wishes; he was the light which flies into the most distant parts of heaven, the mouse which flies before the cat.
>
> —Charles Godfrey Leland, *Aradia*[3]

Deciphering the Mouse Mysteries

It was a wickedly cold night, but my partner, my cat and I were snug in our bright, rather cramped apartment. The three of us watched in idle curiosity, then in amazement, as a mouse sauntered over to the cat dish, selected one piece of cat food, then dashed for cover. Even the cat was too surprised to react. There was no reason to covet the food of the arch enemy, since there was plenty of human food in the apartment that was not touched. The act has to go down as one of the cheekiest gestures of all time. The cat stood guard over her dish for the next two days, until she caught the brazen thief on a second raid.

Mice are as prosaic as bats are mysterious. Mice are common, ordinary. A woman whose looks are unremarkable is described as "mousy." Mice are quiet, plain, timid, unassuming. They breed prolifically and live only a few years in captivity—even less on the prowl, since they have so many predators. Everyone knows about mice.

Mice have been scurrying around my brain for many years, ever since I heard the god Apollo called The Mouse Catcher. Most encyclopedia entries don't even mention this obscure connection, let alone explain it.

Coin depicting Apollo Smintheus with his mouse. Composite drawing, 350–200 BCE.

Years later, mice scooted across my brain with that crazy story about the goddess Diana changing the stars to mice and making it rain mice. The story says she did it to impress other witches, but why mice?

In medieval times Inquisitors considered the mouse a witch critter. Witches supposedly used mice as familiars and changed themselves into mice. The magical connection of bats with witches is obvious. What is so magical about mice, when they're not raining from the sky?

Even crazier is the mouse remedy in English folk medicine curing everything from diabetes to bedwetting. Mice are abundant the world over, but they are not ubiquitous as healing ingredients. If mice did have intrinsic healing properties you would expect to find them prominent in Chinese medicine, where animal derivatives are common. I've found rats as a prescription for hair loss, and I wouldn't be surprised if there aren't some additional medicinal applications for rats and mice, but they aren't a panacea in Chinese medicine, like snakes.

The mouse appears in the Dianic creation myth as Diana from her dark body births the light god Lucifer. As she seeks to devour him into her darkness, he flees before her "like the mouse before the cat." So Lucifer is light, but he's also a mouse. The stars are light. Diana changes the stars to their twin form, mice, and no wonder the witches are impressed: it's a clever conception, as well as a miraculous deed.

But the story still doesn't satisfy. Why is Lucifer the light god also a mouse? Mice are gray or brown. Sure we have white mice today as pets or lab animals, but wild mice are dark, and conspicuous white mice could not survive in an unprotected environment for long.

Turns out, white mice have been selectively bred for a long time. The art of fancy mouse breeding goes back more than 3,000 years, to temples of Apollo along the coast of Anatolia, or perhaps to the worship of an even older mouse god superseded by Apollo. As the cults of Apollo and Artemis spread throughout the Mediterranean, so did mouse worship. There was even a mouse temple in the Greek city of Alexandria, on the coast of North Africa.

It looks like a stellar year for the lucky owners of this mouse. Photo Seweryn Olkowicz.

Church mice may be poor, but temple mice lived a life of luxury. Observers said the mice were given a bed at the foot of the Apollo's altar and permitted to roam freely. The mice were used as a type of early economic forecasting, with more prolific breeding portending a more prosperous year.

Of course the mouse-light god in the Diana story is named Lucifer, not Apollo, but Lucifer is Latin for "light-bearer" and could easily have been a title of Apollo as the god of light. Lucifer is associated with the morning star Venus, and Christians declared him identical with Satan. The old male gods often became libeled as the Christian anti-deity, especially when the cult of the old god proved intransigent.

Before becoming Christianized, the Romans brought the worship of Apollo to their conquered northern territories. Apollo by this time was the god of healing, geometry, music, prophesy and many other things. He superseded the worship of many gods that were probably gods of light or healing. If the mouse association accompanied Apollo to the British Isles, this would explain how the mouse remedy got started there.

Wait, wait a minute, some people are thinking. If the mouse was sacred to Apollo, wouldn't that make it a crime for his followers to kill a mouse, or at least make mice a socially unacceptable meal? What about the death penalty in ancient Egypt for killing a cat? What about the cultural prohibition in India against eating beef?

Let me explain something about the Celts.

The ancient Celts ate anything they held sacred. There are those who contend they even ate the king in ritual sacrifice. There might be conditions on how a sacred animal would be eaten, but it most certainly would be on the menu at some point during the year. This was a way of imbibing the attributes of the animal-god. If Apollo is the god of healing and his sacred animal is the mouse, what would a sick Brit do? Eat a mouse.

The medicinal mouse came onboard with waves of English

and Scottish immigrants to America. The ailments linked with the mouse remedy, though they span a wide province, are most heavily concentrated in areas having to do with bodily fluids, especially lung congestion and bladder problems. A Boston health professional in 1890 discovered a family of English extraction feeding mouse stew to their children to prevent bedwetting. It's too bad the art of mouse cuisine has died out. In my years as a family therapist I've had some bedwetters I couldn't fix, and I'm sure eating a mouse would have cured them.

With the coming of Christianity, mice took on an evil flavor. The Old Testament defames mice as unclean animals, so this could be where Christians got their prejudice. Andrew Lang in *Custom and Myth* states the Israelites themselves became prejudiced against mice during their long stay in Egypt, where mice were reviled. However, Robert Graves, in *The Greek Myths*, asserts the Israelites were reacting to a mouse cult in Palestine, citing passages in the Bible describing or denouncing what certainly sounds like mouse worship.

Why there should be a mouse cult in the first place is puzzling to some, but this is related to the disease and destruction that mice bring. While Egyptians responded to the mouse problem by cultivating the cat goddess, other cultures cultivated the mouse god himself, beseeching him to keep the numbers of his tribe in check. Thus Apollo is not only the mouse god, but the mouse destroyer. Apollo as mouse god steals grain, but he also protects grain. Apollo as mouse god brings disease, but he also brings healing.

The major attribute Christians ascribed to mice, surprisingly, was not disease or thievery, but lust. With the celibate's fascination for all things sexual, clerics used to breed mice in order to observe firsthand the nature of lust. They also maintained that white mice were more "lustful" than dark. It's a good thing we already know about the Apollonian white mouse temples, or we'd have another crazy mouse riddle to figure out. The fact that

Christian clerics associated mice with witches, mice with lust and white mice with greater sin suggests a reaction against the Pagan mouse god. (For the sake of thoroughness, I asked some mouse breeders if their white mice were more fertile. They told me no.)

In seeming contradiction to their notion of mouse hypersexuality, monks touted the mouse as a corroborator of the Virgin Birth, since mice supposedly conceived by licking salt. This notion has been around since at least classical times. Salt has positive associations in Christianity as well as witchcraft, but none that explain its mechanism in parthenogenesis.

The Japanese could have told Christians that the male mouse is necessary, since fancy mouse breeding was already popular in Japan at the time of the first missionaries. Rich men liked collecting varieties of mice, as the mouse was a symbol of wealth and wisdom. The first published work on the principles of genetics came not from Mendel but from a Japanese mouse breeding tract.

For many Native American tribes, the mouse possesses a special wisdom, because her smallness gives her a unique perspective. The mouse's small size also gives her humility, which is an important component of Native spirituality. The mouse plays a prominent role in Hyemeyohsts Storm's novel *Seven Arrows*, about Plains Indians struggling to keep traditions of peace alive while facing the threat of annihilation. The mouse in this story represents the principle of scrutiny. He examines everything closely and reflects on it carefully. In order to get perspective he has to travel long and far, as he can only see one detail at a time.

Maybe that's why the tidbit about the Mouse Catcher nagged me for so long. It was an insignificant piece of trivia that, combined with other small details, added up to something bigger. Mouse magic is powerful; do not underestimate the humble mouse.

The Witch's Queen

This mouse story is from Aradia: The gospel of the witches. *It was published in 1890 from material Charles Godfrey Leland obtained from an Italian* strega *or sorceress.*

Diana was our first mother, the great mother, the one created before all of creation. Her body was the darkness and out of it she created all things. Her first child was Lucifer, the beautiful god of light.

After many eons of creation, Diana decided to live on earth as a mortal woman. At this time she was unknown even to the witches, fairies and elves who lived in the wild places, though she was their mother. Diana endeavored to cloak herself in humility, to live out a mortal lifetime in obscurity, but her greatness would not allow that. The strega flocked about her to learn her magic, thinking her one of them.

One night, when a large number of sorceresses and fairies gathered, Diana felt an impulse to perform a strange magic. She told the congregants she would turn the stars to mice and let it rain mice. The strega murmured that if she could do such a wonderful thing, they would surely crown her queen.

Diana took an ox bladder and a piece of witch money. (This money has a sharp edge like a knife, and with this the strega sometimes cut men's footprints to do their magic.) With the witch money Diana cut a piece of earth from the road and put it in the ox bladder, along with many mice. She blew and blew into the bladder until it burst.

The sky darkened as mice flew from the bladder, and for three days and nights it remained dark, as the heavens rained mice. This is why the devotees of Diana call her Queen of the Witches; Queen of the Cats; and Ruler of Mice, Heaven and the Rain.

The Colony of Mice

Here is the origin of the mouse cult as recorded by Greek historians.

Long before the philosopher Plato, before the great poet Sappho, before the lyric storyteller Homer, before the shepherd Paris of Golden Apple fame, when the Acropolis was still a stony outcrop and the muse Calliope was just learning to spell, adventurers from the island of Crete set out to colonize lands in the east. Being pious as well as fearless, they consulted the oracle of Apollo before they sailed. The oracle told them to settle at the place where they would be attacked by Children of the Soil. The Cretans did not understand the oracle, but they paid attention and kept the words in their hearts. Eventually they landed on the coast of Asia Minor and began exploring. One night, a group of mice stole into their camp while they slept and ate the sinews and leather straps in their bows and shields. These were the Children of the Soil, bringing the long awaited sign.

In this spot the Cretans established what would become the prosperous state of Troy. Here they built temples to their god Apollo and to Apollo's sister, Artemis.

Nor did the Trojans forget to honor Apollo's messengers, the mice. They established luxurious beds of breeding mouse queens, located at the foot of Apollo's altar. Since Apollo is the god of light—sunlight, starlight, moonlight and, of course, the hidden light of the oracle—the mice bred for the temples were light ones. Cradling a mouse bed of Apollo is equivalent to cradling the bed of knowledge, and the most talented soothsayers of the region came to Apollo's temples to interpret messages sent through the sacred mice.

Apollo's temple at Tenedos became home to the celebrated sibyl Herophile, who called herself Artemis. Born in a cave in the mountains of the mainland, townspeople throughout the Aegean boasted that Herophile had slept there. Certainly she passed through Delphi from time to time, but only Apollo Smintheus

Tenedos could rightfully claim this priestess as their own. It was Herophile who correctly interpreted the dream of Queen Hecabe and predicted the fall of Troy.

Coins from regions near Troy are assumed to represent Herophile. Notice the laurel leaf hair, an emblem of Apollo.

The Athenian conquerors knew they could not remain in the region without Apollo's approval, so they continued to support the temples, maintaining the sacred mouse tribes at state expense. The Greeks even exported Apollo's mice to other temples in their far flung colonies.

But the Greek empire eventually fell, as all empires are destined to fall. Perhaps the mice changed their allegiance; if you have in your possession a colony of white mice, you can ask them. Perhaps mice are not omnipotent; only very, very strong. It is a certain truth, however, established millennia past by the oracle on Crete, that no empire can establish or maintain itself without obeisance to the tiny mouse.

Mouse Review

Magical Qualities:
prolific breeding, small, nocturnal, good at hiding, propensity to hoard

Magical Applications:
healing (especially toothache, diabetes, cough, water retention, bedwetting), victory in battle, prosperity, prophesy (especially economic forecast), acquisition of knowledge

Other Associations:
paradox, light, the male principle, small details, thievery, humility

What Is A Magical Animal?

Biologically speaking, an animal is any multi-celled organism that moves and eats other organisms. In plain speaking, an animal is any mammal that isn't human. Pagan magic accepts and expands the biological definition of animal, including birds, reptiles, amphibians, fish, arthropods, non-human mammals and humans in the animal category along with mermaids, unicorns and dragons.

"What separates us from the animals" has long been an important question for biologists, psychologists, theologians and philosophers, and the characterization of that separation changes over time. Tool use, art, language, presence of emotions and other onetime demarcations are no longer useful, now that wild monkeys are using tools, elephants are playing musical instruments, dogs and cats are painting pictures, African gray parrots are speaking in syntax and the gorilla Koko has cried over the death of her pet kitten. The very question of "what separates us" implies that there is a fundamental separation and that the separation is important.

Anthropomorphism—the projection of uniquely human characteristics onto animals—is considered the gravest error a researcher can make, and scientists bend over backwards to avoid the charge. At one point, it was impermissible to draw any conclusion of consciousness, intelligence or emotion in an animal if the data could possibly be interpreted in any other way, however implausible. This bias was upheld to avoid polluting the body of scientific knowledge with unproven assumptions. A conditioned response to stimuli was considered the only thought an animal was capable of, even as animal rights' activists and some scientists correctly pointed out the shaky assumptions embedded in this view. In recent years the rules against interpreting data on animal intelligence in an intelligent manner have lost traction, mainly because the dumb beast bias has become impossible to maintain, even with the bar set ridiculously high.

Research into animal intelligence focuses on language acquisition, problem-solving and mirror recognition, since these involve abstract reasoning. Humans are believed to be the most intelligent animal because, to our knowledge, no other animals come close to us in abstraction. The magical sciences also include abstract thought in intelligence, but there is a high value placed on other forms of cognition, especially perception. Animals like the hawk are admired for their superior eyesight. Animals like the deer are admired for their superior intuition. To the Pagan mind, intelligence is not ranked with humans at the pinnacle, other apes second, corvids third and so on. Rather, intelligence is viewed as incomplete in humans and complete only in nature as whole. Thus we look to other animals to compliment our own intelligence.

From a magical perspective, animals possess intelligence through innate physiology and through lifestyle. For example, raccoons have extremely sensitive hands and gain knowledge through touch, a form of intelligence that is useful for massage therapists. Raccoons also have an intelligence gained from rifling garbage cans to find Fruit Loops, and this intelligence can be utilized in finding treasure.

In the Pagan view, anthropomorphism is not a failing, but a magical skill, one that has applications for healing. I once used the giraffe to cure a problem I was having with my throat. I had more instances of strep throat than I can remember, and my voice was very soft. I also didn't say much. I decided to work with the giraffe to correct these problems. I thought about giraffes a lot, and I kept giraffe images around me. Now, I knew that giraffes have long prominent necks to reach arboreal vegetation, not to "speak their truth." Even so, through focusing on the giraffe my throat problems cleared up, and I found my voice.

In magic, as in biology, animals are separated into categories such as "mammal," "bird" or "insect." However, these are not sufficient. There are also animal gods, familiars, mythical beasts, fairy animals, divine animals and animals beloved of the deity. Animals in the last category would include the bee (beloved of Cybele, Ishtar and Aphrodite), the dog (beloved of Diana and Hecate), the pig (beloved of Cerridwyn) and the raven (beloved of Morrigan). I call these animals "sponsored animals," because they enjoy special status by virtue of their affinity with the deity. Usually a priestess will not eat the sacred animal of a goddess she is devoted to, although traditionally the rules in this regard have been nuanced. The mice in Apollo's temple, for example, were never harmed, but other mice might be eaten. The hare, sacred to the Cailleach, would only be eaten on Beltane. A follower of Cerridwyn would eat pork regularly. In ancient Egypt, killing a cat, sacred to the goddess Bast, was absolutely forbidden.

Often the deity will shapeshift into the form of her sponsored animal. Morrigan likes to shift into ravens, and some would even call this deity a raven goddess, although she is known to take other forms and could be called a shapeshifting goddess. Sometimes the lines between a shapeshifting deity and an animal deity are blurred. The god Pan, however, is clearly a goat god, and Cernunnos is a stag god. Ancient Egyptian deities are mostly animal gods and goddesses, while European deities—especially goddesses—tend to shapeshift or take human form. The goddess is still often pictured with an animal, usually interpreted as her familiar. Perhaps long ago she was the goddess of that animal, and she changed into human form.

An animal familiar is an animal used as a vehicle for magic. The animal can be incarnate or a discarnate spirit animal. The relationship between a familiar and her mistress is a close one, but not all pets or animal companions are familiars: they must be used in magic.

Sometimes an animal deity takes a physical form and becomes a divine living animal. The rare European white stag is considered a divine animal. The white buffalo calf Miracle, born in Wisconsin in the 1990s, was considered by many Native Americans to be divine. The ancient Egyptians were skilled identifiers of divine animals. Their temples often housed a divine animal, such as the temple of the crocodile god Sebek at Crocodilopolis, where the divine crocodile named Petsuchos lived. Other animals might live in the temple of the Egyptian animal god, enjoying special status, but divinity was extended to one animal, or perhaps to one pair.

Pagans sometimes pray to discarnate divine animals, either by the name of the animal god, such as Pan, or (still using goats as an example) by the title Goat God. I once cleared out a cockroach infested apartment by appealing to the Cockroach Goddess. She was an extremely large roach, somewhat scary looking, though she did not threaten me in any way. She reminded me of a hairy overweight hausfrau in a mussy house dress, though she wasn't wearing any clothes. I think it was the strong bitter-almond fragrance that made me think of dirt. She stood motionless, listening without comment to my petition that she move her children to a vacant apartment. By the next day, all the itty bitty roaches had left, but the adults were still scuttling about. I had to call the goddess back a week later and explain that I meant the grownups, too.

Appeals can be made to animal groups as well as individual animals or animal deities. In addressing my cockroach infestation, I could have spoken *en masse* to the cockroaches which were inhabiting the apartment, or I could have directed my comments to all the roaches in the world. If I had been bothered by insects that are highly organized, such as ants, I could have appealed to the ant queen, as head of that particular ant nation.

Mythical beasts, such as dragons, mermaids and unicorns, exist only in the spirit realms. Thousands of these types of animal have been named, and who knows how many more are unknown. While maligned in Christian and Greek mythology, dragons and many other (but not all!) mythical beasts are highly regarded by modern Pagans.

Closely related to mythical beasts are fairy animals, which are animals who live with the fairies, belong to the fairies or behave in a fey manner. Particularly prized by fairies are their herds of white cattle with red ears. At one time, farmers preferred dark cows to white, since the white cow might wander back to the fairyland at milking time. Deer are often considered fairy creatures, since they have a knack for appearing and disappearing at will.

There is another type of animal that should be mentioned here, although it is not a Pagan one. This is the animal archetype, which comes from psychology. An archetype is a well-known image with widely agreed upon characteristics. It is not the same as a deity, although a deity can contain an archetype. The deity is much bigger and more real. For example, the cartoon dog Snoopy is an archetype, but the dog Cerberus, who guards the passage to the underworld, is a deity. Cerberus may belong to that archetypal club of guardians at the gates of death, but Cerberus is not solely an archetype.

Gender is an important human construct, so animal sex may also be significant in magic. Stag, bull and ram can mean something very different than doe, cow and ewe. Conflation of animal sex has caused confusion in magical studies. For horned animals, you would think no mistaken assumptions would be made, but think again. Sheep, goats and cattle have been selectively bred to eradicate horns on females, in order to minimize injuries for humans and animals. Reindeer, which have horns on both sexes, have moved to the far northern reaches of Europe only with the decline of the present Ice Age, and early cave paintings are dated to the time when Europe was much colder. Of course, sometimes sex is unambiguous. An animal drawing may have a penis or a shaggy beard or both. Male and female animals may be drawn together, with the male ruminant larger horned, darker, larger bodied or more muscular. The further back in time you go, the more difficult it is to determine the sex of even a horned animal in religious art.

Erroneous assumptions about sex can have profound influences on our understanding of the ancient sciences. Some believe that Aries, the first sign of the zodiac, was originally a ewe, not a ram. If you think about the cardinal feature of Aries as being the leader, this actually makes more sense, as a flock of sheep is led by one of the senior ewes, not by the ram. Other features ascribed to Aries—head butting, go-it-alone attitude—seem to be taken from the character of the ram. Could the commonly perceived personality of Aries be based partly on an erroneous interpretation of the sex of its symbol?

Wrong beliefs about animal sex, along with the attendant mistaken conclusions, have been made in both directions. In medieval times monastic scholars would demonstrate the plausibility of the Virgin Birth by pointing to the "fact" that vultures are always female. Vulture deities are almost always female in cultures around the world, so the monks' inability to conceive of a male vulture is understandable.

Animals can be understood, categorized and defined in many ways. The understanding of biology and psychology is not exactly wrong, but it is too limited for our purposes. Interacting with the vast menagerie of creatures that inhabit the worlds requires expanding our conceptions, acknowledging our similarities with other animals, and allowing them to teach us their wisdom.

The Pride of King Solomon

Solomon holds a unique place in Western religion. He is revered in all three of the dominant faiths—Judaism, Christianity and Islam—yet many Pagan traditions trace their lineage back to him as well. It would seem that Solomon was the greatest being ever to roam the earth. But was he?

Solomon, the son of David, the King of Israel, enjoyed unparalleled blessings from the creator. He held power over land, air and sea, and over the beasts, birds and fish that resided there. The genii and the demons all performed his bidding. His wealth was legendary, and included not only physical treasures but magical ones too. He was particularly fond of his flying carpet, with its richly embroidered green silk. It covered 360 square miles, when unfurled to its greatest length, yet it could be folded to fit inside a pocket. Solomon liked to ride the swift moving carpet while sitting on his throne surrounded by his army. There is nothing like riding on a magic carpet with an army to make a man feel important.

He was flying over a deep valley one morning, returning from breakfast in Damascus, when he heard a little voice below cry out, "Hide yourselves from the destroying army of Solomon or you will be crushed!" Solomon ordered the wind to move his carpet downward and hold him stationary a few feet above the earth.

"Who called my army a destroying one?" he demanded.

"I did," a thin voice replied.

"And who are you?"

"I am the Ant Queen."

"Why do you malign my army?" Solomon demanded again.

"Where do you come from, Solomon, that a person who asks questions sits above the person who answers them?" Solomon commanded his demon to place the Ant Queen on his carpet in front of him, but this did not satisfy her. "You are still above me on that throne of yours."

Solomon placed the Ant Queen in his hand and held her at eye level. "Now, tell me why you told your subjects to hide."

"I did not want them to be distracted from their glorification of our creator by the spectacle of your presence," she replied.

"I don't see them glorifying anything," said Solomon. "Your ants just look like they're working."

"Work is the purest form of prayer," said the Queen. "Idleness makes one think too much about his own importance."

This talk made Solomon uncomfortable. He had to do some work in governing his country, but his days were spent as much as possible in idle pleasure. "Tell me little Queen, is there anyone anywhere who is as great as I am?"

"There could be thousands and thousands for all I know," said the Queen. "I am just an ant, and I only know of one living soul that is greater."

"And who would that be?"

"That would be me."

"You?!!"

"Solomon, you are holding me in your hand above the earth. If you were greater than me, I would be suspending you in the air." Solomon dropped her on the carpet unceremoniously.

"That doesn't change things," the Ant Queen continued. "One day you will lie in the ground, and I will command my own army to devour you. Solomon, Solomon. Every man succumbs to the ant in the end. Tell me again about your greatness."

Solomon returned the Queen gently to the ground and flew away. It would be nice to say that the meeting changed him totally and completely, but that would not be totally and completely true. To his credit, however, instead of playing with his carpet the next day, the King took out his recording utensils and wrote down the wisdom of the ants.

Musings on the Magical Beast

1) A mouse cult of sorts still exists, with the success of Mickey Mouse and other cartoon mice, as well as the prominence of mice in many children's books. To what do you ascribe the popularity of the mouse today?
2) A creature can be sibling to his mother only if his father and grandfather are the same. But Diana was "the first created before all of creation." How can Lucifer be her son and brother?
3) In Germanic belief, the soul of a dead person leaves the body through the mouth, in the shape of a mouse. A mouse also leaves the mouth of the priestess while she lies immobilized in trance. Can you explain why the soul traveling to the land of the dead would take a mouse form?
4) What are some of the ways humans are the same as other mammals? Other non-mammals?
5) Here is an exercise for those who know a little about astrology. Go through the zodiac and reverse gender for the symbol of each sign. How does your interpretation change?

a. How do you see Aries, when symbolized by the ewe?
b. If the moon-and-horns symbol of Taurus stands for Hathor, the cow-goddess, what characteristics does Taurus have?
c. What if the Gemini twins are boy-and-girl, not two boys?
d. Does the crab for Cancer have an implied gender?
e. What if Leo is a lioness who hunts for the pride?
f. What if Virgo is not the grain goddess, but the dying god of the grain?
g. What if the scales of Libra are held not by a graceful woman, but by a bearded hierophant?
h. What if Scorpio is a mother scorpion with babies on her back?
i. What if Sagittarius is not the Centaur but the horse goddess Epona?

j. What if Capricorn is a nanny goat, with floppy ears and udders swinging with milk?
k. What if Aquarius is a village woman returning from the well, the large urn on her head mirroring her full figure?
l. Fish are often associated with goddesses, since their scent is evocative of the vagina, but the god Dylan was a fish and Gwion assumed a fish form as he fled from Cerridwyn. What gender would you ascribe, if any, to the fish sign? How does this affect your interpretation of Pisces?

6) Medieval monks may not have known about the male vulture, but presumably every culture with domestic felines has known about the tomcat. Why do you think the domestic cat is commonly referred to as "she"?
7) In the north of Scotland, giants keep their own herds of deer. How would you categorize these animals?
8) Draw a line linking these animals with their magical category.

A carefully selected kitten pampered in a temple dedicated to Bast	animal deity
A dolphin in a painting of Aphrodite	familiar
The winged beaked lion known as a griffin	divine animal
A toad who lives with a witch and does magic for her	sponsored/beloved
A wild white hare who stands and speaks to a human in words	mythical beast
The Sumerian Ninsun, whose name means Lady Wild Cow	fairy animal

Chapter 4

Creatures of the Dream World

O forest beauty, 'forest gold'! thou splendid creature of the woods, go circling round the cattle ground, steal past the pasturage of cows, avoid the clanging of the bells and flee from the shepherd's voice.
—Charm protecting livestock from bears, from *Magic Songs of the West Finns* by John Abercromby[4]

Bear Dance

The bear surprised me.

Usually rodents guide me in the space between the worlds. Sometimes bugs or birds appear the gentle kind. I would not be surprised by any reptile. But not bears. Bears have puzzled me by their relative absence in my inner landscape, because I've known so many people who were bear crazy. You never hear anyone bragging about their ant or gopher medicine, but bear people are passionate about their affiliation.

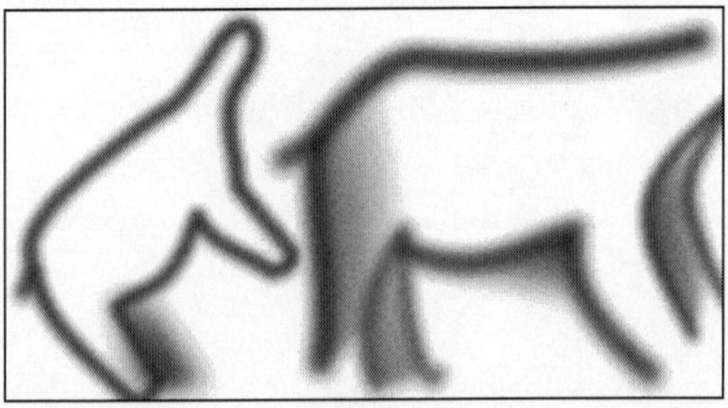

Bear mother and cub rock carving. Ekain Cave, Spain. 14,000 BCE.

For many people, bears carry warm fuzzy memories of childhood and their favorite toy. President Theodore Roosevelt started the teddy bear craze by refusing to shoot a cub under what he considered unsportsmanlike circumstances, an incident that made an impression on journalists of the day. The teddy bear was initially pandered to exploit Roosevelt's popularity, but today the teddy is loved even by people who hate politics. I admit that I have a teddy myself that I've carted around for years.

This teddy came in a curious way. It was a stormy night, and I was living alone in an isolated cottage. I opened the door to find an acquaintance standing in the pouring rain. He pushed past me to get out of the wet and proceeded to my table with a brown package. Inside the package was a teddy bear that he ripped open, pulling out a mess of cash instead of stuffing. He began counting money into piles. There are many speculations I could have made about this unexpected development, but under the circumstances I decided not to ask questions. My acquaintance gave the teddy to my cat and handed me forty dollars as he left, so I "wouldn't feel left out." "I didn't do anything, did I?" I asked. For some reason he thought this was hilarious. "No," he assured me, "you didn't do anything."

Bears excite fear as well as affection. I'm often warned against going into the woods alone because of bears, a warning that annoys me. I'm skeptical because I believe bear warnings are used to scare girls. My skepticism was especially high the time I bumped into a group of mountain bikers on the trail and the last of the six told me, "Watch out, there's a bear back there." Uh-huh, I thought. Half a dozen bikers have torn through the trail, and there's still a bear back there, hoping to steal a bicycle. Most men are accepting and even encouraging of women who take an interest in nature sports, but there is the occasional male who views this as an encroachment on manly turf. Anyway, I'm not easily rebuffed, so I continued on my way until, a half mile further, darned if there wasn't a Black Bear, just sitting on the path.

By the bear's posture, I guessed she knew I was coming.

They're pretty nearsighted, but she could hear or smell me, and she was probably waiting for a closer look. Curiosity is the most typical reaction in a bear-human encounter.

Black Bear. Photo Steve Maslowski, U.S. Fish and Wildlife Service.

I'm not going to quote the nature channel too liberally in this section because years of living in bear country has taught me that nobody really knows bears. They're supposed to go to bed at night, but don't believe it. They're supposed to go berserk if anyone approaches their cubs, but mama bears actually send cubs into human camps to forage. They're supposed to hibernate in winter, but bear footprints in snow are incontrovertible evidence of sleepwalking (or hibernate-walking).

I could say bears are unpredictable, but that would be hypocritical, because so are we. Humans and bears are similar in so many ways. There is a theory that the reason cougars shy from humans in deep wilderness is that they suspect we might be a type of bear. Possibly due to our bipedal stance. Bears sit on their heinie the way we do. They have similar feet. I know this because the partial skeleton of a cub was found on a playground not far from where I live, and the village got in a titter for a day until the bush league forensic specialist ruled that it was not a child.

In the twenty-first century, bear and human interactions have become adversarial. Only a hundred years ago, if a Black Bear stumbled on a homestead, lured by the smell of food, this was a piece of good fortune: a bearskin rug, bear grease for household ingredients and a plethora of meat to share or trade. Not anymore. Bears don't stumble on campgrounds, they live there. They want backpacks, they want coolers, they want trash cans, and they know how to execute a heist. The trick of hoisting food on a rope between trees doesn't work anymore. The first generation of bear-proof canisters was a flop, although the current ones seem to be working. Bears are smart. They're strategic and adaptable, changing their methods quickly to meet new technology.

Yogi Bear in many ways exemplifies the bear fascination with junk food. Yogi's shenanigans strike an endearing chord because they're so human. Only a bear could be as human as Yogi. He's always scheming for stuff he shouldn't have. He has brilliant ideas that turn out to be not-so-smart when they're executed. He's definitely got brains, just not as many as he originally thought. Yogi is the cartoon animal who behaves most like a person in his unwarranted self-confidence and his logical non-logic.

But Yogi is a bear archetype, not the real bear deity who appears in the guided meditation. This bear comes only to help, never to rob. The bear that surprised me in meditation had a mature, maternal air about her.

"I came because you've been frightened lately, and my size is reassuring to you," said the bear.

I explained that I was trying to figure out where I could lead an important ritual. I was worried about taking tenderfoots to a wilderness setting where they might get hurt.

"Didn't you see the sign I left you?" she asked.

The sign ... The sign ... Oh, yes. I remembered.

I was hiking with my blueberry basket one morning and got up top before anyone else, or at least before any human. The views from this mountain are stunning, but on this particular morning the most conspicuous landmark was a big pile of bear poop perched on the summit. Had this bear decided she wanted some nice scenery while she squatted? Soon a ranger on patrol joined me and we giggled together. "I guess this solves the question of where they go," he said. "They go anywhere they damn please!"

As I headed down the mountain I passed a tourist family and was amused to hear their disgusted squeals of "eeewww!" from the summit.

That was a sign?

"That mountain is too popular with tourists," I objected. "And it's too treacherous for a group to navigate after dark."

"Go early in the morning," the bear explained patiently. I suddenly understood that the bear had come because I needed to bend on this issue and adapt to the circumstances.

My metaphysical bear-poop encounter reminded me to heed my own experience. Before this reminder, if anyone asked me to explain the magical significance of the bear, my reflexive response would have been to list the traditional associations.

The bear is associated with motherhood and protection and is a special animal to Artemis. This goddess had a bear sanctuary in Crete, inside a cave with a stalagmite shaped like a bear. This shrine was re-dedicated to the Virgin Mary as "Our Lady of the Bear."

Artemis also had a bear temple complex at the coastal city of Brauron, near Athens. It was dedicated to preparing young girls for the festival of Brauronia, held every four years. The girls

Natural bear stalagmite. Shrine of Our Lady of the Bear. Arkoudospilios Cave, Crete. Photo Wolfgang Sauber/Wikimedia Commons.

performed bear dances, ran footraces and offered gifts to Artemis in this pre-menarche rite of passage. Bear masks, saffron robes and ritual nudity were important aspects of the ceremonies. The complex at Brauron included a spring, an older pre-Hellenic temple site, a shrine to Iphigenia and a small cave that had collapsed by Classical times. A wide variety of offerings have been recovered from the spring, including mirrors, vases, spindle whorls, toys, jewelry boxes and statuettes of children of both sexes. The clothing of women who died in childbirth was brought to Brauron, and women who were pregnant or who had recently given birth brought offerings.

Artemis became merged with an Arcadian bear goddess the Greeks called Callisto. This goddess shares Artemis' function as midwife and mistress of the wild. Callisto is associated with the bear constellation Ursa Major, where she was banished after losing her skirmishes with the Olympians.

In Finnish mythology the first bear came from Ursa Major, rather than being banished there. She was created by the forest goddess and protector of animals, Mielikki. The bear is a sacred animal in Finnish Paganism, and there are circumscriptions

Ursa Major constellation. Drawing Sidney Hall, 1825. Library of Congress.

around naming (and sometimes even drawing) this creature.

Inscriptions to the Celtic bear goddess Artio have been found in Germany and Switzerland. A charming second century statue of Artio being offered fruit by her priestess shows a graceful side to this goddess. Switzerland is home to tantalizing evidence of a Neanderthal Cave Bear cult: a cave filled with carefully arranged Cave Bear skulls. Bear worship has evidently been part of this region for a long time.

Thousands of years later, German settlers brought a curious vestige of bear worship to the United States. Settlers believed that a bear would appear at Candlemass, February 2nd, to inform farmers of weather patterns for the remainder of the winter. As forest was cleared in eastern Pennsylvania for farming, no bears remained, so the honorary role was transferred to the groundhog, another animal which stands on two legs and a sacred animal to the Lenape Indians of the area. The biggest

Lady feeding fruit to bear. Base is inscribed to the goddess Artio. Bern, Switzerland, second century CE. Photo (adapted) Sanstein/Wikimedia Commons.

hitch in transferring allegiance to the groundhog was that the groundhog is a true hibernator, not awakening at intervals in late winter like the bear. An animal had to be captured in the fall and prodded awake on the designated day to obtain the forecast.

For the Native American Ojibwe people, the bear is associated with community protection and information about the medicinal uses of plants. Bears, remember are mostly vegetarian.

There is a plethora of legend, history and tradition about the bear, yet in magic personal experience trumps all. For me, the bear is a furry black shadow, a rival and a worthy opponent. She is almost as smart as I am, and much more determined. She is about thievery and mysterious unreportable events with criminal overtones. She is about humor that is indecent or macabre. She is not a predator, but she requires attention nonetheless.

These are my associations; I don't offer them as universal truths. By pooping at the sacred mountaintop, the bear taught me the importance of giving credence to my observations rather than automatically deferring to tradition. As you continue this guidebook, remember that the information presented here is meant to supplement your experience, never to replace it.

A Priestess for Artemis

Iphigenia means "mother of strong children" and is probably an early name for Artemis or another bear goddess who became merged with Artemis. It later became an honorary title for her priestess. There are conflicting versions to the following story, but this much is not in dispute: The hero Agamemnon, leading an offensive against Troy, made little headway with his fleet due to unfavorable winds sent by Artemis, whom Agamemnon had offended. After consulting an oracle, Agamemnon offered Artemis his eldest daughter Iphigenia, thus earning the implacable wrath of his wife, Clytemnestra.

King Agamemnon of Mycenae was on the wrong side of Artemis from the start. His father had failed to honor a vow that he would sacrifice a prized lamb to the Huntress, and there is no record that the son felt an obligation to make good the pledge. Agamemnon, so capable in manly pursuits, once slew a white stag with a single arrow and boasted that Artemis could do no better. So true this boast: the beast was a member of the Virgin's chariot team, and she would never have slain it.

When Queen Helen ran away with the Trojan prince Paris, Agamemnon took command of the retaliatory mission. Here was a chance to lead a great coalition and gain heroic stature. So much more the pleasure of Artemis, whose sympathies were inclined toward the Trojans, in thwarting Agamemnon's plans. As the fleet readied to embark, an unfavorable northeast wind stranded them in the harbor of Aulis for weeks. Some say the goddess was miffed over the killing of a hare and cursed the whole expedition. Impatient to sail and bewildered by the persistent bad wind, Agamemnon called for an oracle. A chicken was gutted and the seer declared Artemis must be coaxed with a sacrifice of Agamemnon's oldest daughter.

At first Agamemnon demurred. His wife would never surrender the girl, he protested. The military cohorts devised a scheme: send a messenger to the mother explaining that the demigod and prince Achilles wished to marry the princess, and she must come at once.

Clytemnestra, whose ambitions were wholly channeled in securing an advantageous match for her beautiful daughter, hastened to Aulis with Iphigenia, where a comedy of errors—or perhaps a tragedy of errors—awaited them. Agamemnon's secret letter to Clytemnestra exposing the ruse had been intercepted, and the strong-willed matron arrived against her husband's expectations demanding a marriage contract. Achilles, innocent and uninformed of the subterfuge (and married to someone else besides), was protesting there had been a mistake. Priests were completing preparations for Iphigenia's dedication. The bamboozled daughter was balking at the plan, and her mother began begging Agamemnon and then threatening him. Surely there was a face-saving way out of the mess, by declaring Achilles an unknowing partner to deception if nothing else, but the fact remained that ships were stuck in harbor and men were itching for war.

Iphigenia, realizing her father's ambitions and her country's future revolved around her, finally stepped forward and declared she would go to Artemis. Iphigenia was as loyal, devoted and obedient as she was beautiful. Or maybe filial duty and patriotism were just a piece of it, and Artemis herself seduced the girl. Perhaps Artemis promised her adventure in a far flung country. She could be mistress of a great temple. The possessions of rich ladies who died in childbirth were sent to this temple, and Iphigenia's beauty could be displayed against the finest fabrics and jewels.

Iphigenia's acquiescence stirred a whirlwind. At the altar of Artemis the priests raised their knives to slit the girl's throat, but at the last moment a bear cub was switched in her stead, and Iphigenia was swept on a red cloud to the land of Tauris. The same wind that whisked the new priestess filled the sails of the Greek fleet, and they were off to conquer Troy.

In offering Artemis the coveted maiden, Agamemnon was given the favorable wind he requested, but the act never improved the disposition of the goddess toward him. Later she abandoned him to the wrath of Clytemnestra.

It would be inaccurate to say the sacrifice of Iphigenia turned Clytemnestra away from her husband, for he had earned her hatred long ago. There comes a point, however, where dislike becomes disloyalty, and the proud mother had envisioned a greater future for her daughter than being exiled in a remote temple wearing dead women's clothes. That the victorious Agamemnon returned from the war to be trapped in his wife's net should surprise no one.

Iphigenia did not learn of her father's fate for many years, until her brother Orestes was cast ashore at her temple under mysterious circumstances. As high priestess, Iphigenia presided over the slaying of refugees at the altar of Artemis, and during the pre-ceremonial interview learned of his identity.

What was Orestes doing in Tauris? Orestes admitted he was running from the horror of his actions. He had killed Clytemnestra, with Apollo's approval, to avenge her murder of their father. After the filthy deed, Orestes was called to account before the Olympians, where Apollo spoke in his defense. The gods quarreled over his fate along political lines until the goddess Athena cast a vote with Apollo, tipping the verdict in Orestes' favor.

An acquittal won through a brilliant defender and a stacked jury does not automatically erase the pangs of conscience, however, and Orestes had committed a horrendous deed. The Furies, sister deities who rule the conscience, tormented him for his crime until, driven to the edges of insanity, he consulted an oracle for a remedy. The oracle instructed him to steal the sacred statue of Artemis at Tauris and carry it to Brauron, where he was to build a new temple to the goddess. If he was unable to carry out this feat, Orestes declared, he might at as well die in Tauris;

Orestes consulting the oracle. Notice the snakes on the priestess hovering above the tripod. Photo Marie-Lan Nguyen/Wikimedia Commons.

he could not go on living with this torment.

Surprisingly, Iphigenia decided to help her brother. She had grown tired of her exile and longed for the customs, faces and clothing styles of her native country. She told the Taurian king that Orestes and his companion were polluted by matricide and must be cleansed before sacrifice. That much was true; Orestes was not fit to have his throat slit on the altar of Artemis. She further told the leaders of her host country that she was borrowing the statue of the goddess for the purification rites. Iphigenia was certainly the double-crossing daughter of

Agamemnon.

Miraculously, with much adventure and intercession of the gods, the brother and sister eventually reached the ancient shrine in Brauron. A new temple was built, with the sacred image installed therein, and Iphigenia was named high priestess of the complex.

The presence of an important temple to Artemis so close to the city was an honor that made the Athenians nervous, as the wrath of Artemis had already sparked so many misadventures. Every family that could spare a daughter for a year sent the girl to Brauron to attend the goddess and learn the Brauronia ritual. The girls were called little bears and charmed the goddess with their dances. In this way, Artemis extended her healing side to Athens, protecting against plagues and enhancing the survival of infants and their mothers.

Birth of the Honey-Paw

Mielikki is the forest mistress of Finland, creator and keeper of animals. Like so many woodland goddesses, Mielikki is a hunting goddess. Though Mielikki created all the animals, the bear is undeniably her favorite. This is my own version of the myth, styled after traditional Finnish poetry.

The forest mother Mielikki thought of making a great fur creature. The mistress of the flaxen hair wanted a great fur creature, a strong beast standing on two legs.

The bright maiden with the golden buckle drifted through the heavens in her yellow sandals. The clever Mielikki wandered across the sky with the thought of creating a noble beast, a creature standing on two legs.

In her purple stockings, Mielikki ambled past the little red clouds. With golden bangles on her wrists and on her neck, the bright one journeyed into the country of the moon.

From the ether Mielikki gathered wool for her treasure box. From the border of the sky the mother gathered soft hair for her golden purse.

At the constellation of the great animal Mielikki opened her box of wool. On the shoulders of the sky creature the mistress opened her purse of soft hair.

The wool she scattered on the ocean to be washed along the beach. From her vantage in the heavens Mielikki cast hair and wool upon the rivers.

The forest maiden walked the earth gathering fragments of wool and hair. Mielikki wove hair and wool that she gathered along riverbank and seashore.

The resourceful maiden placed the furry bundle in her birch basket and roped it with magic cords. With golden chains the mistress bound her furry bundle to her woven spell basket.

In the upper branches of the pine tree the basket was tied secure. In the highest realms of the tallest pine the bundle of fur was safely sheltered.

Nurtured with pollen and honey the fur baby grew and prospered. Suckled in sweetness, blessed with golden pollen, Mielikki's fur child grew large and strong.

At last full grown, Mielikki's beloved stood before her on two legs. The great brown creature moved gracefully and rose before the mistress of the woods.

Mielikki saw that her work was almost done. Mielikki's work would be done when she endowed her child with teeth and claws, the gifts of all furred creatures.

Mielikki hesitated here, for was it safe? The wise mother wondered if so large a creature should be trusted with teeth and claws.

The mistress brought her honeyed fur beast to the sky father Ukko. Mielikki made the fur child stand before the one who splits sky nails, whom all creatures hold in terror.

Mielikki commanded the beast to kneel before Ukko. The good mother made her child swear before the sky father, made him swear he would not use his teeth or claws for evil.

Trembling before the sky father, the creature took his oath. The giant furred one swore before the splitting thunder that he would not use his teeth or claws for evil.

Satisfied, Mielikki took pine bark and branches for teeth and claws. The clever mistress fashioned solid teeth from bark and curving claws from branches for her honey-paws.

So endowed, the fur beast wanders the woods and marshes. The magnificent honey creature lumbers through the forests and meadows of his bright mother.

Mielikki you have made a lovely creature. Golden mother, the grace and strength of your honey child speaks of your power.

Great fur child of Mielikki, remember your oath to Ukko. Remember by the sound of thunder how you swore never to do evil, how you swore to use your teeth and claws only for good.

Bear Review

Magical Qualities:
curious, intelligent, hibernating, adaptable, likes honey, climbs trees, dens in caves, females protective of young, fierce when threatened, stands on two legs, physique vaguely human-like, varied plant diet

Magical Applications:
protection, problem-solving, abundance, healing (all kinds, but especially infectious diseases, gynecological problems, diseases of early childhood, safe delivery), divination

Other Associations:
motherhood, sisterhood, sweetness, meditation, nurturance

The Animal Guided Meditation—part one

Many priestesses have enlightening experiences through animal guided meditation, also called trance meditation, trance journeying or shamanic journeying. In this meditation an animal helper appears to lead and protect the priestess as she travels beyond physical reality to obtain wisdom.

Before beginning your animal guided meditation, consider your intent. Do you have a specific place you want to go, an animal you want to meet or an issue you need help with?

Plan your meditation for when you can relax. Feeling expectant is okay, maybe a little excited, but you must not be too angry or frightened. You do not need to quiet your mind or still your mind or empty your mind. Just forget about your mind. In the unlikely event that you feel uncomfortable during the meditation, open your eyes, sit up and stop the music. Touch the floor and breathe until you feel calm. If you are seriously depressed you may (or may not) project negative thoughts into the experience. If this happens, wait until you are feeling better to try again, and consider practicing the meditation with someone else. If you have a psychotic disorder or have had transient psychotic symptoms in the past, seek the support of a therapist before doing your animal meditations and stay with the structured voice meditations. Visualizations that turn frightening or hostile are a sign of self-projection.

The amount of light in the room is an individual preference. I like to have a small amount, such as a candle or nightlight. Daytime or nighttime meditation is possible, although many find it easiest after sunset.

Most people choose to lie on their back, but you can sit in a chair or cross-legged on the floor if this is more comfortable. Choose a place and a time where you will not be interrupted in a jarring way. Turn off or muffle the phone. Even more important than noise is the issue of touching. Being touched unexpectedly when you are in this type of meditation is traumatic, so you must take adequate precautions. Have someone guard your body, or remove animals from the room and close the door. Alert people you live with that you need to be approached gently if it is necessary to interrupt you.

Once my cat Samhain jumped on me while I was in meditation. I'm still surprised she did this, because Samhain is an exceedingly polite cat who waits patiently for an invitation before she even hops on a lap. I believe she was confused by my trance state and looking for reassurance that I was all right. I survived the interruption, but it was days before I felt like myself again. Bach Rescue Remedy, a homeopathic concoction available at health food stores, helped immensely.

A voice guided animal meditation is available for download at www.invokinganimalmagic.com. The degree of structure needed varies greatly with the individual. A clear intent and a single monotonous drumbeat may be enough. Drumming is only one option. You can listen to any pleasant repetitive sound, such as a noise machine. You can also listen to soft, uncomplicated instrumental music. You can even sit in a quiet room and simply close your eyes. The animal meditation is "guided" even if you are not listening to a human narration—you are being guided by your animal ally.

Start your meditation with a prayer for openness, safety and guidance. Next begin the audio or the drumming. Close your eyes and breathe normally. When you are relaxed and ready, an animal guide will appear and you will travel together to a place where you will receive knowledge. How and where you travel matters only in the context of the meditation. You may go down into the ground. You may also go up or forward. You may travel by land, air or water. You may walk, fly, swim, ride a horse or paddle a canoe.

The meditation must be given an outside time limit, ordinarily no more than thirty minutes. Otherwise there is a possibility of staying under too long and feeling tired or out of sorts when you are finished. The soundtrack you are listening to is a natural cue to come back. Otherwise, you will need a timer.

When you open your eyes, move slowly and gently reintegrate with your surroundings. Thank your spirit guides for their wisdom and protection. Remember to give yourself time and space to become readjusted to your everyday world.

A meditation with animal guides is an intimate and unique interaction that can be joyful, whimsical, poignant, reassuring, cathartic, revealing or surprising. It can bring clarity or provoke new questions. It is the only direct contact a priestess will ever have with certain animals. It is a way of receiving wisdom beyond the limits of everyday life.

The Fish King

This tale is from Brittany, but in Nordic as well as Celtic belief the afterlife of those who die at sea is in the watery depths. It is a beautiful place, filled with every luxury imaginable. A few people have been lucky enough to travel to this world while still alive and return to tell the tale.

The old fisherman was poor, but wise and experienced in the ways of the sea. When the small fish spoke from inside his net, he did not display alarm but listened carefully. The puny fish claimed to be the King of the Fishes, and he promised to send a net-load of fish everyday if granted freedom. The fisherman accepted the deal and returned the fairy fish to the ocean.

The Fish King remained true to his word, filling the nets daily without fail. Yet one day it looked as if the King would be released from his pledge, for a frightening storm arose, capsizing the fisherman's boat under wild seas. But the fisherman did not drown, because the Fish King swam up to him with a magic flask. Holding the flask to the man's lips with his fairy fish fins, the King imparted a drought that would make the fisherman's lungs function perfectly under water.

The fisherman accompanied the Fish King to his underwater home, a large castle of shimmering beauty. The halls were paved in gold, and there were gemstones piled in every room. The fisherman grabbed what riches would fit in his pocket, and the king did not rebuke him, but gave him a fat gold purse to hold his wealth.

The fisherman wanted to stay with the rich fish in the underwater castle, but he worried about his wife and children. If he did not return, they would think he had come to harm. The Fish King obliged the fisherman's request to return home by summoning an immense tuna. The tuna flattened her back so the fisherman could climb astride, clinging to the giant fin. In this way the fisherman was conducted from the watery depths to the shore of his village. He felt sad to leave his interesting new friends, but the fairy tuna assured him that he could return to the Fish King's castle whenever he chose.

Musings with an Animal Guide

1) Write your own bear story here. What does your experience teach you about the bear?
2) The Finns say the bear was created from the sky and the Greeks say the bear goddess lives there now. What magical quality does the link with the sky give the bear?
3) Honey-glazed Bear Claws

For ritual offering or just for fun. Contains all of Honey-paws' favorite foods. For ecological reasons, ritual offerings are no longer eaten by incarnate beings—the next day the bear's piece goes into a bear proof compost pile or the trash.

1 cup water
1 ½ cups sucanat
3 tablespoons mild tasting oil (canola, safflower or ghee)
½ teaspoon salt
1 ½ teaspoons baking yeast
3 ½ cups whole wheat pastry flour
4 apples, diced
¾ cup dried blueberries
1 ¼ cup sliced almonds
1 tablespoon lemon juice
2 teaspoons arrowroot dissolved in 2 tablespoons water
2 tablespoons carob
2 tablespoons honey (or brown rice syrup)
2 tablespoons Earth Balance margarine

Combine flour, water, oil, ½ cup sucanat, salt and yeast in bread maker on "dough" setting. (If you don't have a bread maker, mix ingredients together, knead for ten minutes and let rise for 1 ½ hours. Add flour if dough is too sticky.)

While dough is rising, combine apples, blueberries, 1 cup

sucanat and lemon juice in a small pan. Heat on the stovetop at low temperature until apples soften. Turn heat to medium, add arrowroot and stir until thickened. Allow to cool uncovered for at least half an hour.

When dough is finished, turn out on floured surface and shape into 9 inch by 18 inch rectangle. Dough should be stiff and easy to work; if too sticky, add more flour. Spread apple mixture evenly over dough, then sprinkle almonds over surface. Fold dough about 2/3 of the way over along the long side. Fold dough in half again from the other side so that the dough is one long 18 inch strip. Pinch ends to seal. Cut the dough into 8 sections. To make claws on these eight paws, cut three incisions about 2 inches long on one of the uncut sides of each paw. Bake on greased cookie sheet at 400 degrees for about 20 minutes.

For glaze, melt margarine in small pan over low heat. Remove from heat and add honey and carob. Let bear claws cool 30 minutes. Place a dab of carob mixture on each bear claw.

4) So you won't feel too silly about it, have a little girl help you do a bear dance. This is an all female ritual that can be done indoors or out. Get some sweets together for a bear offering. Start with bear noises—snuffling, snorting, growling, grunting, squealing, howling, roaring, cooing, moaning, etc. Roll over in the grass. Walk and lumber like a bear. Pretend to be clawing trees or walls. Bears like to rub their back on things. When you're warmed up, each of you call to the bear goddess, asking her to dance with you. Your dance can be to music, drumming or the sound of your own bear noises. When you're tired of dancing, hold hands and jump up and down together making bear noises, then raise your arms straight up and yell. Ground the energy by putting your front paws on the floor or grass and grunting quietly for a moment. Let the little girl raise the offering plate, inviting the goddess and her bear friends to partake. All bear dancers get a treat.

For this ritual you need:

Girl companions
Space to dance
A sweet offering

5) Let's do a guided animal meditation. Go to www.invokinganimalmagic.com and download the Bear Meditation audio. You will need a notebook and pen close by you. Wear comfortable, loose clothing that allows you to breathe deeply.

Begin by establishing yourself in sacred space. If you know how to cast a circle, you can do so. Call upon a special deity or protector. This could be a goddess, a god, an angel or a nature spirit. Explain that you are about to begin a guided meditation and ask your protector to keep you safe. Pray for openness to receive and understand the lesson. Lie down on the floor with a blanket covering you or nearby in case you get cold.

Now turn on the audio meditation and follow instructions.

At the end of the meditation, sit up and turn off the audio. Thank your protector for watching over you. Remember to open the circle if you cast one.

Write down what you just experienced. Include feelings and thoughts that occurred during the meditation.

Chapter 5

Creatures of the Night

It was the owl that shriek'd, the fatal bellman,
Which gives the stern'st good-night.
—William Shakespeare, *MacBeth*

Owlingkraft

Hiking the Sunrise Trail at Midsummer, I had the woods completely to myself. The trail led up a moderate peak to a view of a larger, more interesting mountain across a ravine. I knew a steady stream of people would be climbing the tougher peak that day, and this puzzled me, because you can't view the mountain as a whole when you're standing on it. Perhaps this is not a very deep question, but I was entertaining it, when a barred owl swooped over my head and flew between the trees in front of me. The barred owl (also known as the "hoot owl") is the most beautiful of owls, mostly white with brown stripes. We think of owls as nighttime birds, and they are, but in northern climes when the nights are short the barred owl will hunt during the day. This owl appeared to remind me that I can question her when I'm confused or need information—a timely reminder, since there were more pressing issues where I needed counsel.

Barred Owl.

Western traditions regard the owl with ambivalence. She is a repository of wisdom, but a harbinger of death or other unwelcome news. Not only Shakespeare, but Spenser and Chaucer describe the owl as presager of doom, making the verdict of the English literary giants unanimous. Yet the owl only goes visiting if the messages are unclaimed. When the situation becomes dicey enough for her to hunt down the recipient, can she be blamed if the news is dire?

Distinctive in tone, varied in repertoire, hidden under cover of night, owl talk strikes the listener as steeped in significance. In talking to their own kind, owls can be establishing territory, courting, migrating, defending themselves or calling for mother. But of course we know they are mostly talking to us. Not only do owls carry messages, they carry secrets. Spells from archaic Roman and English sources use the owl to pry secrets from a sleeping victim. The owl is an emblem, by admission or reputation, of various secret societies, including the Masons, the Bohemian Grove and the Illuminati. On the corner of the one dollar bill there is a minute figure that *could* be an owl, which people who subscribe to conspiracy theories attribute to an occult fraternity among the Founding Fathers.

The owl's most conspicuous feature is her large eyes, which give the impression of seeing everything. Most birds, including other birds of prey, obtain a field of vision approaching 360 degrees by having eyes located on either side of the head. The owl's forward facing eyes give her excellent depth perception—important for seeing in low light—and make her appear more human. Her flexible neck allows her to turn her face to the rear. She needs large eyes and wide head movements because her eyes are fixed and cannot move, hence the staring that unnerves some people. Her immovable eyes seem supremely confident and all-knowing. Since the owl sees so clearly into the night, she is credited with the comprehension of death, evil, uncomfortable truths, disquieting outcomes and everything else we place in the rubric of "shadow."

In Italian witchcraft the owl is protection against the evil eye. The Italian word for witch, *strega*, comes from the Latin *strix*, for owl. The Romans regarded the owl in a fairly negative light, as a

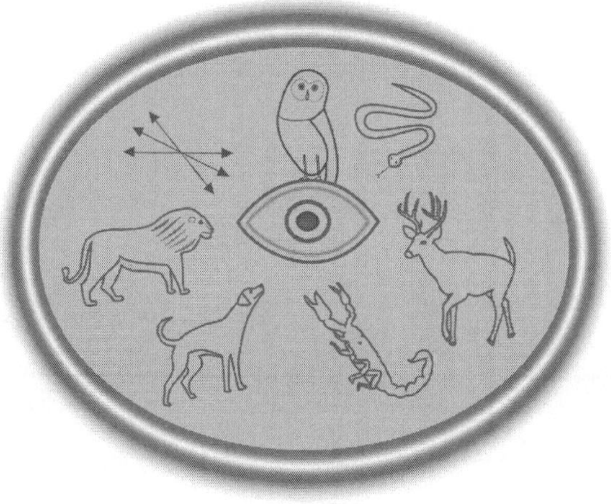

Re-creation of an amulet appearing in Frederick Thomas Elworthy's *The Evil Eye.*

bringer of all kinds of disaster. She was identified with death and wild places, and her visits to cities or ventures into daylight boded ill. The owl is linked, however, with the Roman goddess

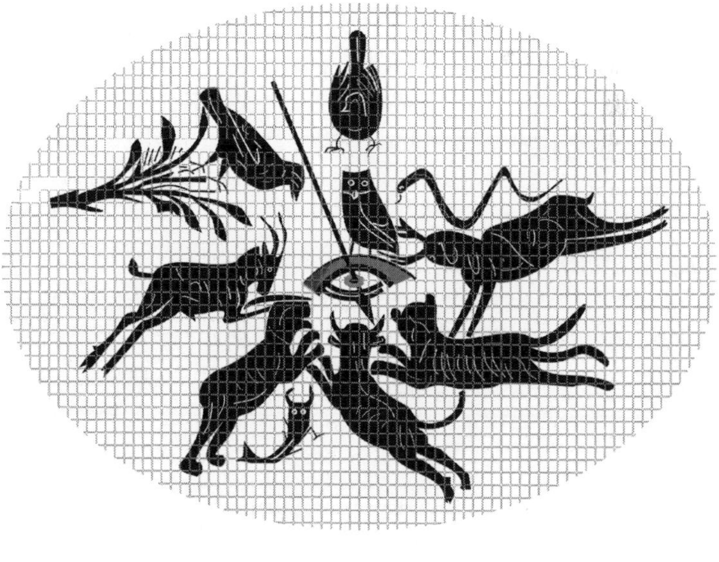

Roman mosaic of owl standing on eye with spear.

of wisdom, Minerva, and her Etruscan forerunner, Menrva. Whether the owl association is intrinsic or a result of her conflation with the Greek goddess Athena is unclear.

Athena was introduced in the first chapter as a snake goddess, but she's also an owl goddess. Bird and snake goddess combinations are common, and archeologist Marija Gimbutas maintains that it is impossible to talk about the snake goddess without the bird goddess. Athena is often pictured with a "screech owl" in her right hand. European and American versions of this owl are classed under different names, but both are small owls with head tufts that look like cat ears. The Eurasian scops owl has a short musical call that may account for Athena's invention of the flute. The screech owls of North America have a repertoire of complex high-pitched trills that many people find spooky. Another name for the American screech owl is "ghost owl."

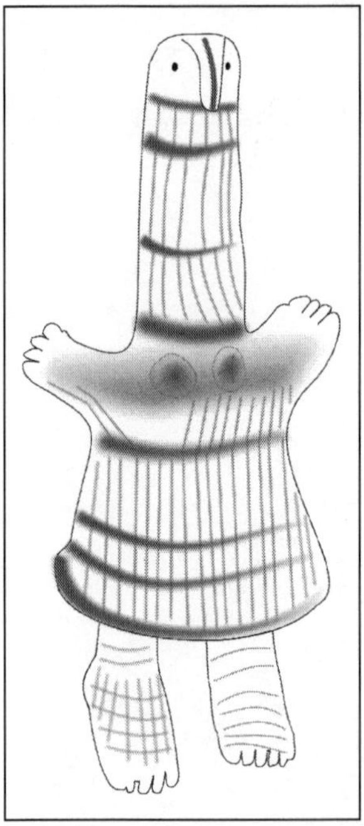

Owl/snake goddess. Boeotia, Greece, seventh century, BCE.

Owls were encouraged to nest in Athena's temple in Athens, where they lived in large numbers. One of Athena's mystery cults was an owl society that persisted into Greco-Roman times. Participants imitated owl voices, dressed in owl costumes and performed owl dances. They also caught scops owls while dressed in owl disguises.

Athena is portrayed in battle with an owl beside her. Greek military forces saw the owl as an omen of victory, unlike the Romans, who saw the owl as a sign of defeat. This difference of opinion was probably convenient if an owl appeared when the Greeks and

Romans were fighting each other, since it allowed them to agree on who was winning.

As patron of the city most identified with democracy, Athena remains emblematic of elected government, and her figure appears on the buildings, seals and coinage of republics around the world. It is therefore fitting that a group of owls is called a "parliament." The word actually derives from a Latin verb meaning "to talk," but this is also appropriate, since owls do a lot of talking.

Coin showing Athena's head on one side and owl with olive sprig on the other. Athens, sixth century BCE. Photo Ancient Art.

Owls also do a lot of listening. Their hearing is the most acute of any bird, and they rely on sound as much as sight to locate prey. In winter the great horned owl will hunt entirely by sound, listening for the scampering of rodents under many inches of snow. Owl ears are concealed—the tufts on the head are for camouflage—and feathers on the face are arranged to help channel sound. Ears are asymmetrical for specialized hearing that pinpoints the exact location of sounds. Owls spend most of their time sitting and listening, locating prey or identifying predators. In the daytime they are readily flushed and so give the impression of perpetual alertness. Hidden in the tree branches, perfectly still, do they ever sleep or is their time of repose a meditation?

The owl can hear everything, but she herself chooses when to be heard. The noiseless flight of an owl seems to come from a vacuum, a product of wing feathers designed to discourage turbulence. The result is a silent motion deadly to rodents and unsettling even to humans. The owl is an ambusher, a deceiver, a stalker, a perfect spy. The characterization of the owl as trickster caused the Mesopotamian and Hebrew goddess Lilith, the defiant queen of desolation, to assume owl form when she entered European culture. In Mesopotamian religion, Lilith is a wind goddess, associated with untamed places and behaviors, probably not associated with owls. Lilith in early Judaism is a demon spirit, a disobedient woman or an inhabitant of deserted places—similar to the Mesopotamian figure. As an owl goddess Lilith developed a reputation as a baby snatcher. Her preferred strategy involved strangling seemingly healthy newborns in their beds as they slept, a phenomenon which sounds suspiciously like the syndrome now known as "crib death."

Accused witch with owl familiar. Detail of seventeenth century woodcut.

The owl was probably suspected of clutching babies in her talons long before Christianity. The owl is the goddess in her crone-destroyer aspect, absorbing life back into her body. Early European tribes practiced excarnation, the placing of corpses on cliffs or platforms for the flesh to be devoured by scavenger birds, the bones being buried at a later time. In the Mediterranean region, vultures were the primary vehicles for excarnation; in northern climates the owl and the raven were more important. Although the Celts buried or cremated their dead, they incorporated earlier Western European beliefs about the owl.

Though unwanted around children, the predatory behavior of owls can be beneficial. Screech owls eat bugs. Barn owls roost in buildings and feast on rodents. Larger owls keep field rabbits in check. This may explain the curious custom, once practiced in England, Germany and France, of nailing a dead owl above the barn door. Sometimes the owl was buried in the doorway instead. In the United States, pictures or carvings of owls are sometimes seen on old barns.

Since owls eat rodents, they are associated with good harvest and thus with wealth in general. In Brittany the owl is known to hoard jewelry in her nest. This is attributed to the owl's superior eyesight, but perhaps it echoes back to Athena's patronage of skilled metal workers.

Amulets for horses go back to antiquity and persisted until the rise of the automobile. The owl image on this twentieth century "horse brass" was particularly popular.

Owls themselves were once hunted for food and medicine. The French, who eat all kinds of things no one else considers food, included owl flesh in haute cuisine to the eighteenth century, though even they were outdone by the British, the most literal of magicians, who actually ate owl eyeballs to improve vision. A Roman charm for ear afflictions involved sticking owl brains in the ears. The most pan-European owl remedy cured or prevented alcoholism with owl eggs. Ideas for the connection between temperance and owls include Athena's reputation for sober thinking and the haggard "owl-eyed" look of the drunkard the morning after. Other owl magic included remedies for whooping cough (English), tendonitis and hemorrhage (Roman) and arthritis (Polish).

In Mesopotamia, women wore owl effigies during childbirth for safe delivery. In French folklore, the hoot of an owl portended the birth of a daughter. Owls are almost invariably female in Western European symbolism. Eagles are usually male, hawks and falcons can be either, but the owl is a maiden, a sorceress, a seductress or a crone.

In a Welsh tale involving an owl-woman, King Math and the magician Gwydion create a lovely maiden from the flowers of oak (symbol of longevity), broom (mild hallucinogen) and meadowsweet (funerary flower). The flower maiden is wed to King Llew Llaw Gyffes, and she subsequently conspires to kill her husband with the help of her lover. Gwydion eventually exposes Blodeuwedd's perfidy and changes her into an owl, so that she will be hated by other birds and hide in shame by day.

The hatred of birds for Blodeuwedd refers to a practice known as "mobbing." Gangs of small birds sometimes attack or harass an owl, since owls prey on smaller birds. Various species will join in the assault. The owl is seldom hurt by the mob; its purpose is to encourage the owl to move to another neighborhood.

Bird mobbing on misericord in Gloucester Cathedral. England, fourteenth century. ©www.misericords.co.uk.

Late November is considered the special time of the owl. Nights become long and frogs and crickets are silent, allowing the voice of the owl to carry. The full moons of early winter are especially linked with owls, but any moon is owl territory. At nighttime, in the wildest places, the owl's light of vision comes from the moon. No animal can see in total darkness. Because she grapples with the undependable light of the moon, the visual and auditory sections of the owl's brain are the most developed of any bird. Most of this animal's intelligence is concentrated on perception. Doubtless her psychic centers, nurtured in the rhythms of the moon, are equally well developed.

Owl scent bottle. Greece, seventh century BCE. Photo Marie-Lan Nguyen/Wikimedia Commons.

Among Navajo Indians, the owl is regarded with suspicion. Creator gave owl the power to tell humans their future, but the owl is used by evil sorcerers to wreak havoc. The owl's link with death carries the many death taboos that are part of Navajo culture.

In Tohono O'odham custom, owl feathers are buried with loved ones to help them cross over. The owl then brings messages from the ancestors. The idea of owl as guide to the next world is echoed among the Ojibwe, where death is referred to as "crossing the owl's bridge."

The Shoshone Indians have a story about the owl as predator of children. Four children are hounded by an owl, when they come upon a buffalo calf, who rescues them. As the children hide behind the calf, she tosses the owl into the air with her head. The owl lands on the moon, where she remains to this day.

In African American folklore the owl is regarded as an unsettling omen. Suspicion of owls could come from European or Native American sources, but West African taboos around owls are especially acute. The owl is again the bird of evil witches and sorcerers, bringing bad luck. Among some Nigerians, the owl is not even referred to by name, instead being called "the bird we are afraid of."

The association of the Hindu goddess Lakshmi with the barn owl seems out of character at first. Lakshmi is a goddess of beauty, love, abundance, friendship and all-round good luck. The barn owl is a rodent predator, however, nesting around human populations and protecting against the theft of grain. Unlike that other mouse eater, the snake, the owl is harmless to humans, making her presence an unmitigated boon. There is also a story about the owl involving Lakshmi's consort, Lord Rama. The vulture and the owl vie for possession of a certain cave, and when they cannot resolve the issue they appeal to Rama. The vulture claims she must have the cave since she has lived there since the birth of humankind. The owl claims she must have the cave since she has lived there since the first plants. Rama rules that, as plants appeared before humans, the owl has the longest tenure, and is therefore the legitimate owner of the cave.

Basic interpretation of the owl is similar around the world. Whether she is good or evil, treacherous or trusted, depends on attitudes toward her areas of power. Her pedigree is ancient and her wisdom undisputed. No wonder witches woo the owl, seeking her knowledge instead of running from it.

The Owl of Cwmcawlyd

The owl-land in the story is pronounced koom-COW-lud. The search for the oldest animal is a prominent theme in Celtic lore.

Every word in this story is true, though it happened long ago. It relates to the quest of the Eagle of Gwernabwy for a worthy bride, though why this eagle had not married before is unknown. He was already very old when he sought his wife.

In his travels to find a mate, the Eagle took a fancy to the Owl of Cwmcawlyd, but the Eagle was careful in all his affairs, and he undertook to learn the age of the Owl before committing himself.

He searched out the Stag of Rhedynfre in Gwent, for he believed the Stag to be very old, and put to him the question. The Stag confirmed that he was an ancient creature.

"See this stump beside me?" said the Stag. "It is withered and gone, without leaves or branches. You would never know it was once an oak, but it was a great oak. I spied it first as an acorn atop its parent tree, and watched the seed fall to the ground. For three hundred years it grew, another three hundred years it stood in the prime of life, and now in its decline it has passed two hundred and sixty years, with only another forty left before the ground reclaims it."

The Stag continued, in the way old timers have of answering a short question in a long manner, "As old as I am, I would have to guess at the age of the Owl of Cwmcawlyd, for she was already very old at my earliest thought. Nor do I have kin who could remember that far back. But go to the Salmon of Lyn Llifon, who is my friend and older than I. Perhaps she can tell you with certainty the age of the Owl of Cwmcawlyd."

The Eagle went to Lyn Llifon to seek the counsel of the old salmon. She, too, knew herself to be very old, with a year of living "for every egg in my roe." She still could not give the Eagle a firm answer, "for I have never known the Owl of Cwmcawlyd to be anything but ancient, nor have I ever in my youth heard an elder mention her age. I do know of one, however, who may have the information you seek. The Ouzel of Cilgwri is an old old creature and a friend of mine, who possibly remembers further than I. Go and ask the Ouzel the age of the Owl of Cwmcawlyd."

The Eagle went to the Ouzel of Cilgwri, an animal so old no one knows what it is anymore, and inquired about the Owl. The Ouzel shook his black feathers and shifted slightly on the small rock on which he perched. "See this hard flint I now sit on?" he asked. "It was once so large that three hundred oxen could not have budged it, yet it has been worn to a pebble by the beat of my wings as I land and the strike of my beak as I clean my mouth. That is how long I have made this rock my home, and yet I know nothing of the age of the Owl of Cwmcawlyd. She was old when I first arrived. Still, I think I know of a creature who can tell you about the Owl. That would be the Toad of Cors Fochno. The Toad was much older than I when we first became friends. The Toad of Cors Fochno will have the answer you seek."

So the Eagle of Gwernabwy sought the counsel of the Toad of Cors Fochno, who certainly looked spotted with age. The Toad reflected a long time before speaking, then offered these words.

"I have eaten the dust of this place for many a year. I only eat small mouthfuls, for fear I will gnaw through all the earth before I die. Once this depression was a hill, like the many great hills that surround me, but now it is a bog, though I am only a toad with a small appetite. The Owl to me has forever been a gray hag, hoary with age, who spoke in a frightening voice when I was young, as she does today. How old is the Owl of Cwmcawlyd? None can tell you, for none are as old as she."

The Eagle had at last the answer that satisfied him. The Owl and the Eagle were married, and have lived happily since. Generations of oak have lived and died, the roe of the salmon have multiplied, many boulders have worn to flint and countless hills have been eaten away to bog since the pair wed. From the courtship of the Eagle and the Owl we now know the oldest animals of the earth. They are, the Eagle of Gwernabwy, the Stag of Rhedynfre, the Salmon of Lyn Llifon, the Ouzel of Cilgwri, the Toad of Cors Fochno, and the Owl of Cwmcawlyd. Of all of these, the oldest of the old is the Owl.

Why the Owl Hunts by Night

There are many tales explaining mobbing. A few have beauty as the rationale. An English fable has the owl mobbed for stealing a rose set aside as a beauty prize, while in a Polish tale the owl must hide from other birds bewitched by her beauty. In an Aesop story the owl's intellect provokes the jealousy of mobbing birds. Another Polish tale claims the owl is mobbed because she once got too drunk and obnoxious at a wedding. The following story comes from Brittany.

Who should be designated king of the birds is not easily detected at first. Would that be the biggest bird, the prettiest, the bird with the sweetest voice? If the king of birds is the wisest, perhaps that would be the owl, but she suggested the honor go to the bird which could fly the highest. The other birds flocked to this suggestion and agreed the one who could fly the highest should be crowned king.

The owl and the eagle, as giant birds of prey, were the main contestants for this prize, but the wren, unbeknownst to anyone, decided to enter the contest secretly. She hid in the feathers of the eagle and rode far up in the sky. When the eagle, having passed the owl, tired and could fly no higher, the wren sped out of her hiding place and climbed as high as she could go. "I'm it!" she cried excitedly. "I'm king—queen—leader—whatever you call the best of all birds."

The other birds puzzled over this development, but there were many witnesses to the feat, and the wren was duly crowned.

In most tales, the story ends here. But there is a sequel, because birds are not fools. The owl had not seen the wren pass her, and the eagle had felt the wren's wings beat against him. Through much discussion, the bird kingdom spotted the ruse and confronted the wren, who was immediately imprisoned. The owl was given the job of guarding the wren in her hole while the other birds determined punishment.

It took them a very long time. Everyone had something to say about the trick—a suggestion to make or a desire to spout off about the indecency of the stunt. As the hours dragged by, the owl began to get sleepy. Her eyelids became heavy and she lapsed into a doze. The doze became a snooze and the snooze became a slumber. The wren jumped out of her hole and flew away.

Oh, the other birds were mad! All of the fury they had saved for the wren became directed at the owl. They flocked around her and pecked and menaced and screamed, and the owl had to fly very high and very far to get away.

They are still angry about it. To this day the owl hides by daylight and does not leave her roost until all the other birds are asleep.

Owl Review

Magical Qualities:
superb night vision, wide range of vision, staring eyes, forward looking eyes, nocturnal, superb hearing, silent flight, good hunter

Magical Applications:
psychic penetration, understanding, enlightenment, divination, inspiration, healing (especially alcoholism, whooping cough, poor eyesight, bleeding, poor hearing, arthritis), protection (especially infants and mothers in labor), prosperity, predicting/managing weather, revealing secrets

Other Associations:
deception, omens (good and bad), death, ancestors, full moon, early winter, night, shadow, wisdom, truth, meditation, spying, education, science, inventions, secrets, democracy, politics, women, forests, fair weather, justice

The Animal Guided Meditation—part two

Many priestesses wonder whether they have truly communicated with an animal spirit or whether they "made it all up."

If you suspect your visions during meditation are the result of imagination, you may be right. However, this does not invalidate your experience. You are the imaginer, so look at what you're imagining. This is your belief or wisdom.

Many priestesses wonder whether they have truly received a piece of animal wisdom or whether they are succumbing to "wishful thinking."

If you suspect your messages during meditation are the result of wishful thinking, you may be right. However, this does not invalidate your experience. You are the wisher, so look at what you're wishing for. Acknowledging a desire can be an enormous breakthrough.

Many priestesses wonder whether they have truly interacted with an animal guide or if they were being "guided by expectation."

If you suspect your observations during meditation are being molded by expectation, you may be right. However, this does not invalidate your experience. You are the expecter, so what do you expect? This is your template, based on your experiences and culture.

Many priestesses try to invalidate their experiences with animal guides. They try, they try, they try so hard. If you are able to visualize things you "make up" through "wishful thinking" to "conform to expectations," you have the potential to penetrate hidden realms. With time and practice, you will be able to differentiate between messages from guides and your own projections. In the meantime, you are getting valuable information. Scrutinize it, cherish it and allow yourself to profit by it.

What if "nothing happens" during your guided meditation?

First, examine whether in fact nothing is happening. Do the

meditation again, and notice how you feel before and after. Take note of any impressions that arise. Write something down after each meditation, even if your initial thought is that nothing happened.

If you find this type of meditation pleasant and relaxing, look at your first sessions as a "breaking in period." Hold off judgment on whether or not this is working. The power of your intention, along with the time and space you are allowing for this process, may be opening your mind and strengthening channels in ways you cannot fathom. Remain open and be persistent.

Consider the possibility that information is coming to you in an unexpected manner. Some people lack the ability to perceive inwardly in pictures, but fortunately not all inner perceptions are visual. Some are auditory, tactile or even olfactory. Other times senses do not seem to be involved at all, but information comes seemingly from nowhere. Some people get a sense or a feeling that contains a message.

Setting up time and space for an encounter with your animal guide does not mean that information necessarily arrives spontaneously. You may get information later in the day or the next day. Pay attention to your dreams.

Here are some ideas for making the guided animal meditation more effective:

1) Make sure you're relaxed. Relaxation is the most important ingredient in successful meditation. It's possible that the beginning relaxation portion is not long enough for you. Try another form of relaxation before you begin, such as soft music or yoga.
2) Utilize crystals. A cluster of clear quartz or amethyst works well, or use several small crystals. (Do not point a large quartz crystal facing your head, or you may get a headache.)
3) Utilize water. Place a cereal bowl of water near your head, far enough back that it does not get tipped over. You might

try visualizing yourself on a raft or boat at the start of your journey.

4) Utilize fire. Place a lighted candle on your altar, several feet away from your body. Make sure the candle cannot be brushed by your legs or the blanket. A tapered candle is not safe to burn while you are in meditation. Use a tea light inside a votive holder, and make sure there is nothing above or around the holder that could catch fire. If burning a candle while you have your eyes closed makes you nervous, this method will not be productive.
5) Smudge the room and yourself with sage, or burn frankincense or sandalwood incense. Don't get the room overwhelmingly smoky or smelly, or it will have the opposite effect.
6) You can try a few different guided meditation tapes, but when you find one you like, stay with it. Repetition enhances the probability of eventual success.
7) Do the guided meditation with a friend. You may ask, how will that change anything? The answer is simply that it does. Try it.
8) Take a workshop that involves guided meditation, in addition to your efforts on your own.
9) Try the meditation on an empty stomach, before your meal.
10) Take stock of your alcohol, tobacco, drug and caffeine use. All of these substances have been used in various cultures to enhance visioning, but in excess they tire the mind and close the channels. Cannabis, especially, can disrupt things, since it accumulates in the body and takes so long to clear the aura.

If you have been trying for some time and feel you are not making headway, consider giving up, at least for now. If you are going forward, but progress is slow and frustrating, also consider giving up temporarily. Concentrate on other aspects of animal magic, such as spellcasting. You can always come back to animal guided meditation at a later time.

Many priestesses have questions about how to interpret their experiences. Here is a general formula that you can apply to encounters with a variety of animals. Feel free to use it sporadically and inconsistently; it's not an overarching theory.

When interpreting your animal encounter, look first at your own experience. The goddess and her animal friends speak your language and want you to understand what they're saying. Believe that your experiences are relevant.

Suppose a lion appears in your meditation. You've never seen a lion, except maybe in the zoo, and that recollection is hazy. You might say, I have no lion experience to draw on. But maybe you saw the lion movie *Born Free* seven times as a child and it made a deep impression. You associate lions with themes in that movie such as freedom, destiny and acceptance of risk. If so, the lion could be speaking to you about these issues. Or maybe you never saw that movie. Still, that lion means something to you personally. Wild lions are now found only in circumspect places in Africa and India, but nearly everyone in the world has some personal association with lions.

Second, examine the animal's meaning and symbolism in your culture and subculture. Again, the goddess speaks your language. In Western belief, foxes are smart and good at hiding. A sexy woman is called a fox. But foxes are also called sly and devious. There are negative and ambivalent associations with many animals in Western culture, so when interpreting an animal guided meditation, we take the positive slant and say, for example, that the fox appeared in meditation to share knowledge, not to outfox anybody. Remember, your meditation was guided by protecting spirits who care about you. Since the snake would not appear in a Pagan meditation to reinforce Christian dogma about sin, we turn to pre-Christian belief when interpreting the appearance of a snake.

Going back to the lion example, there have been no native

lions on the British Isles for a long time—if ever—but lion imagery abounds in Britain. Lion symbolism is among the most ubiquitous in the English language. To be "lionhearted" is to be brave. A great writer is a "literary lion." The lion could be coming to your meditation to speak about courage, greatness or having the "lion's share." If you are knowledgeable in the area of astrology, the astrological meaning of the lion sign should be considered.

Third, look for information outside your experience and personal knowledge. This can be information from biology or history, or symbolism from other cultures. The goddess speaks your language. She knows the books on your shelf, the people you talk to and the magazines you read. Making a heroic effort to unravel all angles of a guided meditation is silly, but don't be lazy about it. Sometimes a message is cryptic to pique our interest and open us to more knowledge.

Returning to the lion example, suppose you don't feel satisfied with the explanations you come up with on your own. Or perhaps the encounter was so charged that you feel inspired to learn everything you can about lions. Going to a nature site on the internet, you learn a bit about lion communication. They greet each other by rubbing heads. They not only roar, but hiss, purr and meow. Maybe this brings a new dimension to your meditation; maybe it's information that you file away for another encounter. Consulting the index of a book about goddesses, you learn that lions are often pictured with the goddess Inanna. This is exciting, because you recently read the story, *The Descent of Innana,* and it made an impression on you. Going further than your fund of knowledge will deepen your experience and help you better interpret future interactions.

If you're still confused about the meaning of your meditation, wait for things to become clear or for the information to come to you in a different way. You can go back in meditation and ask your animal guide for clarity, but often it's better to wait. I like to pray for clarity and trust in serendipity.

An animal guided meditation is never "done," in the sense of settled and interpreted with finality. It is there waiting for the next action, the next development, the next piece of wisdom to be linked to the other pieces. Allow for continuity by remaining open to new understanding and keeping conclusions tentative.

Telling others about your guided meditation is fine. You'll remember it better that way, and fewer details will fall through the cracks. Getting insight from your friends is valuable, provided you don't accept the ideas of others to the exclusion of your own. Write down or share aloud your own thoughts and guesses before asking for feedback. If you have a problem with being too dismissive of your intuition, just ask friends to listen.

It's important to be perspicacious about who you tell. Information about a guided meditation is best shared with supportive, intimate friends. Make sure others want to hear about your experience and that they're not just humoring you. Sometimes your intuition will tell you that your experience should be shared only with a journal for now.

A "spacey" feeling following meditation that persists throughout the day or even into the next is a cause for concern, since it leaves you vulnerable to mistakes and accidents. If this is a problem for you, here are some suggestions:

1) Time your meditation so that you eat a meal or snack within a half hour following.
2) Allow time for a longer integration period after you finish your meditation.
3) Hold a large smooth river stone in your hand for a minute or two before you stand up.
4) Stay with structured, narrated meditations for now, since they help with reintegration.
5) Plan your meditation for a time when you will not be rushed or jolted into a fast paced day. Usually this means evening

when the kids are in bed. Don't go to bed yourself immediately afterwards, however. Have your snack and do something else for at least 45 minutes.

6) Make sure you're getting enough sleep. Who decided eight hours is the right amount? A hundred years ago, people slept an average of nine. Non-human primates sleep at least ten.

When guided meditation with a structured narrative becomes easy for you, begin experimenting with other approaches. Try a simple drumbeat and see how that works for you. A drumming audio works well, although having someone drum for you is wonderful. A Celtic or Native American style drum is fine. If you choose a Celtic drum, don't get too fancy with the rhythm. Keep it monotonous and simple.

Animal guided meditation is difficult for some, while others seem born to it; most become competent with a little persistence. Interpreting meditations becomes easier with practice. Remember to keep safety issues in mind: don't mix meditation with drugs or alcohol, avoid being touched en route, be cautious with candles, have a definite return time, pray for protection before takeoff and make sure you're not spaced-out when you return.

The Spinster's Vision

Prolonged spinning of thread produces trance, so goddesses associated with spinning, such as Brigid, Holda, Andre Mari and the Moirae, are linked with visionary wisdom. Another place of intersection with the otherworld is the hearth.

The old woman was spinning and spinning and spinning and spun far into the night. As she drowsed at her wheel, she heard a tap at the door. "Who's that?" she cried, a bit confused, for it was a dire windy night. But no answer came except another tap at the door.

"Who's there?" she asked again. And again, another tap.

"Who is at the door?" the old lady demanded, a tad annoyed at this point. "Judy, Judy, let me in," called a voice, for the intruder knew her name. "It is cold, cold out here and I am hungry. Give me some milk and let me warm myself at your fire."

The old lady thought the thin voice sounded like a child, so she opened the door hastily, and a large black cat with a white bib slipped in, along with two kittens. They immediately perched on the hearth, warming and grooming themselves and purring. Judy went back to her spinning.

"You ought not spin so late in the evening," the mother cat remarked finally. "The fairies have been eager to hold council at your hearth, and you have been holding up their supper. They are peeved enough to hurt you terribly, but I said, 'Hold off—I will go and talk to her.' Mind you don't stay up so late again. Now where's that milk?"

As soon as the milk was lapped up, the cat and her kittens scrambled out by the chimney. At the hearth Judy spied a pile of silver coins, enough to pay for a month's worth of spinning. Judy put the money in her purse.

Then, she went to bed.

Musings from Another Dimension

1) Why did the eagle want an old bride?
2) Disguising the voice as an owl is a favorite pastime, even today. Listen to owl sounds (some can be found at www.invokinganimalmagic.com) and practice on your own. When invoking the owl goddess, begin by calling in your owl voice.
3) How does the owl's reputation as a bringer of fair weather fit into the Blodeuwedd story?
4) How do you interpret the Spinster's Vision? Why were there three cats, and how did they leave by a chimney with a fire going?
5) As a charm to augment an alcohol abstinence program charge an owl-key ring. You can use any key ring that has an owl on it, or an earring or bracelet charm can be modified. You will need a blank key, which you can get at any hardware store. Begin by washing your old keys, the blank key, the owl charm and the key ring in soap and water to purify them. Charge the key ring and the blank key by placing them under the light of a full moon for one full night.

Cup the ring, key and owl in your hand and pray to Athena for sobriety. Attach the key, saying "This key holds knowledge of my past, my path and myself. With this key, I can open many doors."

For this spell you need:
Soap and water
Owl charm
Key ring
Blank key

6) If you have not already done so, this is the time to get a notebook to record your meditations. Think about how often you're willing to commit to meditation and figure out when

you can set aside time.

7) Read over the bear meditation you recorded. Write possible meanings from the standpoint of your personal experience and your culture. Next talk to someone or consult a reference book and record a new insight about your experience.
8) There are many reasons for referring to a deity in an oblique way: for poetic effect (*La Belle Dame Sans Merci*), to avoid provoking the deity's interest ("Speak of the Devil and he will appear"), or to show respect for the sacred character of the name (the Jewish practice of leaving out the consonants of the supreme deity and writing G-d instead).

A deity can also be invoked in a cryptic way to move between the worlds, emphasizing that separation between physical and nonphysical space. Take a piece of paper and write "who cooks for you." This is what birders claim the barred owl is saying in her most common cry. Draw mice in four corners of the paper as an offering. They don't have to be well drawn; a stylized representation is usually better.

Write a special name or descriptive title for yourself. If you have a personal sigil, write that. If you have a name you only use in spiritual contexts, print that. Otherwise write a short description of yourself. For example, if your name is Deborah, you could write Lady of the Bees, or The Bee Girl with the Brown Hair, or something to do with bees, since the name Deborah is derived from a Hebrew word meaning "bee."

Write the word WISDOM in capital letters below your name. Then write when you are planning your next animal guided meditation. It can be a regular calendar date or something slightly more cryptic, like "Taurus full moon."

Now call the owl goddess. Do not mention her by name, but approximate the barred owl call for a few minutes to invoke her. Address her as Lady, Goddess, Flower Maid or some other suitable title. Tell her that you, The Bee Girl with the Brown Hair, will be in guided meditation on such-and-such a date and would appreciate some wisdom sent your way.

Fold the paper many times and leave it on your altar. When the time comes for your meditation, unfold the paper and call the goddess again with your owl cry. Proceed with the meditation. Discard the paper when you are finished.

For this ritual you need:

Paper and pencil

9) When you are able to easily follow a narrated animal guided meditation, try meditating with a repetitive nature sound. Write your intention for the meditation here. (For example, I am going to meet with the owl goddess and ask her to help me find a job. Or, I am going to meet with the owl goddess and listen to what she has to tell me.)

In guided meditation without a narrator, it's easier to have a stock visualization to start with. For example, you could begin by visualizing the opening sequence on the voice guided meditation and follow an animal ally across the bridge. (If you do not see in pictures, this will be an intention rather than a visual projection.) Outline your starting point here.

Relaxation helps immensely with guided meditation (and just about everything else). To move into a relaxed space, you could listen to the relaxation portion of the bear meditation at www.invokinganimalmagic.com; you could listen to another narrated relaxation tape; or you could listen to music, to give a few suggestions. Write how you will relax before starting the guided portion of your meditation.

Now begin your animal guided meditation using a steady, unstructured sound. Remember to first pray to your goddess for protection and receptivity. Record your experience below.

10) Here is a partial list of Athena's characteristics, achievements and titles. Which would you attribute to her owl manifestation and which to her serpent?

Characteristic	owl	serpent	neither
Negotiator			
Bringer of peace			
Patron of textile arts			
Patron of universities			
Inventor of the plough			
Inventor of wind instruments			
Messenger			
Advisor/counselor			
Goddess of democracy			
Goddess of cities			
Giver of wealth			
Loyalty in friendship			
Rational/logical thinker			
Even tempered			
Giver of vision			
Goddess of the olive tree			
Inventor of the sail			
Moon goddess			
Patron of metal workers			
Lady of the Glittering Eyes			

Chapter 6

Creatures of the Long Journey

Sweet are the uses of adversity,
Which like the toad, ugly and venomous,
Wears yet a precious jewel in its head;
—William Shakespeare, *As You Like It*

The Toad Queen

I've heard so many fairy tales about toads that when I encounter one in the forest I can't trust that the toad is really a toad. It might be a witch. It could be a handsome prince. A medieval belief was that a toad was the transmigratory soul of a Christian who died on pilgrimage. I like this story best, because toads always look like they're going somewhere. They hop to the side of the path and let you pass, like a slow driver on the highway, then continue intently on their way. When they finally reach the sacred spot, will they be transformed back to a Christian? I often encounter toads when I'm climbing a mountain, and mountaintops are sacred places. I'm tempted to ask people I meet up top, "Did you used to be a toad?"

The toad is linked with that most magical of plants, the mushroom. I always assumed this was because both have hallucinogenic properties, but I learned recently that toads or frogs are connected with mushrooms even in places where hallucinogenic mushrooms are absent. Clearly there is more going on than meets the psychedelic eye.

The most psychoactive portion of the toad is in the venom, although the skin can have psychoactive properties as well. Toad venom rests mostly in glands behind the eyes, the "horns" of the toad. These glands, when dried, are the legendary toadstones of folk magic. The venom is usually "milked" from a live toad. I haven't tried it myself, but knowing the symptoms of intoxication and the chemicals that have been synthesized from toad venom, I would guess that the reputation of toad venom as toxic is well based. The altered state is reportedly noticeable, but not dramatic, and accompanied by numerous unpleasant symptoms. Whether it has any spiritually enlightening properties I couldn't say. One spiritual man I know, who attends religious meetings where hallucinogenic substances are ingested, tried venom from one of the more psychoactive toad species and went back to his other practices. I have seen toads or parts of toads as ingredients in flying ointments, but always in combination with strong hallucinogenic plants.

Physician extracting toadstone. Illustration Johannes de Cuba, 1497.

Toad venom was at one time prized for its anesthetic properties, and toad venom, warts, skin, saliva, blood, bones and legs were used in healing concoctions. Toads warded off bubonic plague and alleviated complaints of the kidneys, such as water retention and stones. They had a reputation for helping heart problems, tuberculosis, thrush, excessive bleeding and menstrual complaints. Chemical studies have confirmed the existence of antibacterial, antifungal and other medicinal qualities in common toads, while tropical frogs are still studied in hopes of discovering new medicines.

The heart of the toad/mushroom connection is that they're both used in *healing*, for a wide variety of ailments. With a toad and a toadstool an old-time witch could probably heal most of the diseases she encountered.

But while the medicinal qualities of a mushroom can be extracted easily using heat, a toad is more challenging. Sometimes toads or toad parts were boiled, but for some ailments this didn't work. Toad venom could be dried and pulverized, but this was difficult and messy. Fresh toad venom could be applied directly to the skin, but this was highly caustic. The easiest way

Detail from The Ripley Scroll by fifteenth century English alchemist George Ripley. Photo courtesy of Yale University Rare Book & Manuscript Library.

to extract the medicinal components known to be present in the toad was through magic. Dried toads or toad legs were worn in silk bags around the neck, or a toad could be tied under each armpit (presumably because bubonic plague affects the lymph nodes in obvious ways). The toadstone, long lasting and durable, was the preferred way to go. Toadstones were often set in rings or pendants. Probably this is where the idea that some toads contain a jewel in the head comes from.

Toads have a reputation for being aphrodisiacs, and ceremonies to Aphrodite once incorporated them. The most celebrated priestess of Aphrodite went by the name *Phryné,* which means "toad." Toad bones were often used for this purpose, although any part of the toad was fair game. Toad bones could be worn as amulets and toad blood added to love potions. A drink made from toad boiled with certain fungi gathered under the full moon could bring a lover, if the right incantation was spoken at midnight.

One intriguing love spell, for women only, involved holding a communion wafer on the tongue until encountering a toad, then placing the wafer in the toad's mouth. Would such a thing work? The idea was so intriguing I was tempted to test it. Communion wafers could probably be purchased at a Christian supply store, I reasoned. If not, I had a health food cookbook with a recipe for whole wheat communion cakes.

Detail from statue of Aphrodite by Praxiteles with legendary beauty Phryné as the model. This is a first century copy. Statue was defaced by Christian vandals. Photo Ricardo André Frantz/Wikimedia Commons.

The problem still remained that toads are strictly carnivorous—to the point of disliking any food that isn't still wriggling when it enters the mouth. The way around this, at least in theory, would be to get a wafer that had been used in communion—after all, it would be the living body of Christ. But would this be in keeping with the Wiccan injunction to "Harm None"? I spoke to a minister who assured me that imbibing a communion wafer did not constitute conversion, and no animal could be converted to Christianity at any rate. So there was no worry about a toad that was not already a Christian being involuntarily converted.

But getting a blessed communion wafer meant going through a lot of rigmarole, and what if the toad sent me a Christian lover? I knew I could put a teenager up to this stunt, but word was sure to leak out, and I was pretty sure my Christian neighbors would be offended if word got out that I gave the Eucharist to a toad. I reluctantly gave up the idea as impractical. I have tried to be scientific about the material presented here, but the proclivity of the toad to play matchmaker in exchange for a piece of the Christian god will have to be taken, as the Christians say, on faith.

The healing applications of toads are straightforward, even the kooky ones like stuffing toads in your underpants (there are lymph nodes in the groin, after all), but what is the magical connection between toads and El Amor? Maybe it has to do with the applications of toad venom in women's medicine. Toads were used in treating menstrual complaints, so perhaps toad chemicals regulate women's hormones.

Where there are love potions, there are charms for conception and childbirth, and toads are featured in both. Toads have a reputation for stanching blood flow, always a useful tool in childbirth. The association of toads and childbirth spans thousands of years. Effigies of toads in birth positions from Neolithic sites are on the one side of history; effigies of toads as fertility offerings to the Virgin Mary in Eastern European churches are at the other.

Let's look at the fertility and life cycle of the toad herself. Toads and frogs lay eggs in water, where they hatch into tadpoles. Tadpoles grow from tiny legless threads to adult toads in a few months. Like human fetuses, they start out with a tail, but lose the tail in the course of their development. The adult toads soon begin living on land, and this change of environment puts them in the class of amphibians, which is Greek for "two lives." The profound change in both appearance and living environment gives toads their transformative properties. If you think about it, it's no more incredible that a person should change into a toad, than that a legless fish should change into a walking land creature.

Standing terra cotta toad. Notice the venom glands resemble breasts. Serbia, Fifth millennium, BCE.

Toads are distinguished from frogs by the presence of skin protrusions that look like warts and leathery skin adapted to drier environments. Toads have a special gland for their venom, although the skin of all toads and frogs is venomous to a greater or lesser degree. In temperate climates they are not dangerous to the touch. Just wash your hands. Some languages make a distinction between toads and frogs; others do not. Biologists do not find the distinction useful, because it is not a predictor of evolutionary origin, the organizing feature of modern taxonomy. It is impossible to distinguish frogs and toads in archeological relics.

When toads are ready to mate, most species trek back to their place of birth, sometimes hopping many miles past other perfectly suitable ponds. Migration, again, brings the wisdom of changing perspectives. Mating takes place in water, and the male attracts females with his powerful voice. Vocalizations are also used as territorial markers. Since toads and frogs are so talkative, they naturally have a lot to say in fairy tales. Their melodic voices link them with musical study. Sometimes they have a high pitched voice, like a flute. Other times their mating calls are complex, like singing. At times the sound is more vibratory, like a loose guitar string. There are at least two musical instruments with parts named after frogs: a piece of the violin stem and the percussion piece of the bodhran drum.

Toad crossing sign in the Netherlands. Photo Aliq/Wikimedia Commons.

Toad mating does not sound like a lot of fun, at least from the female perspective, as males and females often get stuck together. Sights of female Colorado River Toads hopping with males stuck to their backs are familiar in the Senora Desert. In the common *Bufo bufo* toad (I love that name), many males attempt to mate with one female, and it is the job of the male who is first on the scene to keep his rivals at bay. If he fails, the female usually drowns. The availability of drowned female toads explains how dead toads could be used as charms in cultures that forbade killing them. There is a Romanian saying to the effect that a man who would kill a toad would kill his own mother, and Serbian culture has similar taboos against killing frogs.

Toads and frogs are prodigious breeders, laying thousands of eggs resulting in thousands of tadpoles. The fishy incarnation, like the adult, is poisonous to most predators,

Zee *Bufo bufo*. Photo Dr. Holger Krisp/Wikimedia Commons.

ensuring that large numbers of grownups emerge from the ponds to pierce the night with their collective chorus. Animals that have copious offspring are associated with fertility.

As the moon is connected to birth, it should be no surprise that there is a toad association with the moon. The moon rules not only birth but menstrual cycles and sexual desire, giving us another basis for the toad's power as an aphrodisiac and fertility agent.

The toad's reproductive cycle holds another powerful magic. Certain species of male—including the American Toad and the *Bufo bufo*—have a rudimentary ovary that is activated only if the male reproductive organs are damaged. This can happen during the brutal competition to mate. When the transformation is complete, and the male-to-female transsexual toad has mated, the eggs only hatch into males, since the new mother lacks the genetic female makeup. Sexual ambiguity of any kind—homosexuality, bisexuality, androgyny—is linked magically with the power to enter transformative states.

Mating is over by late July, and who knows what toads do during the month of August? When it starts to get cold—or dry, in the case of desert toads—hibernation takes place. Hibernation is the time when animals travel to the world of the dead to gain wisdom and prophesy, and toads and frogs are "true hibernators," meaning they don't wake up even to stretch their legs. Toads generally hibernate in groups underground, while frogs hibernate alone in the ground, under the silt of ponds, under logs or bark, or even in ice. Animals which congregate become symbols of human social groups. The toad was the emblem for the southern Greek city of Argos, associated with Hera and Dionysus. The Frankish King Clovis had three toads on his flag before his conversion to Christianity.

Toads were once believed to inhabit rocks, and the source of this idea has long puzzled biologists. It's tempting to dismiss this as superstition, but anecdotal reports of finding toads in rock have persisted to the twentieth century. The only explanation that makes any sense is that a young toad slips between the fissures of a large rock pursuing insects, then finds herself too big to leave the way she came. The toad is able to reduce her metabolism drastically and could conceivably live inside a large rock for a considerable amount of time.

The inside of a rock may be the ultimate hiding place, but toads and frogs are also masters at hiding in the open. They must conceal themselves, as their relatively slow movement not only makes them vulnerable to prey, it presents problems for catching insects. The skin of toads and frogs generally matches their living environment, blending with bark, leaves or the debris at the bottom of ponds and forest floors. Some species of frog can even change color to match their choice of location, rather than having to seek out inconspicuous environments. Tropical frogs sometimes have ultraviolet coloration that makes them virtually invisible to snakes or birds with the same color perception, while remaining perceptible to humans, who lack these color receptors. Camouflage is a magical quality having to do with protection and ability to synchronize to the environment.

Some frogs adapt to a change in environmental coloration by shedding skin, and all frogs and toads shed skin as they grow in size. During hibernation they enclose themselves in an impermeable skin-like sack designed to retain moisture. Frogs and toads do not leave their sloughed skin behind them, like snakes, but eat it instead. The shedding of skin is associated with death and transformation. Animals linked with death are employed to communicate with ancestors, and witches use toads to call up spirits of the dead.

Toads get some of their association with death from their venom. Ancient Greeks thought toads terribly poisonous, although frogs and toads outside tropical climates are not lethal in most forms of contact. Perhaps a more poisonous variety did exist in southern Europe at one time. When Dionysus rows across the River Styx to the underworld in Aristophanes' play, *The Frogs,* he is serenaded by a chorus of dead frogs, whose voices he finds irritating and distracting. The frogs sing of their association with Apollo, Pan and other musical deities. Hecate is not mentioned, although her role as lunar and underworld goddess would seem to connect her with them. Leto, mother of Artemis, changes the Lydians to frogs. Artemis was honored with toad effigies at her temple in Sparta.

The connection between Hecate and toads probably began during the Greek occupation of Egypt, with Hecate's name being conflated with the similarly named frog birth goddess Hek-at. By this time the Greeks demoted the powerful and complex Hecate to patroness of the diabolical forms of witchcraft. In central and northern Europe it would have been natural to link the witch goddess Hecate with the magical toad. Wherever and whenever this Hecate/toad connection got started, she seems to like the association, and pictures or statues of toads are a welcome addition to Hecate's altar.

Devotees of the German goddess Holda were reputed to keep toads for magical purposes. Holda's connection with the underworld would make the toad her logical emblem.

Marija Gimbutas has suggested that some "Sheela Na Gig" representations are anthropomorphized toads. These squatting figures with prominent genitalia were carved above doorways, outside churches and on castle walls until the sixteenth century. They can be found throughout Western Europe. Attempts to explain their origins are complicated by the simplistic categorization of any "lustful" female representation as a Sheela Na Gig, but these figures probably belong in many categories, with no explanation fitting all of them. The most well-known Sheela's splay their almond shaped vaginas with their hands as they grin back at the onlooker. A place of worship can be viewed as the womb of the creator, and the vagina is analogous to the door. A person's home can also be viewed as a womblike retreat.

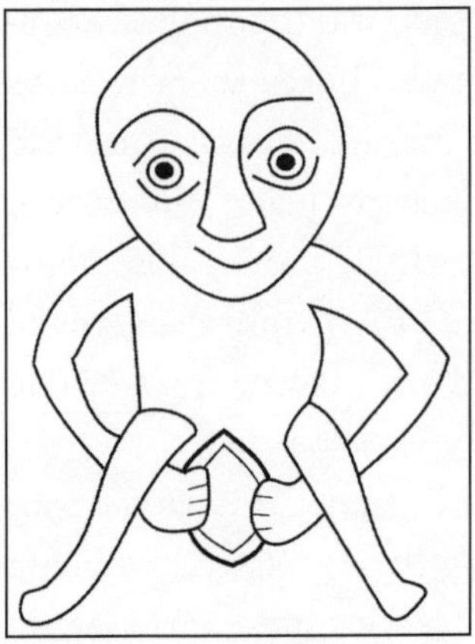

Sheela-na-gig. Twelfth century. Corbel of St. Mary's and David's Church, Herefordshire, England.

Today some people, not necessarily Pagans, like to place a porcelain toad by the front door. Could toad effigies at the door have contained magical significance at one time? Actual dried toads, or even portable toads, would not have survived, but stylized toads carved into the foundation of buildings certainly would. In the Pagan mind, hanging a toad at the door would ward off disease, ensure fertility, provide protection in childbirth, bring wealth and guard against lightening.

The Lithuanian Ragana is another important toad goddess. Ragana's name is synonymous with "witch," but it is derived from a root word for divination. Ragana embodies aspects of the goddess that evoke fear. She halts bloom and growth in plants, cuts the light of the moon through cyclic waning and eclipse, and exhausts men's sexual energy. However, she also decides when the waning cycle is complete, at which point she stimulates growth again. In her toad aspect she foreshadows death or brings healing. A toad who wanders into a Lithuanian household brings good fortune —unless she croaks, in which case she only stopped by to announce that someone in the house is going to, well, croak. Such are the subtleties of animal divination.

Toad planted at an entranceway.

Toads are sometimes credited with owning treasure, and they

will share their wealth with humans who treat them kindly. Are they rewarding their human friends for allowing them to keep the "jewel" in their head? In folklore there are admonitions to treat toads kindly, because they are really human. The type of human varies. Sometimes they are the unfortunate lost souls wandering on All Hallows Eve. Sometimes they are the souls of dead children. They may be Christian sinners undergoing penance. And, of course, they can be witches.

Toads were either treated cruelly or with excessive deference during the witch persecutions. A witch could reincarnate as a toad, she could temporarily shapeshift into a toad or the toad could be a witch's familiar. The toad could also be a personal extension of the witch herself. Variations on this general story circulated: A man would have some odd interaction, good or bad, with a woman he did not know. The woman was either old and ugly or young and beautiful. After taking leave of the woman, he would have an odd interaction with a toad that appeared on the road or in his house, boat, et cetera. He would consult a wiser, more experienced man who would provide specific instructions on how to dispose of the toad. Later, the woman would be discovered with the same injuries given to the toad.

Inquisitors in Sweden, France and the Basque region noted that children of witches were put in charge of herding flocks of toads. Inquisitors came up with all sorts of ridiculous notions, but if a quantity of toads needed to be readily available for medicine or spells, the care of these toads would be just the sort of job that would be delegated to children. The other tidbit, that may be related, has to do with toads being dressed up in silk or velvet, with bells, to be baptized at a sabbat. During the trials a Basque woman confessed to seeing toads awaiting baptism dressed in black or red velvet, with bells. This has to be taken with a grain of salt, since torture or the threat of torture was always present in these interrogations, but if you were keeping a flock of toads, it would make sense to put bells on them so they wouldn't hop away, especially if the spell was being consummated after dark.

On the subject of odd toad customs the Toadmen deserve a mention. These were country people in England who had the power to rule horses. When and how they appeared is a mystery, but they were popular in the early twentieth century, disappearing by about 1940 with the rise of the mechanized farm machinery. Women were circumspect about how they achieved this power (and they were known locally as witches, not Toadmen), but some men claimed to be initiated through a ceremony involving running water, the full moon, a bone from a toad's skull and a struggle with the Devil. The toad bone was supposed to resemble a part of the underside of a horse hoof called "the frog." English farm people retained an aversion to toads and considered the Toadmen spooky, but they were sought as employees nonetheless.

Sheela-na-gig at Kiltinan Castle, Ireland holds a horseshoe in her right hand.

Devil and toad are the same word in many Romani dialects, according to Charles Leland in his 1891 *Gypsy Sorcery and Fortune Telling*. Perhaps this is meant ironically, since Leland also says the Gypsies were amused by the toad phobias of the time. According to Leland, Gypsies found toads easy to tame, useful facilitators of fortune telling and a general source of good luck.

In Appalachian folklore, witches are believed to keep flocks of toads that they whip to encourage chickens to produce more eggs. Witches might keep toad flocks in lieu of chickens, as the witches can make the toads lay. Although associated with witches, toads should never be killed because that will make the cows give bloody milk. From the Ozarks comes a remedy to avert the curse of an accidentally killed toad: seven pebbles are thrown over the left shoulder at sundown into a well.

Around the world the toad is incorporated in healing a variety of ailments, particularly bleeding and skin diseases. Sometimes the toad herself is used—especially in China, where relatively sophisticated methods for extracting ingredients in animals have been utilized for centuries. Other times the toad, dead or alive, is an agent in charms or a participant in healing ceremonies. Parallels between European witchcraft and toad magic in other cultures include association with mushrooms, the moon, death, ancestors, shamanic mastery and long life. Toads are used in visioning with or without imbibing the venom. Toads are used magically to shapeshift, increase fertility, protect from lightening, ignite sexual desire, bring true love, bring wealth, improve agricultural productivity, bring rain and give victory in battle. The toad and horse connection seems peculiar to the British Isles, but the toad has a spiritual twin in Siberia with the bear, in North America with the coyote, in Ancient Egypt with the wolf, and in Mexico with the jaguar.

Some toad traditions have no equivalent in European folklore. Toads or frogs feature in creation myths in Ancient Egypt, the Pacific Northwest, parts of South America and Mongolia. A frog or toad swallowing motif appears in Namibia, Australia, the Andaman Islands and Mexico. Usually the toad or frog swallows water, but sometimes she swallows people or the sun. The toad is a wise trickster in Tibetan stories and in one Navajo story outsmarts the coyote. Toad venom is one ingredient in a special Haitian voodoo powder used to induce a temporary deathlike coma. As in flying ointments, the venom is not considered by chemists to be the most potent ingredient in the powder. In an interesting reversal of the "she changed me into a toad" theme, the Arawaks of Guyana claim humans were originally toads who became transformed into people.

In the 1970s a paper by Marlene Dobkin de Rios rocked the anthropological world by suggesting Mayans employed the toad for hallucinogenic purposes in shamanic rites. The idea met with both excitement and skepticism, with detractors pointing out that there was no evidence of such practices, from Spanish colonialism to the present.

Except that closer examination revealed that there was a written record of these practices, from Spanish colonialism to the present. Not only that, the prominence of the toad in Mayan language and art suddenly became significant. Might the difficulty scholars have had in recognizing what was in plain view have anything to do with discomfort regarding European witchcraft?

The toad's importance in Paganism cannot be overemphasized. The toad queen is ubiquitous, good natured, unobtrusive, powerful and wise. There's nothing intrinsically ugly about her, though she is a little goofy looking. After all the changes she's been through, she still refuses to take herself too seriously. She teaches us to do the same.

The Three Feathers

This tale from the Brothers Grimm highlights the toad's magical qualities. How many can you spot?

An old king had three sons but one kingdom, and therefore saw trouble ahead. He wanted no quarrel amongst the three, so he devised a test of mettle for the prince destined to take the crown.

He brought the three to the meadow beyond the castle and threw three feathers high in the air. "Go, each one to follow a feather in his chosen direction, and bring me back a fine carpet." One feather flew to the east, the other to the west. The third feather did not fly at all, but sank soberly to ground.

Now it must be said that the three brothers were not equal in merit. You see, the older two were very very smart. Which was the smarter would be hard to fathom. The third—well, he followed the feather that sank to the ground.

The young prince was slow to understand what a feather on the grass had to do with a carpet. Then he noticed a door on the ground tangled in weeds. He opened the door and descended many stairs to another door. He knocked politely.

A low deep voice called out:

Maiden little, maiden green
Limping like a little fiend
Hop hop hop down yonder hall
Tell me who has come to call

The door opened to a large hall. In the large hall was a huge toad. Around the huge toad were many little toads.

Big Toad rasped at the young prince:

Why do you come here, why today?
Why all alone to the land of fey?
State your mission, state your claim,
State your ambition, state your aim.

The young prince stammered that he wanted a carpet.

Big Toad rasped to her sycophants:

Maiden little, maiden green
Limping like a little fiend
Hop hop hop and do not rest
Bring me out my best gold chest

The carpet the huge toad selected was beautiful, more lovely than any the prince had seen before, a tapestry of shimmering color that could never have been woven in the land above.

The prince thanked the generous toad and brought the carpet back to his father. The old king was astonished, all the more so because of how his youngest son's gift measured up to those of the older two.

You see, the eldest brother said to himself as he wandered in the east, "My brothers are too dumb to even find a carpet, let alone a fine one. I'll purchase the first carpet I can and end this silly game quickly." The eldest purchased a burlap carpet from a shepherd woman and hurried back to the castle.

Smart minds think alike, and the second brother said to himself as he wandered in the west, "My brothers are too dumb to even find a carpet, let alone a fine one." The second brother spied a discarded carpet by the side of the road and sped off with it, sparing himself even the cost of a purchase. Now that was smart!

The old king looked at the gifts and shook his head. "If there is justice in the world," he said, "my youngest son has earned my crown."

But the older two could not accept this, and clamored and quarreled and yelled "unfair," creating just the scene the king had hoped to avoid with his feather game.

"Peace!" intoned the king. "I will devise another test. The son who brings me the finest ring will have my crown." So there would be no quarrel among them, he brought the three to the meadow and threw three feathers in the air. The first flew to the east, the second flew to the west and the third fell limply to the ground. The three princes were off to claim their kingdom.

This time the third son immediately looked for the door to the hall underground, and he traveled eagerly down the steps. There was knocking, there was rhyming, the young prince asked for a ring, Big Toad called for her chest.

The king was astonished to see the ring. It was gold, of course, exquisitely detailed and encrusted with the finest sapphires, rubies and diamonds. It was the sort of ring that could only be crafted in the world below. The eldest son, on the other hand, had purchased an unremarkable ring at the market, while the second son had cleverly pounded the nails out of an old carriage ring. "If there is any justice in the world," the king proclaimed, "my third son will wear my crown."

But of course there was no justice. The three feathers were thrown a third time. They flew east and west and simply down.

The third prince opened the door in the meadow and traveled to the underground. There was knocking, there was rhyming, the young man asked for a beautiful woman, Big Toad called for her chest—Er—no, she didn't. "I have no woman here," she told the young prince. She didn't even bother to make it rhyme. "Here, take this hollowed yellow turnip," she said. "I will fasten three pairs of mice to the front of it and you may place the little green maid of your choice in the center." The prince grabbed the nearest "green maid" in a desultory manner and left with six mice, a toad and a turnip. He had come to expect great things from Big Toad, so his disappointment was immense.

When he reached the land above, the prince put the toad in the turnip as instructed. The turnip was immediately transformed into a golden coach, with six groomed white horses harnessed to the front. And inside the coach—an exceedingly beautiful woman dressed in the finest gown. The third son proudly escorted his maid to the castle to meet his father, who said "If there is any justice in the world"—no, not this again!

The elder brothers also brought back maidens, but we will not bother to enumerate their faults. The two princes prevailed on their father to agree to a test for the three women. A hoop was erected in the castle hall, and each maid was to display her grace by jumping through the hoop. The two brothers had devised the test themselves, reasoning that their younger brother's maid was too dainty to jump so high.

The maids the elder princes had brought were able to jump through hoops, but they were clumsy creatures who landed heavily and broke bones. The maiden of the youngest prince sailed easily through the hoop, then hopped to the ground as gracefully as a toad.

"If there is any justice in the world," proclaimed the old king—but at this point the older brothers saw the story was getting too long, and they conceded the kingdom. The youngest son eventually became king, and he ruled the land for many years in a manner justly and wise—well, justly, at any rate.

The Frog Princess

I admit that I've fleshed this story out a bit, adding a few details of my own and combining elements of the German and Italian versions. I will swear on a stack of toadstools, however, that this is a one hundred percent true and honest fairy tale.

Children bring sorrow to their parents always, even more by their absence than by their deeds. There was a couple in a far flung village who had tried many years to conceive, without success. They had dreamed of their son becoming a great artist; of their daughter marrying a prince. Later they dreamed of having a clever and handsome child. Still later they said they would take any child at all. Finally they said they would take any child, without condition.

What did they mean when they said, "without condition"? Did they actually resort to mysterious ways, pay a witch to make a frog charm? Did they make a bargain with the fairies, known to deal in tricks or place conditions of their own?

Whatever the meaning of their words, the couple got their wish, and the wife soon gave birth to a little baby frog.

The frog child grew into a life of privilege, for the parents were well off and treated the frogster kindly. Noticing the frog liked to sing, the couple taught her music, until her voice surpassed the finest soprano in the land.

A handsome and unmarried prince, happening one day to pass the house in the remote village, heard the astounding voice and wondered why such a well trained singer would live so secluded. The prince tarried under the shady trees enjoying the lovely music. At last he decided he had to meet the great soprano.

Her father said it was impossible. You see, the father had told no one that his child was a frog.

The prince went away, but he could not forget the beautiful voice. He returned to the village and asked permission to marry the singer.

Her father said it was impossible. The prince would not be dissuaded. "At least ask your daughter if she will marry me, and if she will not I will go away."

To her parents' great surprise, the frog girl agreed to marry, at least under certain conditions. She must go alone in a closed carriage to the royal castle and enter the bridal chamber unseen before the wedding. The prince agreed.

When the day of the wedding arrived, the prince strode into the bridal chamber, eager to meet his mysterious singer. He was disappointed to find the room empty. He waited and waited for her appearance, and eventually fell asleep.

Around midnight, the frog crept out of the pillow she had been hiding under and crouched on the prince's chest. The prince woke and, not understanding why there was a frog in his bed, threw the frog singer across the room. She was greatly offended and hopped away in disgust.

It would seem this betrothal was finished, but the prince was a man of rich discernment. During the ensuing weeks of reflection, he realized that his true love was an enchanted frog. Not revealing that he had guessed her secret, the prince returned to her parents' house to renew his proposal.

The frog girl again accepted, this time without condition. When the day of the wedding approached, she headed out alone in a small wooden box that she had fashioned into a wagon. To the box was harnessed a large white rooster.

As she drove her rooster along the road, the frog youth encountered three witches. The first witch was blind, the second was hunched almost double and the third had a thorn caught in her throat and could not speak.

"Where are you going in your little box, little frog?" asked the second witch, the one who could see and speak.

"I'm driving my rooster to the city," replied the frog, "so I can marry a handsome prince."

The three witches burst out laughing. The first witch laughed until she cried, and the tears washed away her blindness. The second witch rolled on the ground laughing, and her back straightened. The third witch expelled the thorn with her laughter, and she could speak again.

"You must be rewarded for healing us," said the first witch. "I will rid you of this ridiculous box and rooster, and you shall have more suitable transportation to your wedding." The witch waved her magic wand, and suddenly the frog was sitting in an exquisite carriage, harnessed to a handsome white pony and attended by a liveried driver.

"You must have something for your expenses," said the second witch, and with a wave of her wand a fat purse appeared in the carriage, loaded with gold coins.

"You still look ridiculous," said the third witch. "I will have to transform you."

With a wave of the third magic wand, the little frog became a lovely woman in a splendid gown. She rode eagerly to her wedding and married her prince. The two then lived happily together, without condition.

Toad Review

Magical Qualities:
amphibious, poisonous, hibernating, group affiliated (tadpole and dormant phase), transsexual (injured males), vocal, migrating, good at blending with surroundings

Magical Applications:
healing (especially menstrual complaints, water retention, excessive bleeding, contagious diseases, skin conditions, fungal diseases), easy childbirth, control over weather, control over horses, protection from lightening, fertility, love, agricultural abundance, psychic ability, shapeshifting, trance, invisibility, transformation, good luck

Other Associations:
ancestors, birth, death, pilgrimage, mushrooms, stones, the underworld, women, the moon, altered states of mind, transformation, generosity, music, wealth

What Kind of an Animal are You?

In reality, of course, you are not an animal at all, not even a human one. You are a spirit enlivening a human body. In the physical world we possess humanness along with other attributes that are rigid, like sex and race. Yet there are worlds that are far more plastic. The world of imagination, the dream world and the world of magic are a few examples of these other worlds. Because we are not limited to one world, we can enter others; and because at core we are not our human definition, when entering these plastic worlds we can take other forms. Quite often, we take the form of another animal.

Keep in mind that taking the form of an animal, borrowing power from an animal or understanding the magic of an animal is not about taking your identity from an animal. You already have an identity, which is you; something that is hard to describe but does not need definition. You can be described by various labels—some transitory, some carried until death—but in any case the label does not define you, but you define the label.

Many people (not all people) who are attracted to animal magic lack a stable sense of identity. They seek to compensate for this by identifying with an animal they admire. People who lack core awareness of identity believe that at times they lack identity. This is a perception, not a fact. They feel this lack most acutely when faced with an important loss—a job, a relationship, participation in a favorite sport—but they feel it at other times as well. When others disagree with their beliefs or when they lose a power struggle, they anguish over "feeling erased." While periods of confusion and indecision are a part of life for everyone, they will say they have a more difficult time than most people figuring out what they want. They feel incomplete without an intimate relationship, but complain that in relationships they "lose themselves" in the process of change that accompanies the merging of two lives.

If any of this describes you, you're in the right place. Animals can be helpful guides in the process of learning to recognize yourself. But if you do not already possess a strong sense of yourself, there is a pitfall in working animal magic. That pitfall is identification with the animal you choose to work with.

Identification with an animal diverts energy toward feeding a persona rather than nurturing the core self. It provides an outward projection of invulnerability at the expense of inner security. It diminishes authenticity.

In the past, many people would attach to an animal totem in order to shore up an insecure identity—itself a problem—but in recent years it has become fashionable to claim identity *as an animal*, perhaps even attempting to reify this identity into words like "therian" or "otherkin." This is very harmful. Moving efficiently between worlds requires acceptance of laws operating on the various planes. Denying who you are on the physical plane confuses the energy about you and makes you magically clumsy. On a physical plane, you are human. On a metaphysical plane, you are not fettered to constructed "identities" like therian.

If you have an insecure sense of identity you need to recognize this and consciously avoid identifying with a favorite animal. If you choose to work with bear magic, for example, you will need to view yourself simply as a friend of the bear or a person who is working with the bear, not as a "bear person" or "bear mother" or "bear shaman." To do otherwise will strengthen a false sense of identity and intensify fear of identity loss. As you continue to work with the bear, you will understand her power and use that power, but that power will not strengthen any true sense of self. Power is great, but power is not self. Power is power, and it can be taken away.

One of the most important stories about the nature of power and identity is the Descent of Ishtar/Inanna to the Underworld. This popular story is frequently mischaracterized and misunderstood. Although the story is not about sexual politics, it is often reinterpreted as an allegory of women regaining power and deposing the patriarchal interloper. The story is also portrayed as a journey into depression and a return to life. Most commonly, the story is interpreted as the loss and regaining of self. The first interpretation ignores the complexity of the myth's exploration of power. The second two are simply wrong.

If you are unfamiliar with this myth, or it's been a while since you've read the whole story, take a moment to review the synopsis presented here.

Inanna initiates her descent to obtain power—the power over death—and finds, to her dismay, that she must relinquish other powers to do so. Inanna's surrender of an emblem of power at each gate illustrates that the powers she has accrued in the upper world are irrelevant below. When she finally stands naked before Ereshkigal, about to get the sixty diseases, she lacks even the power to defend herself. Yet she does not lose herself: she loses her power.

Inanna can initiate her transformative journey because she knows that without status, without wealth, without the perfume the text calls "let him come," without being the all-powerful lady and instead being the lady who must be rescued, she can still compare herself to boxwood, silver and lapis lazuli. Inanna is still Inanna, even with her body on a meat hook. She does not identify with power, even while she craves it.

Inanna experiences hardship in her descent, but her journey is not about suffering and misery. She is surprised and dismayed as her crown and other possessions are taken from her, but she accepts the situation and continues on. Being on a meat hook is not a happy occurrence for her, but if she were in the depths of despair the text would say so. Sumerian mythology is not circumspect about feelings; its emotional vibrancy is distinctive. Compare Inanna's reaction to Dumuzi's, and the way Dumuzi whines about his state of affairs for many lines. I left most of it out, because we don't have time for it.

Dumuzi's fatal mistake is that he misuses power, although not in the manner of the despot. He does not recognize that his power comes from the goddess, mistaking it for an immutable part of himself. He draws on external associations, like high status relationships, past deeds and possessions, rather than his intrinsic value, as he attempts to escape his fate. This reaches the height of absurdity when he invokes his status as Inanna's husband to get food and drink. Dumuzi further misuses power by asking it to do what it cannot. He asks for snake feet and hands, gazelle feet and hands, and secret hiding places. None of these things can save him. Snakes cannot hide from death and gazelles cannot outrun death. Notice that he never asks for safety. When Dumuzi encounters the grandmother as he flees, he only asks for bodily sustenance, which again cannot make him immune to death.

I don't mean to sound unsympathetic to Dumuzi's perspective. He is a victim, albeit of his own mistakes, whereas Inanna consciously confronts hardship in order to gain something. Dumuzi asks first to hang on to what he already has, then seeks only the power to save himself; Inanna is audacious in the scope of her ambition. In the end, Dumuzi, like Inanna, receives the power of life and death, yet this is a power he did not pursue, and so its uncertainties and hardships are more sorely felt.

We all wish to identify with Inanna, because she is the heroine of this story, but how many of us consciously assume risk to expand our power? Power comes to most of us, male and female, as it does Dumuzi: as a change and a loss to be resisted, kicking and screaming, until eventually we accept it because we must.

Many women are uncomfortable with power. They do not want to seem pushy, and it is hard to wield power and not appear bossy. Some women have seen too much abuse of power and believe it is inherently corrupt. Some women say they themselves have abused power and want to stay away from it. If you do not feel ready to pursue power, you need to honor that. However, there are several points that merit consideration.

The first is that there are many types of power. What we most commonly think of as power is authoritative power. This type of power comes from things like recognized position or expertise. Training a dog or a horse involves wielding this type of power, at least occasionally. Often authoritative power is backed by coercive power, which might include not only physical force, but withholding something, such as refusing to start the car until Rover settles down. Authoritative and coercive power can be abused and overused, but these powers have a beneficial place.

An often overlooked power is the power to elicit cooperation. Voluntary, uncoerced cooperation. It is a power gained through charm, virtue and self-assurance. Inanna uses it when she plans her rescue effort. Women draw on this power extensively, rather than immediately resorting to authority, which is one of the reasons (but not the only reason) women also tend to be more effective magicians.

Another type of power, which may be cooperative or authoritative, is earned, as opposed to gifted, power. The power that you are accruing through the exercises in this book is earned power. By earning magical power you understand it better than the powers you were gifted with. You value it more and guard it better. Earned power can still be abused, but it's more likely to be used responsibly.

Many women like the idea of having power and thinking of themselves as powerful, yet are unwilling to consciously use power. But power is not a pretty bauble to be kept in a hope chest and taken out and looked at occasionally. If you have power and are not willing to use it, do you really have power?

The pursuit of power is often denigrated as "unspiritual," yet the spiritual traditions which renounce power practice under a special array of circumstances. Where renunciation of money, status and position occurs in a monastic setting, the devotee is under the protection, support and authority of the collective. Within tribal cultures which do not view power in individual terms, power is a shared responsibility and a shared benefit for members of the community. In both of these situations, the individual exists in a nurturing environment. For witches and other Pagans, centuries of operating in a hostile climate, often in isolation, has fostered a different perspective on power.

Western magical traditions view animal magic as a way to gain personal power, yet the pursuit of power also involves risk. One of the greatest risks is identification with an animal power, yet this is a known danger that can be recognized and met. Let the power of your animal helper nurture you; don't try to make it become you.

Inanna's Descent to the Underworld

There are two versions of this story, now believed to be essentially the same: a Sumerian and a later Akkadian version. I have relied mostly upon the earlier version, because it is more complete, although I could not resist adding a few gems from the later one, such as Ishtar's zombie threat and Ereshkigal's arm disease. In this story the goddess known to the Akkadians as Ishtar is called by her Sumerian name, Inanna.

Inanna, the queen of heaven, began to think about the world below. The beloved lady of the cities began to wonder about her sister's kingdom in the world below, the land known as Irkalla, where the dead dwell in their abysmal state. They have wings and feathers like birds. They sustain themselves on clay and dust. They live in darkness, without light. Inanna decided she would visit this place. She would attend the funeral of her sister's husband. She would visit the great Ereshkigal.

Inanna reflected carefully upon her journey. She arranged her hair in curls across her forehead. She wore her jeweled crown, her small lapis beads, her double-stranded necklace, her gold bracelet and her breastplate. She carried her lapis rod and wore her finest dress. Still reflecting on her journey she called her priestess Ninshubur to her side. "Ninshubur! If I do not return in three days, this is what you must do. Listen carefully to what I say."

Inanna then traveled to the gate of Irkalla. Inanna knocked loudly at the first gate of the underworld and declared, "Let me enter this great land, or I will tear down the gate. I will shatter the bolt. I will raise the dead and let them devour the living, so that the dead will outnumber the living."

The gatekeeper replied mildly, "Do not do that, Inanna. I will go and tell the great lady Ereshkigal that you are here."

Ereshkigal, on hearing the message, was incensed. "What refreshment do I have for the gods of heaven? Do they come to eat clay and dust? What hospitality do I offer those from above?

I have no tears for the man taken from his wife, no pity for the woman torn from her lover, no mercy for the child wrenched from his mother's breast. Tell Inanna the rules are no different for her. She will come to my chamber bowed low."

The gatekeeper returned to the gate and said, "Enter my lady, and let the underworld rejoice at your presence." Then he took the crown from Inanna's head.

"Why have you taken my crown?" Inanna protested.

"Great lady, you are in Ereshkigal's domain, and this is her rule."

At each of the seven gates it was the same. Inanna was required to surrender something as she passed through the gate. Her lapis beads, her double-stranded necklace, her breastplate, her gold bracelet, her lapis measuring rod and her robe were taken from her. Each time she protested. Each time she was reminded, "You are in Ereshkigal's domain, and this is her law." Every gate was slammed and bolted behind her, as if to underscore the finality of her decision.

At last Inanna stood naked before Ereshkigal and the judges of the inner chamber. The judges awarded Inanna the same fate as any other being who crosses that last gate: ignominy, eternal imprisonment, total loss. Ereshkigal commanded her minister to unleash the "sixty diseases" against Inanna. The eye disease was perpetrated upon her eye, the heart disease was perpetrated upon her heart, the head disease was perpetrated upon her head, the arm disease was perpetrated upon her arm, et cetera et cetera. Inanna had become a rotting corpse that could be hung on a hook like a slab of meat. According to the laws of Irkalla, the journey was now complete.

Meanwhile, the earth's surface had become a place of mourning and sterility. Inanna's sons wore sackcloth and wept in the temple. There was drumming and wailing in the assembly places. There was no conception for humans or beasts. Men and women slept apart, and even the bull would not mount the cow nor the ass mount the jenny. Ninshubur, Inanna's devoted priestess, donned beggar's dress and entered the temple of father Enlil, as she had been instructed. She gave Enlil Inanna's message.

"Save the life of Inanna, your dear daughter Inanna. Do not let your fragrant boxwood be cut by the woodworker. Do not let your precious lapis become pulverized by the mason. Do not let your shining silver be flung in the dust."

Enlil responded angrily, "My daughter should have been content with the powers of heaven. Death is the price of challenging Irkalla."

Ninshubur entered the temple of father Nanna, as she had been instructed. The moon god Nanna was also angry. He was unswayed by Ninshubur's eloquence and said Inanna only got what she deserved.

Ninshubur finally left for the temple of father Enki, who as Inanna predicted could not let his beloved daughter remain in Irkalla. Enki devised a plan for coaxing Ereshkigal into relinquishing the corpse of her rival.

Enki took dirt from his fingernails to mold two asexual creatures. He gave them the food and water of life to take into the underworld, instructing them to slip through the gates unnoticed "like flies." "In the inner chamber, you will find the lady of the underworld shrieking with the pain of a woman giving birth," said Enki. "Moan with her as she struggles, groan with her as she sighs. The lady will be pleased, and she will offer you any favor in her power."

The plan unfolded exactly as Enki envisioned, at least at first. The two creatures slipped through the gates like flies, finding Ereshkigal in pain, as predicted. They let out sympathetic wails and cries, until Ereshkigal stopped in labor and pressed them to accept gifts. The two refused everything offered, finally saying they would accept the corpse hanging from the wall hook. Ereshkigal hesitated at this, protesting "that corpse belongs to

Inanna." But she granted the request.

The creatures sprinkled the flour and water of life on what was left of Inanna's body. The food and water from Enki did its magic, and Inanna's body was restored. Inanna was ready to leave the underworld.

But not so fast. The judges of Irkalla had already passed their sentence and demanded a replacement. Inanna must send someone else to the underworld in her stead. The judges imposed seven galla to enforce their decision.

The galla are demon-birds who cannot be bribed. They do not eat, drink, feel sexual desire or take gifts. They have no parents or siblings. Their only pleasure is obedience to their master. The galla accompanied Inanna through the gates as she accepted back her robe, measuring rod, gold bracelet, breastplate, double-stranded necklace, lapis beads and crown.

In her splendor and power, Inanna walked again through her kingdom. At the gates of her temple she embraced her loyal priestess Ninshubur in love and gratitude. The galla seized Ninshubur for abduction. "Walk on, Inanna," said the galla. "We have found your surrogate."

"No!" exclaimed Inanna. "Ninshubur is my advisor, my warrior, my faithful friend. Ninshubur saved my life. You may not take Ninshubur as my replacement." The galla released her.

At the city of Umma, Inanna met her priest-son Shara, still dressed in sack cloth, prostrating himself before her. The galla would have taken him, but Inanna would not let them. In the temple in Badtibira, Inanna met Lula, the loyal son she calls her right and left arm. Dressed in soiled robes, Lula prostrated himself before Inanna in the dust, inspiring her with love and gratitude. No, she would not let the galla take Lula. It began to look like Inanna would not send anyone to Irkalla in her stead.

Finally Inanna reached her main city of Uruk, visiting first the magnificent tree outside the city walls, the tree where she had often made love with her husband, the shepherd god Dumuzi.

Dumuzi was there, sitting on his throne, but he did not rise and run to her. His hair was neat and tidy. He was not dressed in sackcloth. He had not been mourning the loss of Inanna.

Inanna fixed on Dumuzi the eye of death. "Take him! Take Dumuzi!" she told the galla. They flew at Dumuzi, beat him and gashed him with axes.

Dumuzi fought for his life. He wept and cried out to the sun god Utu, Inanna's brother, for justice. He appealed to family ties, his past gifts and Utu's merciful nature. Dumuzi asked that his hands be turned to snake hands and his feet to snake feet so he could escape the galla. Utu obliged.

The snaky Dumuzi escaped to the wilderness, filled with terror and despair. He felt desolated by the loss of his throne. He beseeched the hilly landscape to weep for him. He asked the crabs in the river to weep for him. He asked the frogs in the river to weep for him. He sought out his sister Geshtinana, goddess of the flocks, and told her about his troubling dreams.

In Dumuzi's dreams the reeds trembled and the tall trees loomed above him. Water poured on his hearth and the bottom of his milk churn tumbled. His drinking cup dropped to the ground and his shepherd's crook disappeared. An eagle grabbed one of his sheep and a falcon snatched a sparrow from its perch on a reed fence.

Geshtinana said the eagle was the galla who would scratch Dumuzi's face. The falcon was the galla who will capture him behind his fence. Geshtinana told Dumuzi that the lapis beards of their goats would drag the ground and their sheep would scratch the earth with bent feet. Milk would dry up and the cup would shatter as Dumuzi disappeared. The sheepfold would be opened to the winds. This was the interpretation of Geshtinana.

The horrified Dumuzi called his good friend and his sister to him and made them promise not to reveal his hiding places to the galla. The two swore they would never reveal his hiding places, or may Dumuzi's shepherd dogs devour them. Dumuzi slid away in the grass.

The galla seized Geshtinana and asked for Dumuzi. She would not tell them where he was. They offered her many gifts and she would not take them. They tortured her and tore her clothes and still she would not tell them.

The galla brought gifts to Dumuzi's friend, and he told them right away, "Dumuzi is in the grass. He is hiding in the big plants. He is hiding in the little plants. He is hiding in the ditches."

The galla found Dumuzi, bound him and beat him. Dumuzi again appealed to Utu, this time for the hands and feet of a gazelle. Dumuzi escaped a second time.

Dumuzi ran on his gazelle legs with the galla in hot pursuit. He ran into the house of an old woman, demanding food and drink, on the grounds that he was the husband of Inanna. The woman fed him, but she did not stay and protect him. As soon as she left the house, the galla entered and chased Dumuzi to his sister's sheepfold. The galla climbed the reed fence of the sheepfold, where Dumuzi was penned. The first galla scratched his cheek with a nail. The second galla hit the other cheek with the shepherd's crook. The third galla smashed the bottom of his churn. The fourth galla tossed his cup from the peg. The fifth galla smashed the top of the churn. The sixth galla shattered the cup.

The seventh galla proclaimed, "Dumuzi you must come with us. We have captured your sheep and lambs; we have seized your goats and kids. Take off your crown and your power robe. Throw your royal scepter to the ground and leave your sandals behind. You will come with us naked."

As the sheepfold opened to the winds, Inanna began her mourning for Dumuzi. She sang a long lament. She lamented that the sweet lovemaking was over, that the jackal slept in her lover's bed and the raven pecked in his sheepfold. She sighed over the silence of the reed pipe.

Dumuzi's weeping mother searched for her son and found his

body in the desolate wilderness. She could not find his spirit, however; only the body of Dumuzi lay like a slain bull among the wild grasses.

Dumuzi's sister Geshtinana could not be consoled. She mourned Dumuzi more than anyone, so much that she determined to go where his spirit had fled. "If only I could comfort him," she wept. "If only I could be with him and share his fate." As Geshtinana rambled through the city calling Dumuzi, Inanna was moved with pity. She told her sister-in-law the galla had taken Dumuzi's body and had pursued him to some unknown place. Inanna did not know where he had gone.

A fly overheard the conversation and said to Inanna, "If I tell you where Dumuzi is now, what will you give me?"

Inanna told the fly, "If you tell me where Dumuzi has fled, I will allow flies to gather in the taverns and in all other places where people congregate." The fly told Inanna where she could find Dumuzi.

Inanna and Geshtinana found Dumuzi's weeping spirit wandering the rugged steppes. Dumuzi's spirit wandered the steppes in desolation and despair. Inanna took her husband's hand and said to him gently, "You must go to Irkalla, where you will remain for half of every year. Since your sister has asked to share your fate, she will stay there for the other half year. During the time that Geshtinana is in the underworld, you may return here." And so Inanna sent Dumuzi to the land of Ereshkigal.

Great is the Lady Ereshkigal. All praises to the mighty Queen of Irkalla!

Musings on a Fairy Toad

1) If you meet your power animal on the road, kill it! This means
   a. Some kind of Pagan Buddhist psychobabble.
   b. You're having hallucinations.
   c. Leave some road kill for the holy ravens.
   d. Depends on whether you're on the high road or the low road.
   e. Other
2) What does identity have to do with animal magic?
3) Here is a spell to help you acknowledge your identity. It is deceptively simple, so try it before making up your mind. (Note: This spell is not recommended for males.) After combing your hair in the morning, stand before a mirror that shows at least your whole face and run a comb through your hair three times, repeating each time "Thou art Goddess." This spell will strengthen not only your identity, but your beauty. Do you believe that you are a goddess? Do you believe this in your mind, but have trouble feeling it? If the spell is uncomfortable at first, try continuing it anyway for several weeks. It will eventually become tolerable, then enjoyable. Record your initial feelings after doing the spell here, then record them again at three weeks and at six weeks.
   Initial
   3 weeks
   6 weeks

4) Old women who appear in myth are usually a goddess in disguise. Which Sumerian goddess do you think gave Dumuzi food and water at her cabin?
5) What magical characteristics would you attribute to the fly? What gives Inanna the authority to expand the fly's domain?
6) In the Akkadian version of Inanna's Descent, instead of

asexual beings entreating Ereshkigal in the underworld, a cross-dressing homosexual entertainer is sent to amuse and soften the goddess. Does this change this part of the story or leave it essentially the same?

7) The tropical frog is invisible to certain snakes because it emits light that blends perfectly, from the snakes' point of view, with the environment. Could we humans be sharing space with animals whose existence we are unaware of because they emit light patterns imperceptible to our eyesight, sounds in frequencies beyond our ears, scents out of the range of our nostrils? Is it possible that animals of significant size gently lope out of our path as we walk, leaving a rustle in the grass that is ignored because it seems to make no sense? If so, how would you characterize these animals? Would they occupy the metaphysical realms, or would they be classed as inhabitants of physical reality?
8) As the toad is transformed from witch to toad to prince to toad to pilgrim to toad, does it become different beings, or is it the same being through all its transformations?
9) What magical quality would you ascribe to an animal that lives in stone?
10) Toads are not aggressive, damaging to crops, carriers of disease, damaging to human habitation or annoying. Why are they disparaged?
11) Why do so many people get changed into toads, as opposed to other animals?
12) What do the mice in the Three Feathers story symbolize?
13) What is the magic inherent in the following characteristics of the toad:
    Migration
    Hibernation
    Sloughing skin
    Amphibious development
    Hallucinogenic qualities

Toxic secretions

14) What magical quality would you assign an animal who hibernates in ice?
15) The blind witch and the hunchbacked witch are common in fairy tales, yet a thorn in the throat sounds odd. Does knowing that the third rune is called "thorn" add meaning to this story? Who are these three witches, and what would be their relationship to the frog?
16) Do you prefer deodorant in your armpits or a few toads? Now you don't have to choose! Make a photocopy of the toad below, cut it out and tape it to a container of natural deodorant. Ask the toad queen to come to you, then repeat the rhyme.

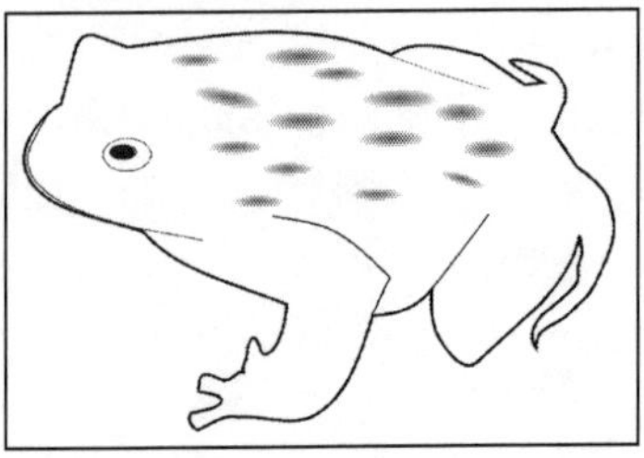

Toad so lovely, toad so strong,
help me smell good all day long.
In rest and action, cold and heat,
may my underarms smell sweet.

Your deodorant now has a boost. You can tape the rhyme to the bottle and repeat it aloud each time you apply it, for extra protection.

For this spell you need:
Copy of toad drawing
Deodorant
Tape

Chapter 7

Creatures of Silence

Spider, O my pretty spider,
Blessed be thou!
The web which thou weavest,
Leave it in my house!

The web which thou makest
Make it lucky...
—Italian charm in *Etruscan Roman Remains* by Charles Godfrey Leland[5]

In Search of Spider Gods

Curtains of dense fog nestled in the holler at night, back at the farm. In the morning fields and trees would be sopping wet—wetter than if it had rained, because the droplets beaded tightly on the leaves. Zillions of spiders' webs sparkled across fences, bushes and trees, and it seemed deliciously wicked to me that the fog, which hugs the earth at night to obscure vision, would expose these traps that are normally hidden.

The spider makes her nest not on the ground, not in the sky, but somewhere in between. She lives in a place that is "neither this, nor that" and so epitomizes the area between the worlds, which we call magical space, a place not apparent to the casual eye.

The spider is secretive in her habits. She hides in obscure places, making herself small or disguising herself as debris. She doesn't talk and she makes no noise when she walks, exemplifying the magical principle of silence.

Silence envelopes energy and keeps it from dissipating. Silence guards objects, ideas and information from those who might steal these things or abuse them. Silence protects an initiate's truth. When a truth is exposed to those who ridicule, ignore, trivialize, miscomprehend or diminish it, this truth fails to deliver its power. Speak a disregarded truth often enough and eventually it becomes hidden in plain view, like the forgotten clutter on an end table that is never cleared, with much less chance of being noticed than if it were locked away in a safe with a secret combination.

Speech competes with reflection and observation. This is why many monastic orders observe silence as a spiritual practice. The proverbial witch living alone in the forest also has long periods of silence in which to gather wisdom.

Silence aids the development of projects. Every time we talk about what we're planning to do, we trick ourselves into thinking we're actually doing it. Take a week to observe the people who talk about their projects constantly and you will notice that these are the people who do the least.

Orb weaving Cave Spider. Photo Dr. Holger Krisp/Wikimedia Commons.

The spider is a productive lady. She constructs an elaborate house that requires frequent upkeep. The common orb spider, who builds a perfect wagon wheel, takes down the crosshairs of her web every night, leaving only the foundation. She then reproduces the sticky circular portions. The old silk she eats rather than discard, making her a paragon of economy as well as industry.

The spiders' web is a marvel not only of beauty but of strength. The silk strand is stronger than steel, more elastic than nylon and efficient in channeling water. The structure of spider silk has long been studied for applications in textiles, medicine, defense, construction and many other industries. Aside from the superiority of the material, the structure of the web itself produces a strength and flexibility that continues to influence engineering and architecture.

Commercial use of web material has been disappointing. The quantity of spider silk needed to weave cloth makes the cost prohibitive, as most spiders do not live well in colonies. They tend to eat each other. People in some parts of the world do use web material for nets or fishing string.

In folk medicine webs are applied to open wounds. The rational explanation for this would be that the sticky web stops bleeding, but apparently the web has antibiotic properties as well. Another traditional use is application to the bridge of the nose to alleviate headache. The spider's healing web extends into the modern world, as webs are scrutinized in medical laboratories for clues in constructing artificial tendons or in reducing transplant rejection.

The spinning and weaving of webs can be compared to the spinning and weaving of fate. Not every fate goddess is a weaver, however, and not every weaving goddess is a spider. This is a common trap. The Latvian Laima sisters are not spiders, but they do weave cloth and fate, nor should they be confused with the Greek Lamia, the snake goddess who steals children and harasses travelers but has nothing to do with clothing. The fateful Norns weave a multicolored web from the mountains to the ocean, which makes them spiders in function but not in form, while the Greek Moirae spin the thread that spans a life but do not weave it. Athena is the weaver, but she demurs at setting fate. Athena is not a spider, either, but her Etruscan counterpart Menrva has a spidery side. The unequivocal spider goddess is Arachne, who is a weaving goddess of the Anatolian coast. Arachne is Greek to all of us, since her name in that language simply means "spider."

The weaving spider goddess Uttu, from Sumeria, has woven an interesting record. Uttu (not to be confused with the sun god Utu) is the great-great-granddaughter of Ninhursaga, the Mother of Animals. While her grandmother commands the wild places, Uttu rules the household, the weaving of cloth and everything that is exclusively in the sphere of women. She also rules marriage, itself a type of weaving. Uttu is represented in Sumerian writing as a spider. The spider is a common symbol in Mesopotamian cylinder seals, carved stones that leave a raised impression when rolled in moist clay. These seals were used to sign documents and to identify or secure property. The spider is an appropriate emblem for a seal even today, since seals are used to authenticate objects and guard against trespassing.

Cylinder seal impression of three spiders. Mesopotamia, 3000 BCE.

The spider hangs upside down in her web as she waits for her meal. Recall the significance of resting head down from the chapter on the bat. The spider's wisdom comes not only from her inverted point of view, but from all the time she spends patiently waiting for supper to come. For the spider, waiting does not mean going off and doing something else; it means being quiet, poised, alert and ready to pounce.

One bug's opportunity is another's demise. The spider makes her living through entrapment. Ensnarement by invisible stationary webs is the dominant means, but there are other ways. Sticky nets can be thrown over passing ground prey from above.

A ground burrow can be used to surprise prey á la tarantula. Spiders camouflage themselves among flowers, dry leaves, dung and many other things, popping out unexpectedly for the death grab. Some spiders look almost identical to their prey, and they use this disguise to infiltrate insect colonies. Appearances can be deceiving, but so can smells. Some spiders produce manure odors to attract insects while others fake pheromones to lure unsuspecting moths. Sneakiness reaches new heights (or depths) by tapping into the mating codes of other spider species. The imposter goes to a rival's web and taps the mating code on the outer strands. When the female rushes to the edge of the web, expecting sex, she's history.

Sneaky predation is one of the major reasons spiders are classed as villains, the others being cannibalism and venomous bites. Deception and entrapment are certainly not qualities that promote community living, which may partly explain why only a few of the 40,000 known species live in colonies. Yet by dint of the world she inhabits, the spider can become an ally for piercing through deception of all kinds. She does not dismiss the possibility of entrapment and has attained discernment through long memory and acute observation. She does not get caught in her own web.

Cannibalism, specifically cannibalism of female spiders toward males, is another reason the spider gets a bad rap. The Black Widow is a cultural icon, symbolizing sociopathic sexual behavior by cunning women toward hapless men. But how close to the truth is this?

In laboratory settings, Black Widows and other spiders have been observed attacking and devouring males. Since male spiders only seek out females with the intention of mating, it was once assumed that females were exploiting males for sperm and then preying on them.

We now know that spiders behave differently in natural settings, where they tend to be less aggressive toward each other.

Some female spiders, including the Black Widow, have been observed in the wild attacking or eating males, but we don't know how often this happens. Usually the male gets away. The reason for the aggressive behavior of (some) females toward males is poorly understood. In situations where females do attack and kill males, mating usually does not occur. Female spiders are known in the laboratory and in the wild to be aggressive toward males when they are approached after they have already mated. I saw an interesting video recently (*True Adventures of the Ultimate Spider Hunter*) of a Tarantula eating a male. He came a-wooing at her door and she told him she was not interested with a few feint (but pretty scary looking) attacks. When the male persisted to the point of crossing her threshold, she flew outside, killed him and ate him.

Voluntary sacrifice occurs in one species. The Australian Redback Spider offers himself to the female as a meal in order to elicit her cooperation in the mating process. He places his abdomen in front of her fangs and pushes his sperm pouches inside her while she's distracted by eating him. Otherwise, she's not that into him.

The Crab Spider does practice cannibalism during the mating process—by males toward other males. There is heavy competition for an unmated female, and losers get eaten by their rivals.

The male uses a secret code when arriving at a female's house, so she does not mistake him for prey. In ground burrowing spiders, the male taps his feet on the ground in the rhythm of that particular species. The spider's sense of vibration is so subtle that the female can sense the light movement from her underground home. In web building spiders, the male taps his code on a strand of silk at the edge of the web.

Spiders of most species are devoted mothers. A few species actually rear their young while most stand guard until the young hatch. Many die of starvation while guarding the nest, leaving their exoskeleton above the egg sack to ward off predators.

Baby spiders can fly, at least many of them can. They eject a small amount of silk and jump, letting the wind carry them in their "balloon" (which doesn't really look like a balloon). Settling far from home decreases competition for food near the breeding site. No, they can't really get to or from Mars, but, darn, can they go far: spiders can coast hundreds of miles, even across oceans. Recall that migration is a magical quality associated with new perspectives.

Scientific study of one species of hunting spider reveals that spiders do not always act out of instinct, but are capable of learning and adapting. They respond to new situations in ways that reflect a trial-and-error approach to their environment. This may not seem like much of a revelation to Pagans who are familiar with the spider as a symbol of wisdom, but for the field of biology this has been a startling development. Even invertebrates with complex behaviors, such as wasps, are believed to react mainly in reflexive, pre-programmed ways. For an arachnid to display the kind of cognitive functioning previously documented only in birds and mammals is upsetting long-held assumptions about intelligence. Whether the spider is unique among invertebrates in her ability to reason remains to be seen, but at any rate her cleverness rises to a level that can pierce even the obtuseness of highly educated people.

The majority of spiders spend their lives in isolation, though communal living is not unheard of. This can range from living side-by-side, to male/female cohabitation, to actual cooperative colonies where young are raised together and large prey is tackled en masse. Colonizing spiders are found in Africa and South America. Less complex forms of communal living are found in the rest of the world. I've observed many Black Widow spiders living in close proximity, their webs touching like town homes.

Spiders are perceptive creatures credited with psychic ability. In some cases it's hard to know how they know certain things.

Ballooning spiders, for example, seem to have their own weather report, picking days with good updraft for their voyages. Spiders rely heavily on their awareness of movement to conceptualize their environment, and they have a keen and discriminating sense of vibration that humans attribute to intuition.

Spider eyesight varies. Cave Spiders are totally blind and most web building spiders are myopic. The Jumping Spider, a species that hunts rather than build webs, has complex eyesight adapted for perceiving movement, color and depth. This spider sees well at a close and distant range. The Jumping Spider, like many other spiders, has eight eyes facing three directions. Apparently one pair of eyes tracks sun position to aid in navigation. We don't really understand what the visual field of a spider looks like, and maybe this is more than the two-eyed human brain can conceptualize. Superior eyesight is associated magically with clarity of vision.

One spider I find especially fascinating is the House Spider. This is a category of spider that can only exist in man-made temperature controlled environments. Unlike Cave Spiders, which also exist in climate-controlled settings, House Spiders are not blind. They climbed into warm houses or tents sometime in the distant past and thereby co-evolved with humans. The spiders who adapted to human environments are not dangerous, since if they killed us there would be no one to build them houses.

Yes, but what about poisonous spiders? Spiders produce venom to immobilize their prey, and the venom from some spider bites is toxic enough to require medical attention. Brazil, home to the dangerous Wandering Spider, reported nine deaths in 2005. Venomous spiders are not aggressive toward humans unless provoked, and given a choice they will run away rather than bite. I used to catch Black Widow spiders in jars, and then let them go outside. They responded like any other spider. Female spiders have a greater quantity of venom than males and this venom is more potent. The only exception to this is the male Sydney Funnel-web, which has a smaller amount of more concentrated venom. From a magical point of view, venom represents raw power and death. Any substance that can cause death is considered a potential source of healing as well, so representations of venomous spiders are common in healing spells. Spider venom is used in some popular homeopathic remedies, and venom is used in medical research.

The venomous bite of a spider related to the Black Widow inspired a popular dance originating in the German province of Saxony in the fourteenth century. The story goes that a number of people bitten by this spider felt compelled to dance in order to get relief from the venom. This dancing mania, called tarantism, became common throughout Western Europe and persisted in southern Italy into the eighteenth century. Music was used to channel the movements of the dancers in order to dissipate the venom. People not afflicted would join the victims to help them dance in a productive manner. Skeptics maintain that tarantism was a ruse to evade Christian proscriptions on dancing, but medical writers of the time described it as a true illness that may or may not have an incendiary spider bite. One of the spider dances is still performed in Sicily, where it is called the Tarantella.

The Western spider phobia is perplexing, issues of venomous bites notwithstanding. The idea that there's some evolutionary advantage to this fear has been disproven, as fear does not increase precautionary behavior around spiders or any other animal. Almost everyone displays a similar amount of caution around spiders they know to be dangerous, whether they have a fear of spiders or not. Arachnophobia is far more prevalent among Europeans and people of European descent, yet that area of the world has (let's face it) the wimpiest spiders. They're less aggressive when provoked and less venomous when they do attack. I'm not saying they can't be dangerous, but if a South

American, an Australian and a European spider walk into a bar, we all know better than to put money on the eight-legged from Par-ee. She will be served with a slightly dry champagne—it is very tasty, *oui*.

Social scientists trace the prevalence of arachnophobia to a tenth century belief that spiders spread disease. At that time, new, poorly understood epidemics began to sweep Europe. To my mind, this is not an explanation. As the chapter on bats demonstrates, the cultural belief that an animal spreads disease *follows* fear of that animal; it does not cause the fear. Especially in the case of spiders, where there is no objective basis for the disease prejudice, there has to be another explanation.

A biblical rationalization (of sorts) for the fear and repugnance excited by snakes, toads, bats and mice among European Christians can be found; there is no biblical spider dissing anywhere. The closest example is from Job, where a man's faith is disparaged as being insubstantial as a spiders' web. There are a few *positive* Christian legends about spiders. In one story, spiders decorate the Christmas tree with their webs, which is why tinsel is applied to holiday trees today. In another a spider spins a thick web over the cradle of Baby Jesus to hide him from the wicked King Herod. Since Christmas is the most Pagan of Christian holidays, it seems reasonable that some Pagan solstice stories about spiders became woven with Christian themes.

Early twentieth century Christmas postcard. Illustration Carlo Chiostri.

Spiders were strongly associated with witchcraft in the witch trials. Witches were said to transform themselves into spiders. Witches were believed to have spiders as familiars, and these spiders supposedly rested innocuously under the hood of the witch's robe. The appearance of a spider at a trial or in a witch's jail cell was taken as evidence that the familiar had appeared to aid the witch, obviously to no avail.

Today no school Halloween decoration would be complete without fake spiders' webs and pictures of cute spiders. The association of spiders with witches is not misplaced. Though I have never known a witch with a spider familiar (they probably exist), the way we conceive of magic is wrapped in spider talk. We speak of *spinning* magic and *weaving* a spell. *We are the spiders/we are the web*, goes a popular witch song.

Having a spider show up at your witchcraft trial was not a fortuitous event, but a belief that spiders bring good luck persists among many people. There is also the superstition that killing a spider kills good luck. "If you mean to thrive, let the spider run alive," goes the saying. The Romans certainly associated spiders with money. They carried a stone or piece of jewelry engraved with a spider for luck when conducting business. I had a bet with myself that I would find a reference to lucky spiders on a gamblers' website, and I was not disappointed.[6]

As a group, spiders represent each of the four elements. The air element from the ballooning spiders and the earth element from the burrowing ones are obvious. The desert spiders represent the fire element, especially the desert dwelling Sun Spider, who has fire in her name. What about the water element? There are spiders which build their webs over water and eat water insects and small fish. There's even a Eurasian aquatic spider that builds a silk diving bell so she can breathe while hunting under water.

The spider is associated with the number eight, since she has eight legs. Her hourglass body is probably the inspiration for the numeral 8. Although not a traditional association, the spider can also represent infinity, which is symbolized by the numeral eight turned sideways. Eight is the number of solar holidays in traditions with Celtic influence, so the spider can represent the eight spoked wheel of the year. Eight is a recurring numerical theme in Mesopotamian religion, a goddess number, associated with Ishtar and Uttu.

For thousands of years spinning, weaving and other textile arts were considered women's occupations, making the spider a patron goddess of women. The female spider is more powerful than the male, with more potent venom and a better web. Thus, while both priests and priestesses regard the spider as a positive ally, she is a particularly strong symbol of feminine power.

Interpretations of some animals are remarkably uniform throughout the world, but the power and personality of the spider varies across cultures. An enduring aspect, however, is her creative ingenuity.

In the West African Ashanti tradition, the spider is a male god called Anansi who plays the part of the trickster. Anansi is generally admired for his cleverness, although sometimes he invites tricks on himself through his arrogance. Anansi stories are filled with ironic humor that appeal to both children and adults. These stories followed West African slaves to the Americas, where they were transformed into tales about "Aunt Nancy."

In Native American Hopi tradition Spider Woman or Spider Grandmother is a creative force who establishes order in the world and continues to aid humans in solving problems. Spider Grandmother is integral to the continuity of life.

In Hindu and Buddhist traditions, the spider spins the web of the living world. She is the energy behind the manifest world, an emblem of the goddess Maya. The world of Maya is often disparaged as a deceptive and illusive snare that must be overcome in order to attain bliss.

The spider goddess has woven us a world of sorrow and joy, hindrance and help, deception and illumination. It is hard to say she is one thing or another. By watching her tiny emissary, we can perceive the world as it is, never making it exclusively rosy or unrelentingly grim.

The Weaving Furies

Athena is usually gracious and classy in myth, but it's hard to say which goddess comes off looking worse in the following conflict. Some say the back story to this myth involves the textile rivalry between Athens and other city states in the Aegean. This story takes place on the Anatolian coast.

There was in the city of Miletus, in the kingdom of Caria, a young woman renowned for her skill in weaving and embroidery. So luxurious were her fabrics, so intricate were her designs, that eventually the populace could not be satisfied simply viewing the products, but thronged to the workroom to watch the artist herself as she wove.

When even the nymphs of the mountains and the nymphs of the rivers journeyed to the humble home to watch the young woman work, the interest of the goddess Athena herself was piqued. Athena applied gray to her temples, rearranged her features, hunched her body over her cane and limped into the young woman's studio disguised as an old woman.

"I had heard you were taught by the great Pallas Athena herself," remarked the disguised Athena. "I can see by your skill that the rumors were true."

"There is no truth to those rumors at all," declared the young woman, whose name was Arachne. "I was taught by no one, not even my own mother, who died when I was born."

"But the goddess must guide your hand and provide you with visions of your finished work," persisted Athena.

"I guide my own spindle," retorted Arachne, "and the thoughts in my head are my own."

"Such arrogance is unbecoming in a young woman," said Athena. "You must acknowledge the source of your skill and ask the goddess to forgive your rash words."

"Give your advice to your daughters, old woman," replied the young weaver. "I did not ask for your wisdom. Athena would be pleased to have my talent. She is daunted by my skill and will not challenge me."

At this Athena discarded her disguise and revealed herself. The contest began at once.

The spindles whorled and the looms clattered as the ladies labored furiously. Athena's tapestry was magnificent, not only in its execution but in its portrayal of greatness. She chose to depict the clash between Poseidon and herself for the patronage of Athens. There were Poseidon's muscular horses, glorious in war; there were her own majestic olive trees, more glorious in peace. As a companion to her triumph over Poseidon, she wove scene after scene of mortals who had contested the gods of Olympus and suffered for their sacrilege in the end.

Arachne's own tapestry was vibrant, flawless and awe-inspiring in its choice of subject. She chose to depict the Olympians in their most ignominious moments. There was Zeus as a bull for the rape of Europa; there was Zeus again as a swan to rape Leda. In scene after scene, she showed Olympians in poses of trickery, Olympians creating mischief.

Viewing the insulting tapestry, Athena became so enraged that she attacked Arachne with the loom comb, hitting Arachne's face again and again until it tore and bled, until Arachne fled to the rafters and hung herself to escape the abuse.

But perhaps Athena was too impressed by Arachne's skill to let her die, for Athena changed Arachne to a spider. As weavers today are guided and inspired by Athena, so are spiders guided by Arachne in the spinning of their perfect orbs.

The Children of Uttu

This story is from a much longer myth. The clay tablet is fragmented and there are probably crucial details missing from this story, which I have not tried to conjecture. In retelling this story I am struck by how much a story changes when the details remain but the focus is shifted. Usually this is a story about Enki and his virility. With the spotlight on Uttu, it becomes a story about marriage and continuity.

Ninhursaga and Enki were lovers. She of the stony mountain and he of the moisture combined to form many plant children, all of whom were daughters of Ninhursaga. For generation after generation, a plant daughter was born and grew strong, to be moistened by Enki's semen and become fertile again. The daughters gave birth quickly and easily. Each month was one day to each of them, and so they delivered their children in only nine days.

Eventually the daughter Uttu was born. She was born in nine days like all the others, but she was different from the others. As Uttu grew strong, Ninhursaga whispered in her ear, "Uttu, do not let Enki come to you. Do not let him in your house, unless he brings you gifts of apples, cucumbers and grapes."

Uttu did as her grandmother instructed. When Enki came to her door, she told him, "I must have apples with the stems on, cucumbers and clusters of grapes." Enki argued with her, but Uttu held firm.

These gifts were not easily obtained. Enki wandered until he found a gardener in need of moisture for his plants. Enki filled the canals with water and the garden produced an abundance of cucumbers, apples and grapes, which the gardener shared with Enki.

Enki came back to Uttu's house. "I have brought you apples with the stems on, cucumbers and clusters of grapes," he said. Enki poured beer for Uttu. Uttu invited Enki into her house to make love to her, and Uttu conceived.

But Uttu was different from the others. When her time came to give birth, she was in pain. Uttu cried out in pain. Ninhursaga rushed to Uttu's house to help her give birth, and Uttu gave birth to eight children.

The plant children of Uttu were also unique, different from Uttu and different from the other plants. Enki was intrigued by them. As Uttu's children grew, Enki pulled them up by their roots and ate them. Ninhursaga was furious.

"I turn my life-giving eye from Enki," declared Ninhursaga. "He may die for all I care. I will not look at him."

Enki was wounded by Ninhursaga's curse. He was hurt in his hair, his head, his nose, his mouth, his throat, his arm, his rib, his side. In eight places Enki was wounded. As Enki approached death, the land became dusty. Without Enki's moisture the land was dry, and the gods despaired.

As the calamity broadened, the fox smelled opportunity. He went to speak with Enlil, the chief of the gods. "What will you give me if I soften the hardness of Ninhursaga?" the fox asked Enlil. "What will you give me if I bring Ninhursaga to your temple?"

"You will have two shrines in my city," promised Enlil, "and be worshiped always."

The fox anointed his body and arranged his fur nicely. He darkened his eyelids with kohl. The fox went to Ninhursaga and spoke sweetly to her. The fox was flattering and respectful. The fox explained that he needed something that only her greatness could fulfill. All of the other gods—Enlil, Nanna, Utu, Inanna—all of them were willing but unable to help. Ninhursaga was flattered. Ninhursaga was concerned. Ninhursaga was softened, but she did not lift her curse.

Following her meeting with the fox, Ninhursaga hastened to the temple of Enlil, where she met her brother Enki, who was close to death. Ninhursaga would not look at Enki with life-giving eye, but she took his semen in her vagina. Ninhursaga allowed the moisture of Enki to enter her body.

Ninhursaga gave birth to eight children. Each child had the power to heal one of the eight wounds on Enki, but Ninhursaga would not demand that her children heal Enki. Ninhursaga would not ask her children to heal Enki. Ninhursaga would not be responsible for healing Enki.

The children went to work the moment they were born to heal their father. The eight children healed the eight wounds on Enki, brought there when Ninhursaga cursed Enki for eating the eight children of Uttu.

It pleased Ninhursaga that her children healed Enki. She declared that the children would be rewarded. This is what happened to the eight children of Enki and Ninhursaga.

Ab-U became lord of the grasses.

Ninsikila became lady of the island of Dilmun.

Ensag became lord of Dilmun.

Ninsutu married the healing god, Ninazu.

Ninkasi became lady of the wine horn.

Nazi became lady of justice and lady who interprets dreams.

Dazimua married the lord of snakes, Ningis Zi Da.

Ninti became ruler of the month.

Ninhursaga's granddaughter Uttu became lady of the household, lady of the woven cloth and lady of all things belonging to women.

Great praise to our sweet mother Ninhursaga, who nourishes her children richly in all ways.

Spider Review

Magical Qualities:

rests upside down, silent, builds a structured nest, waits for prey, circular nest (Orb Weaver), hides well, entraps prey, venomous, adaptable to new situations, migration (some species), isolated lifestyle (most species), complex navigational skills, superior eyesight (Jumping Spiders), affinity for human environments (House Spider)

Magical Applications:

protection from entrapment, visioning, building psychic awareness, becoming invisible, discerning truth, finding a way out

Other Associations:

Them Lyin' Critters

People like being around animals because animals are emotionally authentic. Whatever they feel, they show. They don't hide their anger, sadness or disappointment to spare your feelings. When they feel affectionate, happy or curious, they're unrestrained with these emotions as well. Emotional authenticity reflects a clear understanding of identity. Feeling one way or another doesn't impact the sense of self or self-worth.

But animals also deceive. They deceive with mimicry: some edible moths mimic the ultrasonic signals of the poisonous moths to deter predatory bats. They deceive with camouflage: the Asian Leaf Frog changes its color to blend with the environment, again to discourage predators. They deceive by hiding evidence: squirrels bury nuts in plain view to throw birds off track, then come back later and change the hiding place. They deceive with language: the ape and bird species that have been taught to communicate with signs, words or pictures have all been documented telling simple lies, the most convincing evidence yet of their ability to think.

One of the most ingenious examples of animal deception I've seen happened when I was a child, back at the farm. We had just finished a cookout, and us kids were getting ready to roast marshmallows—only we couldn't find the bag. We searched at least ten minutes, growing more frustrated all the time because it didn't make sense. If an animal had tried to carry the large bag away, there would have been bits of marshmallow, or at least a mauled and empty bag, at a reasonable distance from the scene. We had reached the point of arguing and accusing each other, when a loud burp interrupted the fight. We all turned and looked at Bill, each of us thinking the same thing.

Bill was a hound trained as the lead in hunting parties. There aren't many creatures smarter than a smart hound. Bill was foresighted enough to lay on top of the empty bag when he heard kids coming back with sticks and patient enough to remain inconspicuous, even in the midst of a sugar rush, while we searched all around him. No doubt he would have gotten rid of the evidence later, and we'd never have been the wiser, if he just hadn't burped.

Bill was containing the energy around his prize to confuse everyone, the simplest and cleanest form of deception, though requiring a degree of thought and planning. The ultrasonic moth, on the other hand, is creatively redirecting energy, otherwise known as lying. She creates a deceptive sound that says, "I'm that other, poisonous moth," directing attention away.

The following Baba Yaga story involves several deceptive strategies. In this story, a cat outwits the dangerous crone in order to save a little girl.

As the story begins, the girl's mean stepmother orders the child to go to her step-aunt's house to borrow needle and thread. The girl is suspicious, reasoning that this wicked lady's sister could very well be Baba Yaga. She feels confused about what to do, confusion being a natural response when exposed to a deceptive atmosphere. The girl handles the situation appropriately by seeking clarity from a person she trusts, in this case her own aunt. The aunt advises her to seek allies from within Baba Yaga's camp and gives her specific instructions for how to do this.

When the girl reaches the hut of Baba Yaga, the crone directs her to weave while she makes preparations for the girl's overnight stay. The girl approaches the loom with trepidation, suspecting these preparations involve cooking her for breakfast. She sneaks Baba Yaga's cat a piece of ham while she weaves and whispers, "How do I get out of here?"

The cat gives the girl a comb and tells her to run away quickly. He takes her place on the loom, and the sound of weaving continues to reverberate in the hut. Being a cat, he is tangling threads instead of weaving them, but he is giving the girl a head start on her race home. Eventually Baba Yaga discovers the ruse, but instead of taking off right away she gives in to her impulse to remonstrate the cat, her maid, the dogs, the birch tree outside and the gate for aiding or at least not hindering the girl in her escape. They in turn upbraid Baba Yaga for her stinginess, arguing that the girl deserved more loyalty, since she gave them a small gift or did them a small kindness.

When Baba Yaga finally takes off in pursuit, the girl is far advanced. Even so, Baba Yaga reverts to her habit of sweeping her tracks with a broom as she travels. Eventually she closes in on the girl. At this point, the girl throws the comb behind her, as instructed by the cat, and Baba Yaga is caught in a thick forest she cannot penetrate. The girl continues running and is soon safely home.

The girl and the cat must resort to trickery when dealing with Baba Yaga because Baba Yaga is more powerful. They utilize several forms of deception, but the most effective is the tangled energy block that slows Baba Yaga's momentum. The thick forest created by the comb Baba Yaga cannot avoid; the argument with her staff is a trap that she characteristically walks into.

Baba Yaga makes herself vulnerable to deception through her disregard for others. The energies she relies on to support her are easily redirected by those trying to outwit her. She behaves in stereotypical ways that are anticipated. She herself is not particularly deceptive, except for erasing her tracks and being secretive about her intention to eat the little girl. Baba Yaga relies mostly on her superior power to execute her will.

Baba Yaga's nefarious intentions toward her child visitor are easily anticipated, since her dangerous reputation is widespread. In a sense, Baba Yaga is only doing her job. It is when people in trusted positions betray their authority that deception becomes hard to penetrate. The "Abduction of Idunn," involves this type of betrayal, as the maiden Idunn assumes that Loki, a member of her own divine family, would not do something that harms his fellow gods. Failure to recognize deception also occurs when people are so blinded by their own sincerity that they are unaware that those around them have ulterior motives. This is certainly the case with Idunn, whose pure and guileless mind admits no thought of harm from others.

Blind sincerity of spiritual seekers focused on their personal quest for knowledge has perversely allowed certain misinformation to become endemic in the Pagan communities over the past twenty years. Misinformation is not limited to religious fundamentalists quoting Bible passages about Satan; some of the most pernicious misinformation has come from erroneous academic scholarship challenging the validity and continuity of our practices. These challenges start from the a priori conclusion that Pagan religions are inventions or reinventions and go on to identify the twentieth century individuals or groups responsible for the invention. These alleged inventors are then used as straw men and women to be torn down in order to expose the shaky foundations of contemporary Paganism. Niggling pieces of evidence (when acknowledged at all) are dealt with by conjecture presented as fact. An example of this would be, the idea of "murrayite covens": early twentieth century covens formed out of the writings of archeologist Margaret Murray. The murrayite conjecture seems plausible to historians, just as the idea of witches flying on broomsticks to satanic meetings once seemed plausible to Christian theologians, but both propositions are lacking evidence and both have problematic assumptions.

Since they are assumed to be reinventions, Pagan religions are naturally criticized for deviating from pre-Christian models—as these models are interpreted by historians, anthropologists and archeologists—denying Pagans the validity of evolving beliefs and practices. The use of the limiting prefix "neo-" is used religiously in order to underline the supposed discontinuity with our past. It is as if scholars were applying a cat's comb to our religion, using research and analysis to obfuscate the truth instead of clarifying it.

There was a time when our opponents assailed us openly. In a sermon on the topic of Pagan soothsayers in the year CE 530, Bishop Caesarius of Arles instructed his faithful: "Even if they tell you the truth, do not believe them."[7] You have to admire the confidence of someone who could actually say, "Do not believe their truth." Today Pagans are in a more powerful position, and strategies to undermine us are less direct.

It is important to recognize and reject the invalidating language that has seeped into our discourse, planted by people who are not our friends, who claim authority they do not have. We do not have invented traditions; we have traditions. We do not have imagined communities; we have communities. We do not have a historical reinvention; we have a history.

Especially harmful is the notion that we have "fragmented" traditions. Fragmented means "broken." According to Random House Dictionary: "1) reduced to fragments; 2) existing or functioning as though broken into separate parts; disorganized; disunified." In point of fact, we have a nature-based system of worship, magic and healing that is very well integrated. It's a bit different than it was in the Stone Age, but it evolved from there to here. No years got left out. It wasn't sent to the Pleiades in a time capsule to return in the Eighties with the New Age. It hasn't been "reconstructed," which implies it's been broken and pieced back together. There is nothing broken about the Western shamanic tradition. It is hidden. Occult. It's been hidden for as long as we can remember, probably long before the Witch Craze.

It is also important to affirm that the truth matters. Doreen Valiente spells out the tough questions about the origin of Wicca in an engrossing book called *The Rebirth of Witchcraft.* Raven Grimassi discusses evidence of practices of witchcraft in medieval and classical times in many of his books, such as *The Witches' Craft*. Ben Whitmore takes on one of the most influential takedowns in *Trials of the Moon*. Max Dashu's "Secret History of the Witches" is available online, so it need not remain a secret to those who seek.

Of course, some Pagan groups do have a discrete date and place of origin and do not claim initiatory heritage. I am a member of one such group. These groups may use psychic or library research for developing practices, but even in these cases it is important to adopt language that affirms connection with the past. It is usually not in our interest to adopt the neo-prefix.

At the opposite pole of those blinded by sincerity are those who make themselves vulnerable to deception through habitual dishonesty. They create a dense curtain of tangled energy around themselves that makes it difficult for them to analyze situations that should be no-brainers.

There are those drawn to magic whose lifestyles require deception. They may be involved in drug addiction, compulsive gambling, scamming or sexual misconduct. Their lives are not working for them, and magic seems like a good solution, but without fundamental changes in thinking and behavior, magic doesn't work for them, either. Their lives stay disorganized and chaotic. They can't focus their businesses and continue to lose money. They attract romantic relationships that bring greater pain. Eventually some bring deception into their magic, doing harmful things that have the effect of further tangling the energy and hastening their downfall. They never know when to stop because in the process of deception they lose the ability to realistically assess a situation that would be clear to those with a modicum of integrity.

In folk tales it's often the fox which trips herself up by her devious thinking. In one Scottish tale, a fox attempts to trick a rooster by claiming to know more tricks. The rooster admits that he only knows three tricks and the fox claims to know seventy-three. The fox then boasts that her grandfather taught her to close one eye and shout. The rooster falls for the trick and immediately shuts the eye facing the fox, crowing loudly. Of course the fox grabs the rooster while his eye is closed and begins scampering off, as the missus of the house runs after yelling. The fox does not know a human tongue, but she can pretty well guess what the woman is saying. The rooster, who lives among human voices, suggests the fox shout back, *Se mo choileach a th'ann*. The fox, ever glad of a chance to be clever, opens her mouth to say those words—and the rooster flies to the top of the house, closes one eye, and crows.

Lying is a harmful practice because with habitual lying words lose their power. This is why in Celtic myth some characters will perform elaborate tricks in order to avoid a direct lie, and why the hero will often follow through on his word even at great personal cost. Cormac mac Airt, the King of Tara, is tricked into giving up his daughter, son and wife by a stranger who says he comes, "From a land where there is only truth." To honor his word, Cormac gives up his family, but he tracks them to this stranger's land, called the Land of Promise, which turns out to be the otherworld. He finds a woman roasting a pig, who tells him a quarter of the pig will be cooked for each truth that is told. To start the process a man describes how the pig will be eaten today and return tomorrow whole and unharmed, to be roasted again. (It doesn't sound like a pig's heaven, does it?) When it is Cormac's turn to tell a truth, he relates how his family was taken from him. Like the pig, the daughter, son and wife are soon restored, and they return with Cormac to his kingdom. One of the gifts Cormac brings back with him is a cup that shatters when three lies are told, but reassembles when three truths are spoken. So important is truth in the Land of Promise that Cormac cannot test the cup there, but must wait until he returns to this world to see it shattered.

The Cup of Cormac is similar to the vessel of crystal that Badurn's wife brings back from the fairyland. While visiting a spring, Badurn's wife spies two fairies linked with a bronze chain diving under the water. She follows them through an underwater opening to the underside of a fairy mound. During her visit with the fairies she encounters a bowl that breaks in three parts with three falsehoods and reunites with three truths. She persuades the fairies to let her bring the bowl back with her, then gives it to her husband the king so that he can refer to it during his adjudications. The crystal bowl becomes known as the Vessel of Badurn. That this measure of truth comes from the fairyland is significant. The Celts have often viewed the fairyland as a place of deception, bewildering in its landscape, full of changeability and, most consternating of all, unreliable in its perception of time. The space we enter for magic has a similar fluidity, with its own rules and surprises, yet it is a source of ever-renewing truth.

To follow a magical path you need to regard truth as your ally while recognizing the machinations around you. Get the masters of deception on your side. The rat knows the maze, as does the snake. No one can dissemble like a cat, mislead like a squirrel or entrap like a spider. Paradoxically, these birds know a lot about truth.

The Abduction of Idunn

This Norse tale comes from the Prose Edda *and other sources. Idunn shapeshifts into a nut in some accounts, a swallow in others. The reappearance of Bragi at the end is my own addition.*

She felt like warm sun on a gentle day, and attention followed her wherever she walked and whenever she spoke. She carried a box made of ash-wood, and inside the box was the gold fruit that brought beauty, vigor and a playful outlook. The fruit was replenished every day, and she was generous, so the gods of Asgard stayed forever young.

Idunn was the lady's name, and she was married to Bragi the Long-Beard, foremost skald in all the worlds. He kissed his wife when he awoke each day, then wandered off with his gold harp to amuse any and all with his eloquence. On the morning of this tale, as soon as Bragi was out of hearing, the god Loki approached Idunn with a proposition.

At the mention of Loki your back stiffens and your breath stops for just a moment, but must you be so cynical? Certainly Idunn, who harbored ill toward no one and was greeted with joy everywhere she went, entertained no suspicions.

Here was the proposition of Loki: that he knew of a copse of berries exactly like hers—more beautiful and tasty even. He would lead her there if she wished, if she was curious. Idunn was curious. Loki reminded her to bring her own box of fruit, so she could accurately compare the two varieties.

Everyone has their motivation for what they do in the world. Idunn's was the sharing of gifts and enjoyment of life around her. Loki's was the need to escape from something—boredom, punishment, obscurity, the derision of others. On that fateful day when he coaxed Idunn out of Asgard, Loki was in a jam.

There was a storm-giant, Thiassi by name, who had tried to kill Loki in a dreadful way. The giant liked to take the form of an eagle, and while in this form Loki had thrust a spear in him. It was the giant's own fault really; certainly it wasn't Loki's. Yes, Loki and his hunting companions had agreed to give the eagle first dibs on their kill if the eagle started them a fire, but who would have known that an eagle could eat three-quarters of an ox? Odin just stood there with his mouth hanging, like he was going to accept that he'd been tricked, but of course Loki wasn't going to let the injustice slip by, and then when the eagle flew off with the spear sticking to his body and Loki still clinging to the spear, what was Loki to do but agree to whatever the giant—oh, forget it, it's a long story and nobody understands. Loki deliberately led Idunn into a desolate place, so the giant storm eagle could swoop down and kidnap her.

Poor Idunn! Too foolish to avoid the trap and too principled to escape it. She would not give the magic of unyielding vigor to a storm giant, so she locked her box of fruit and endured Thiassi's harassment. And it took a while for anyone to notice she was gone. Days and then weeks passed, but finally the gods most obsessed with youth noted her absence. The alarm was raised and the gods of Asgard held council.

Loki was arrested and tortured, though he denied wrongdoing, since most of the gods assumed that if anything went wrong Loki had a part in it somewhere. Loki eventually accepted that he would be killed unless he took a major role in Idunn's rescue, so he borrowed Freya's falcon feathers and took off for the eagle's nest.

While awaiting Loki's return, the gods collected a huge pile of debris. The dead shrubbery, leaves, twigs and grasses were arranged in a stack. Then they stood back and carefully watched the distant sky. A swift moving falcon eventually appeared, with a swallow in his talons. Pursuing the falcon, and gaining on him, was an eagle. The falcon swooped deftly over brush and released the swallow. As the eagle closed in to strike at high speed, the fuel was lit, the pyre ignited, and the storm giant was immolated.

At this moment Bragi reappeared from his minstrel

wanderings, unaware that while plying his harp in distant lands his whole world had been lost and regained. The notes of Bragi's harp transformed Idunn from a swallow to her beautiful shape, and the gods feasted once again on the berries of youth.

Musings on Deception and Truth

1) If Idunn is the goddess of spring, how would you interpret the story of her abduction and return?
2) Why would truth cook a pig?
3) The little girl in the Baba Yaga story seems helpless, but she possesses a power discussed in the last section. Can you spot it?
4) Should we declare ourselves agnostics on the issue of whether there is any historical basis for our magical traditions until there is a validating consensus from historians?
5) Can we avoid falling prey to deception by limiting our awareness of reality to those things that have been accepted and explained by scientists?
6) Finish the summary in the "Spider Review" section, listing traditional associations for the spider.
7) What did Arachne prove by weaving scenes in her cloth that embarrassed Athena?
8) Here is a spell that imitates spider communication, using Morse code. Special codes are an effective way of communicating between the worlds. At one time Morse code was a prosaic form of communication used to conduct business, but it has largely fallen into disuse. Today it is mostly used by children operating in a secret play world. The association of this code with childhood enhances its otherworldly aspects.

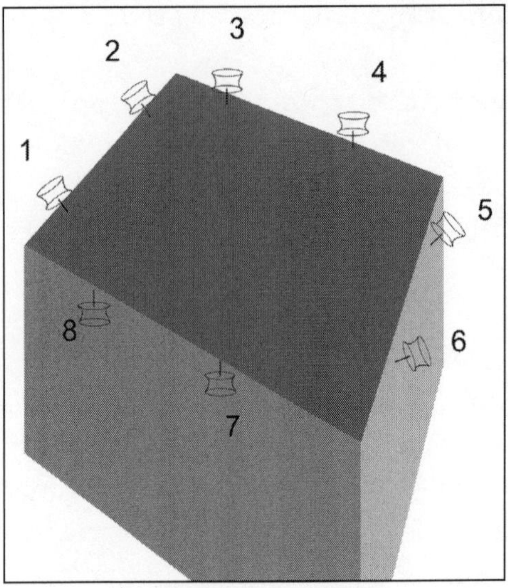

Cut the flaps off a cardboard box, then insert two push pins on each side of the box near the top. The pins should be roughly equal distance apart.

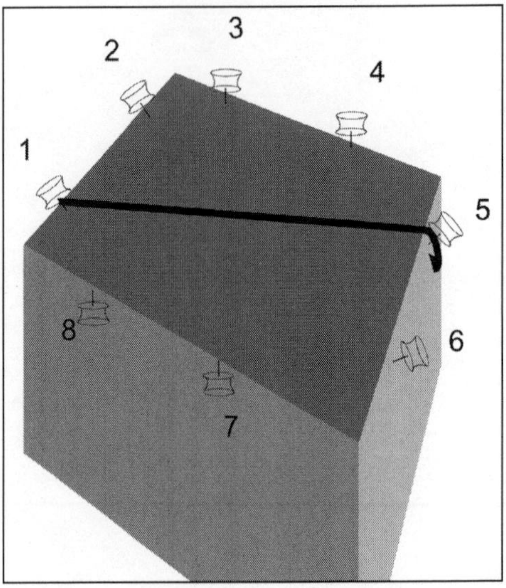

Now cut eight pieces of string each several inches longer than the box. You will be wrapping each string around a push pin and across the open box to the opposite pin to form the foundation for a web. For example, wrapping the first string around pin 1 and pin 5 in the drawing.

Continue tying the strings across the box to form eight spokes that will support your web.

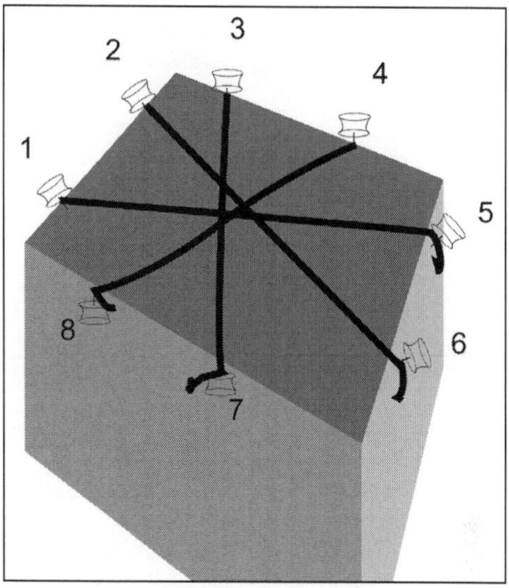

Now drench the strings in school glue. The glue will drip into the bottom of the box, but this doesn't matter. While the glue is still wet, take a long piece of string and lay a spiral across your foundation, starting on the edges and moving inward counterclockwise.

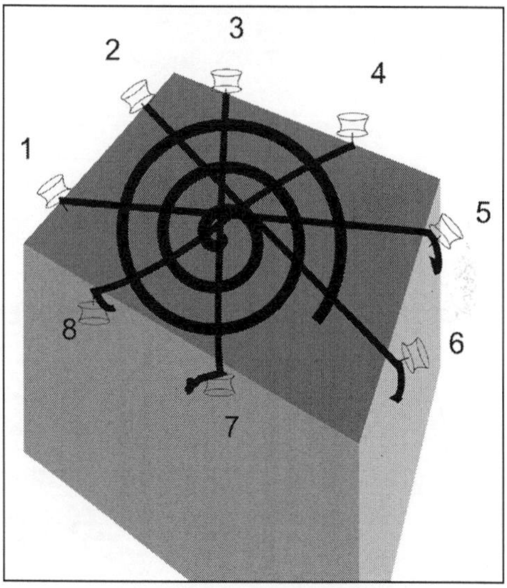

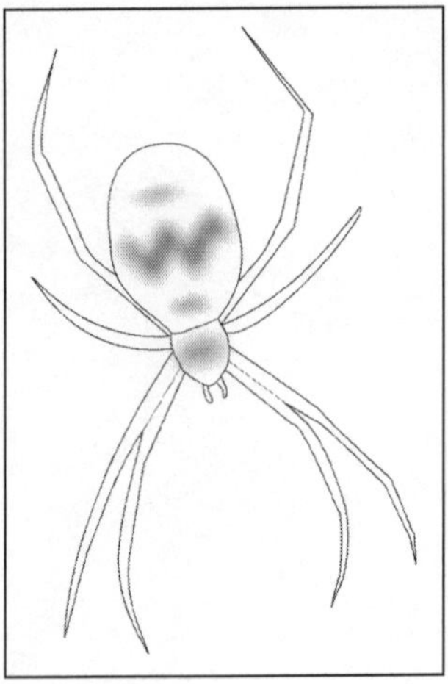

Cut out a photocopy of a spider and glue it to the web.

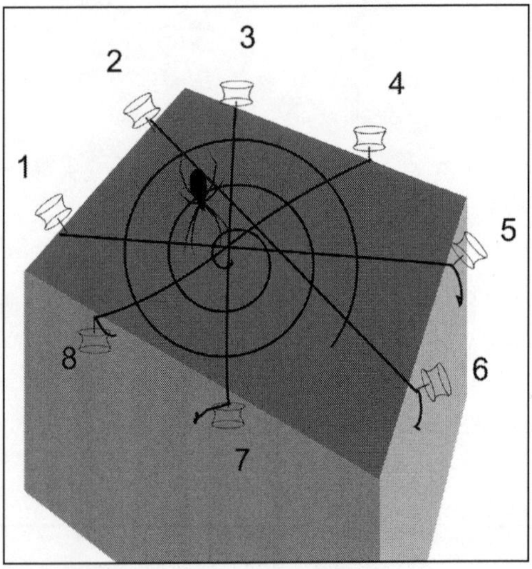

Leave the web alone until the glue dries, which will be at least overnight.

Note: These instructions for weaving a web are suggestions based on actual spiders' webs, but you can weave your web however you want, with or without glue.

Now you are ready for the spell. You will be tapping the web using Morse code. It's easier to write out your message beforehand, along with the written code. The format is simple: name the spider goddess, state your message, and sign your name. Since this is a cumbersome way to communicate, your request will necessarily be short, which will make it more effective.

Morse Code Table

A . _	H	O _ _ _	V . . . _
B _ . . .	I . .	P . _ _ .	W . _ _
C _ . _ .	J . _ _ _	Q _ _ . _	X _ . . _
D _ . .	K _ . _	R . _ .	Y _ . _ _
E .	L . _ . .	S . . .	Z _ _ . .
F . . _ .	M _ _	T _	
G _ _ .	N _ .	U . . _	
1 . _ _ _ _	5	9 _ _ _ _ .	
2 . . _ _ _	6 _	0 _ _ _ _ _	
3 . . . _ _	7 _ _ . . .		
4 . . . . _	8 _ _ _ . .		

Make a short tap for a dot and hold the web down a little longer for a dash.

Honoring the age old tradition of the telegram, my first message to the spider goddess was
_ · · { } · { } · — { } · — · { } { } · — { } · — · { } · — { } — · — · { }
· · · · { } — · { } · { } { } · · · { } · { } — · { } — · · { }{ } — — { } —
— — { } — · { } · { } — · — — { } { } — · · · { } · — · · { } · { } · · ·
{ } · · · { } · { } — · · { } { } — · · · { } · { } { } · · · · { } · { } · — { }
· — · { } — { } · · · · { } { }

I was not disappointed in her response. My second message was
— { } · · · · { } · — { } — · { } — · — { } { } — · — — { } — — —
{ } · · — { } { } · — { } · — · { } · — { } — · — · { } · · · · { } — · { } ·
{ } { } · — · · { } — — — { } · · · — { } · { } { } · · · · { } · { } · — { }
· — · { } — { } · · · · { } { }

For this spell you need:

cardboard box (any size, but 8x8 dimensions are nice)
string
8 push pins
photocopy of a spider
school glue

9) What false doubts do you entertain that weaken your magical power? Where do you tell yourself you're too this or not enough that? Do you say you're not psychic enough, you're not educated enough, you're too citified to be an effective priestess? Do you think real magicians are only found in remote tribal cultures, or in some long ago period of pre-history? Do you realize this is nonsense, but you can't shake the belief? Write down the thoughts and beliefs that weaken you here.

Now make a photocopy of this puppy and use scissors to cut along the circle.

Pick one of the stupidest sentences you wrote above and copy it inside the puppy. You're going to put that puppy to bed. Take a small cloth, like a piece of felt or a small handkerchief, and cover the puppy.

Say out loud, "I am putting the idea that (repeat the wrong belief you just copied here) to bed." Put the covered puppy on your altar, or in another place where the puppy can sleep undisturbed overnight.

The next day, take the cover off the puppy and put it aside to be washed. The piece of paper can be burned or torn up and flushed or thrown away. It no longer has power.

An easy way of repeating this spell is to laminate the photocopied puppy-circle after you cut it. The wrong belief can be written over the laminated puppy with a non-permanent marker. When the spell is finished, instead of throwing the circle away, you can just wash it off so it can be re-used.

For this spell you need:

Photocopy of puppy

Small piece of cloth

Chapter 8

Creatures of Transformation

The stag that bears the covered horn
The beast that hides between the corn.
The creature all men flee in scorn,
The being no one dares to name.
—*Les Nouns de un Levre en Englais*[8]

Bunnies and Rabbits and Hares (Oh my!)

One animal I still haven't glimpsed in the wild is the snowshoe rabbit. I've seen her in summer, in brown fleece, but that doesn't count. Once I met a hunter carrying one he had shot, but that doesn't count either. Snowshoe tracks are ubiquitous in winter, but the animal herself might as well be invisible. I feel a sense of deja vu when I come across fresh tracks, back to when I was a girl in Ohio, trying to find the Easter Bunny. Decades later here I am, still searching for that rabbit.

Snowshoe Hare. Photo U.S. Fish and Wildlife Service.

Julius Caesar noted that the Celts held the hare in such high esteem that they would not eat one. As in most Roman observations about the Celts, this one was only half true. The ancient Celts ate anything they held sacred, but a particularly revered creature would be hunted, killed and eaten only at prescribed times in a prescribed manner. Such was the case with the bonnie hare, which was hunted at Beltane. This event would officially mark a boy's first hunt, which made it a coming-of-age ceremony.

Hare on Irish three pence coin. Mid twentieth century.

The Celts considered the hare a fierce animal, owing to her defensive behavior when threatened. This is one of the conjectures as to why Queen Boudicca released a hare from her garments at the start of her famous campaign to overthrow the Romans. Other ideas are that the hare miraculously appeared (probably a popular explanation at the time), that Boudicca released the hare to bring morale to her troops, that she hoped the Romans would kill the hare and be stricken with cowardice (a consequence of killing a hare during taboo periods), that she wanted to divine the course of the battle from the hare's behavior and that she thought the hare would bring good luck to the campaign. Boudicca invoked the goddess Andraste before releasing the hare, which has led to an association of the hare with this goddess, whose name means "invincibility."

The fierceness of the hare lives on in Irish legends about the "fairy rabbit." This is a rabbit which haunts fishing boats at sea and seeks to drown the occupants with huge waves. The idea that a rabbit, a land animal, would visit the sea sounds strange. However, there is a member of the leporid family who lives not on land but on the moon. This is the "hare in the moon," a silhouette commonly seen in the moon's face. The moon rules the ocean tides and can exacerbate high waves close to a shoreline, potentially wrecking a fishing boat.

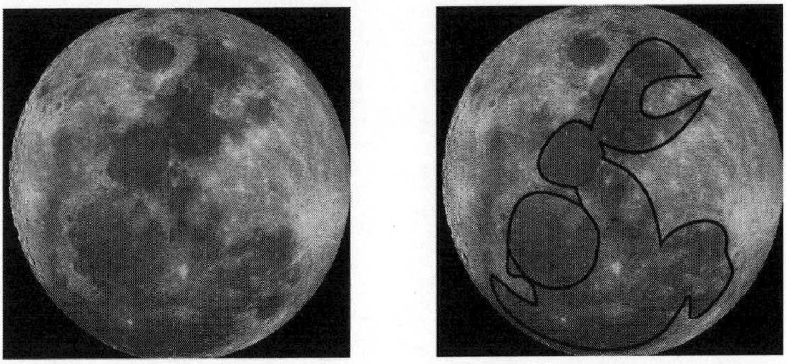

NASA photograph of moon taken in 1992.

The full moon facilitates shapeshifting, which may explain why witches have been said to change to hares more than any other animal. The witch supposedly changes into a hare to steal butter or drink milk from the cow's udder, especially on Beltane. The dairy stealing witch-hare who appears on May 1st is a longstanding and pervasive superstition, recorded in Ireland, Scotland and the Isle of Man. The superstitions of witches stealing milk are legion, but why hares and why on Beltane? Were hares and milk featured in Beltane ceremonies as symbols of rebirth?

In Irish legend the hare is also present at harvest, when the crone goddess Cailleach takes the form of a hare and conceals herself in the tall wheat. Cutting the last sheaf of grain is called "cutting the hare" or "chasing the Cailleach into the next field." Again there may be a moon connection, since the moon in her waning phase represents the sickle.

Sicilian coin depicting hare with ripened grain. A small bird of prey hovers under a sickle moon. Fifth century BCE.

The hare presented a dilemma for early Christians. Jewish dietary law categorizes the animal as "unclean," and Church fathers interpreted this as an indictment of the hare's moral character. The hare's association with the fertility rites of Beltane also made her a dangerous symbol for a religion that rejected sexuality and enforced chastity on its most devout. Early Church doctrine not only forbade the consumption of hare flesh but expounded on the lascivious nature of the beast. A contrary impulse tried to reconcile the sacredness of the hare with Christian tenets. This was particularly true in Ireland, where Christianity was viewed as a culmination of Pagan culture rather than its usurpation. A conscious blending of new religion with existing culture required that many of the old symbols be incorporated into Christian theology. The hare became a symbol of the Resurrection through the rebirth of spring. An apocryphal story arose that the hare waited in the Garden of Gethsemane for Jesus, and at his resurrection Jesus appeared first to the hare, not to Mary Magdalene. The pursuit of the hare by predators became an allegory for the martyrdom of Christ. Most importantly, the hare's ability to give birth through parthenogenesis became a mirror of the Virgin Birth. This misconception, recorded since at least Roman times, was based on limited observation. The female hare copulates when she is fertile or infertile, or even while she is pregnant, and stores sperm in her body. Thus a penned hare can give birth to two litters with no access to a male between births.

By the early second millennium the hare was firmly ensconced as a Christian symbol, and the interesting Three Hares' development emerged in Church architecture. The Three Hares motif is a circle with the heads of three hares pointing to the center. Looking at each hare individually she appears to have two ears, while looking at the circle as a whole the three hares are sharing three ears. The origin of this riddle is unknown. The earliest examples are found in Chinese Buddhist cave temples dating from the seventh century, and the motif appears in many religious sites across Eurasia and the Middle East. The theme is often celebrated as an example of the universality of Buddhist, Christian, Muslim and Jewish beliefs.

Three Hares roof boss in St. Peter and St. Paul's Church, Wissembourg, France, fourteenth century.

In Europe the Three Hares most commonly appear in carved ornaments, called roof bosses, designed to hide the joints in cathedral ceilings. The largest hare cluster appears in medieval churches in southwest Britain, where over thirty examples are incorporated into the building structure and many others appear in floor tiles and stained glass window designs. In Devon, England, the Three Hares church carvings are called "tinners' rabbits." The rabbit has long been the patron of tin miners, and the rabbit is the alchemical symbol for tin. Rabbits tunnel through the earth like miners, and the silvery color of tin suggests moonlight.

Interlocking animal themes are common in Celtic art. Detail from Kinnitty Cross, County Offaly, Ireland. Ninth century. Drawing Henry S. Crawford.

I've been using the words "rabbit" and "hare" interchangeably so far, which is no doubt annoying to some, but the two are so conflated in legend that it's impossible to keep them segregated. For example, while the Irish talk of the "fairy rabbit," nineteenth century British sailors would not say the word "hare" inside the boat. As mentioned before, the "three hares" carving is often called the "tinners' rabbit." To confound things further, many types of hare are commonly called rabbits and vice versa. Some languages do not distinguish the two leporids, but English does have words to distinguish the two, so the issue must have been important to English speaking people at one time.

In biology hares and rabbits, like other animals, are distinguished by their presumed evolution. This distinction involves examining things like teeth, skull formation and bone structure, as well as fossils of existing and extinct species. This way of categorizing animals, so practical from a scientific standpoint, is not always useful for describing groups of animals in terms of appearance and behavior. Let's look for a moment, however, at the distinctions between rabbits and hares that may be relevant to magic.

Hares give birth to around three leverets, which are fully formed at birth, in contrast to rabbits, who may have a dozen kits that are blind and furless. Most hares seem to be able to regulate their fertility to available resources, while rabbits have periodic population explosions that raptors play an important part in controlling. Snowshoe rabbits (which are really hares) also have a baby boomer cycle, however, so the distinction is not universal. Both leporids reproduce throughout the warm months, although the hare does not breed well in captivity and has not been domesticated. Rabbits and hares are common throughout the world, native to every continent except Antarctica and Australia. (In Australia rabbits are considered invasive species.) Aside from mating and raising young, hares are solitary, while some rabbits form extensive social groups. In the wild, at least, the largest hare is bigger than the largest rabbit, but there is considerable overlap across species. Size alone will not necessarily tell the two apart. Hares have slightly larger ears proportionately, although this difference is not as conspicuous in North American hares. The

European Brown Hare is one of the fastest land animals in the world, but all members of this family are quite swift. They are not easily frightened into flight nor do they stand frozen in fear. They move into an inconspicuous place and rely on camouflage when threatened, then run away quickly if pursued. To avoid being tracked, they hop over previous tracks and then jump to break the snow and scent trail. Hares have proportionately larger hind feet, which they use to make sharp turns to flee or confuse a predator. Hares and rabbits are an important food source for medium-sized predators, and adults typically live only a year or two.

Both hares and rabbits will defend themselves fiercely, and they can have aggressive interactions within their own groups. Some rabbits have hierarchical social structures, where males fight for dominance. European Brown Hares can be observed "boxing" throughout the year, especially in early spring, which is where the term "mad as a March hare" comes from. It was once believed that males were fighting over mating rights to females, but most boxing matches are now believed to occur between males and females. It is unknown whether females are fighting off males because they are not ready to mate, or if this boxing is how hares "get in the mood."

Male hares sometimes have antlers, while rabbits never do. At first I assumed medieval pictures of horned hares were meant to convey only the idea of a male hare, but naturalist writings of the time are adamant about the existence of a rarely seen horned hare. There is now speculation that the "horned hare" is really a hare with a pathological boney growth on the head. Other explanations are possible: there could be hares with antlers in nonphysical dimensions, or early artists could have put horns on hares in stylized images to denote gender, and later naturalists interpreted the pictures literally. It does seem like the hare ought to have antlers. Most large grass eating animals do, especially the males. The horse is an exception, but that is probably where the unicorn comes in.

Three hares and a squirrel in an early nature book. Hare in center has horns. Illustration Joris Hoefnagel, 1575.

The absence of antlers is explained in an Aesop story where the hare goes to the god Jupiter and asks for antlers, with disastrous results. Marie de France in her later version has the hare approaching his goddess for a rack, which makes more sense to me, too. Diana would be the logical deity for animals to pray to, especially for antlers. Regardless, the goddess is no more sympathetic to the hare's request than Jupiter. She tells him that he could not possibly handle antlers. The hare will not be dissuaded, however, so at last the goddess crowns him with horns. The hare then finds it difficult to move with the extra weight.

The idea of antlers on a hare will probably always be in the wind. In the American West, where everyone enjoys a tall tale, credulous newcomers are encouraged to keep eyes peeled for the horned "jackalope," which is a jackrabbit/antelope cross endemic to remote desert regions. Postcards of the huge hybrids are common on drugstore racks beside more familiar animals and nature scenes. A popular south-western jazz band of the nineties took its name from the mythical beast.

Most hares and rabbits change color in winter, but several species of hare turn almost completely white. This probably cemented the hare's association with the moon, although the moon association exists even in places where hares are normally gray or brownish. Only domesticated rabbits have white or black fur. In magic, a white or black animal has special powers, usually drawn from the full or dark moon.

Habits of European hares and rabbits diverge in ways not seen in their North American cousins. The European rabbit, ancestor of all domestic rabbits, is native to the Iberian Peninsula. Rabbits were Spain's first major export, and the name for Spain is derived from the Latin word for rabbit. Iberia was an important source of tin from around 2000 BCE, so the first patrons of the tin mines may have been rabbits. As trade expanded, the European rabbit was introduced everywhere in the world and arrived in Britain around the year CE 1000. Thus early Pagan beliefs, outside of Spain and Portugal, were formed around the hare, not the rabbit.

Breeding European hares build solitary nests, which are indentations or "forms" lined with grass, while highly social rabbits build underground burrows called "warrens" to escape predators and nurse young. This distinction is important, because burrowing links this type of rabbit with mining and other wealth below the earth, as well as underworld themes such as death and ancestors. In desert areas of the Southwest and Mexico, Jackrabbits (which are really hares), will nest and rest underground to escape the broiling sun. They commandeer another animal's burrow rather than scraping their own.

The hare doe establishes each leveret in a separate place after birth, moving between nests to nurse. You can see why she limits her family size! The vegetation-lined "form" which harbors the leveret is akin to the nests in which some ground birds, such as the lapwing, nurture their young. Lapwing egg hunts were once a spring event in northern European countries. Germanic folklore about an *Osterhas* or "Easter Hare" that hides eggs may relate to the breeding habits of the Brown Hare. The "hare in the moon" appears to be carrying an egg, and the moon herself is egg-like when full. In America, German settlers crowned the Cottontail Rabbit as the Easter Hare. Cottontails (which really are rabbits), do not burrow but build well developed fur-lined nests on the ground to nurture their young.

Germanic hare symbolism is connected with early spring, which is the Eostre or Ostara sabbat for many traditions of witchcraft. The hare and the Eostre holiday are associated with dawn and the direction of east. Witches say the hare thumps on the earth at the equinox to wake up the sun. The eighth century monk and historian, St. Bede, writes that Anglo-Saxon Pagans called the month of April Eosturmonath after the goddess Eostre. The word "Easter" is derived from her name.

The ancient Greeks didn't have chocolate Easter bunnies, so they gave each other live hares as love tokens. These gifts were not necessarily fertility symbols: homosexuals also exchanged hares as expressions of love. The hare was the preferred sacrifice

Maenads offering hare to Dionysus. Greek vessel painted by Amasis, 550 BCE. Photo Marie-Lan Nguyen/Wikimedia Commons.

to Aphrodite. Artemis is linked with hares as both huntress and protectress of animals. Recall that Artemis keeps Agamemnon's fleet in harbor partly over objections to the crew's sacrifice of a hare.

The German goddess Holda is accompanied by a procession of hares carrying torches. The Lithuanian goddess Medeine, a forest goddess who protects animals, also has a sacred hare. The remains of many of her shrines are called "hare churches." A male hare deity named Hittavainen, originating in Finland and the Karelian Peninsula, is a god of hunters.

St. Melangell of Wales is a Christian figure associated with hares. The story goes that Melangell, born in Ireland to a royal family, left home to establish a hermitage because she did not wish to marry. A hunter-prince happened upon her when a hare sought refuge in Melangell's cloak, and the hounds, recognizing a holy being, refused to continue pursuit. The prince was impressed and ceded the valley to Melangell. Hares began flocking to Melangell's sanctuary, and they became known as "Melangell's lambs."

A holy woman who protects animals, refuses to marry, lives apart from human society and is associated with hounds and hares. Who does this sound like? Of course, the Romans usually re-dedicated the worship site for a local goddess to Diana, so Melangell's church was probably once a shrine to another Celtic goddess, who could even have been named Melangell. More likely this is the goddess Nimue, associated with hares and dogs (among other things), who became Diana's daughter after the arrival of the Roman religion. The only original part to this story is the hare/lamb connection. It recalls Caesar's observation that the Celts kept hares in pens.

There is another hare/lamb connection in a legend from the Isle of Man. A farmer asks a fenodyree, a type of fairy indigenous to the island, to herd his sheep down the mountain and into his barn. The fenodyree appears several hours later, panting, explaining that the job is finished, but that one of the little rams gave him much trouble, leading him three times around the mountain. The farmer investigates and discovers that the "little ram" is actually a little hare, also quite fatigued.

Witch persecutions capitalized on the notion that witches disguise themselves as hares. There is no animal except the cat as closely aligned with witches in the trials, and, perhaps not coincidentally, the Scottish word "mawkin" can mean hare or cat. Witches in hare form were accused of stealing butter and wreaking other mischief undetected. Even more damning was a witness who could testify to having been verbally addressed by a hare. If there was any remaining doubt, scratches or bruises on the accused could be attributed to encounters with dogs while in hare form.

Witch superstitions and fear of the fairy definitely put a dint in the hare's popularity. The nineteenth century Irish folklorist Lady Wilde could find nothing positive to say about the creature: "Hares are considered unlucky, as witches constantly assume their form ..."[9] Encounters with hares on hunting excursions could prove especially sinister, since the witch-hare could seek revenge. Most anecdotes of hare speech occur in the context of hunting. Almost any animal can talk in legend, but hare conversations have been remarkably enduring, recorded by folklorists up to the twentieth century. The hare is not a particularly vocal animal, except when distressed, but animals tend to have a more prominent place in myth and magic if they can stand on two legs, as the rabbit and hare do while they're scouting the field. In one story a hare asks the young man, "You wouldn't shoot your old grandfather now, would you?"

This hare's statement recalls another saying recorded in parts of Ireland, that a person who would eat a hare would kill his grandmother. Remember that the Cailleach sometimes takes the form of a hare. Notice the parallel to the Romanian saying about people who kill frogs, "A man who would kill a frog would kill his grandmother."

The high regard for the hare has created tension and controversy regarding hunting, in Pagan and Christian times. The Celts seem to have resolved this tension by placing boundaries around hare hunting, while in Greek myth disputes among the gods regarding hare killing suggest some type of social disagreement around hunting practices. The Greco-Roman philosopher Arrian maintained that hare hunting, while enjoyable and stimulating, need not involve the killing of the hare, whose screams were disagreeable. Arrian was referring to a type of hunt called coursing, in which dogs are used to chase the hare to a point of exhaustion before the kill. Montaigne, in his essay "On Cruelty," confessed that while he enjoyed coursing, he was repelled by its cruelty. Shakespeare was inspired by this essay to include a description of coursing from the hare's point of view in *Venus and Adonis*. Many other poets and writers, among them Thomas More and William Blake, took up the hare's defense, casting the poor creature as the gentle and innocent victim of man's persecution.

The domestication of the rabbit also played a part in softening the perception of the hare. Domestic rabbits are too small to produce much in the way of meat or pelts, and lack key nutrients, but they have remained a minor source of food and fur. The arrival of the Belgian Hare (which is really a rabbit) changed the course of leporid history.

Emerging in the eighteenth century in Flanders as a cross between wild and domestic rabbits, the animal that became known as the Belgian Hare was originally born of an attempt to produce larger, hardier meat stock. The resulting hybrid remained limited in appeal until British animal fanciers took a liking to the breed's resemblance to the Brown Hare. The Belgian Hare was then selectively bred to closely mimic this hare in appearance and certain behavior traits.

In the 1880s an Albany millionaire imported a few Belgian

Hares as a hobby, and then everybody wanted one. Importing rabbits to America is a bit like importing snow to Alaska, as this is where half the world's leporid population resides, but this is where rabbit breeding finally took off. It was soon discovered that the Belgian Hare, while a bit frisky, has a gentle disposition and makes a good pet. Rabbit breeding became focused on the pet trade, with the aim of producing smaller animals that children could easily handle. New breeds were developed later for meat or wool, but even here good temperament was important, as caring for rabbits is the children's job on a farm. For youngsters involved in rural farm organizations such as 4-H, raising rabbits is often a first project.

By the twentieth century nobody was scared of a bunny. Perhaps even the ancients saw some irony in their characterization of the hare as potent. She looks harmless, but knows how to fight. She looks harmless, but could be a magician or a goddess. She looks harmless, but might be a portent of danger. If so, Monty Python's "Rabbit of Caerbannog" is doubly ironic. In the scene from *The Holy Grail*, King Arthur and his knights rashly battle a giant rabbit (which, in King Arthur's time, would have really been a hare), resulting in the deaths of several men. The scene's humor relies on our perception of the rabbit as gentle. Arthur himself would not have understood what was funny about the scene, and his knights would have been too suspicious of a hare guarding a cave to be taken down.

Another measure of how much the conception of the leporid changed in popular belief can be found in the "killer rabbit" incident of Jimmy Carter's presidency. The President was fishing in Georgia when an unusually large Swamp Rabbit approached the boat, in which he was the only occupant. A Swamp Rabbit is a large Cottontail who spends a good deal of her time in the water. Why this particular Cottontail tried to climb into the boat is unknown—perhaps she just wanted a picture with the President—but Carter and his bodyguards believed it was an attack. The President did an admirable job of fending off the rabbit with his oars, but had the poor judgment to talk about the incident later. The story struck so many as ridiculous that even members of Carter's own party speculated on whether the strain of office was becoming too much. It was hardly the reason Carter lost his re-election bid, but it certainly didn't help.

Aside from the jackalope and "killer rabbit" episode, other dubious contributions to hare culture from America include the lucky rabbit's foot, the girlie pinup and, of course, Bugs Bunny.

Bugs Bunny relies on the conception of the hare as a good natured underdog to create sympathy for his character. The sassiness of Bugs would seem hostile coming from an animal acknowledged as capable in self-defense, such as a porcupine or skunk, and bullying coming from an animal considered fierce, such as a wolf or bear. But far from being just a fluffy bunny, Bugs is a rabbit to be reckoned with. He is smart, self-confident and totally irreverent. Inspired by Groucho Marx, with obvious influences from African and Native American folklore, Bugs' defense in hare-y situations comes from his quick wit, which is an enduring quality of the hare. In case anyone is bothered by the use of the words "rabbit" and "hare" to refer to the same bunny, Bugs thinks you need to loosen up, doc. The creators of the character use leporid appellations interchangeably for Bugs, choosing the name with the most tempting word play for the situation.

The lucky rabbit's foot sounds like yet another emblem drawing on the benign qualities of the hare, but the charm's original purpose was not about luck, but power. The charm comes from African American hoodoo, a synthesis of African, European and Native American magic. The use of animal parts to create charms is part of hoodoo and many other magical systems. The rabbit, however, may not be just any animal. She might be a witch. To ensure that the hoodoo rabbit foot charm comes from a witch, the rabbit is killed in a cemetery at the full moon or the dark moon, or on Friday the 13th, or on Halloween. A silver bullet is recommended, presumably so the "rabbit" doesn't use magic to get away. The left hind foot is the only part taken.

The rabbit is commonly believed to be a Native American symbol of fear. David Carson and Jamie Sams state in *Medicine Cards*, "Rabbit medicine people are so afraid of tragedy, illness, disaster, and 'being taken,' that they call those very fears to them to teach them lessons."[10] I have known people initiated in Native spiritual paths who were taught never to say the word "rabbit" in ceremony for fear of introducing fear into the circle. More positive Native attitudes towards rabbits do exist. In the Plains Indian Sun Dance ceremony, the rabbit represents humility, and dancers wear rabbit fur so they can enter the sacred space with an unassuming nature. Sometimes men who perform certain ceremonial tasks are called "rabbit men," because many believe the Sun Dance was once performed secretly by rabbits. A tribe in the far north takes the name Kawchottine or "Great Hare," out of respect for the creature which has supplemented their diet in lean times. For the Algonquian tribes, originally of the North-east and Great Lakes, the rabbit hero plays an important role in the creation of earth and of humans. In one story, he creates humans from the dead bodies of the first animals, thus assigning humans their animal clan. The rabbit appears as a trickster in legends of the south-eastern tribes, and may have influenced (and been influenced by) the Br'er Rabbit tales.

Br'er Rabbit, the African American trickster of the briar patch, consistently uses ingenuity and deception to obtain food and avoid traps set by other animals. In "Br'er Rabbit Fools Sis' Cow," Br'er Rabbit asks Sis' Cow to butt her head against a tree to shake down persimmons, knowing she will get her horns caught in the tree. Once Sis' Cow is deeply mired, Br'er Rabbit goes home to fetch his children and milk pails, and Sis' Cow is soon milked dry.

Br'er Rabbit has close precedents in Africa. The African hare is cunning and resourceful, often tricky, occasionally overconfident. In one tale the hare trips himself up by volunteering to take on a message the slow-moving ant is carrying for the moon. But the hare relays a mixed-up message. Instead of saying, "As the moon wanes, dies and grows again, so will you," the hare tells humanity, "As the moon grows, wanes, and dies, so shall you." The hare is struck by the angry moon in retaliation, receiving his characteristic split lip. Stories of how the hare got the split lip or bobbed tail are common all over the world.

The association of the hare with the moon is especially strong in East and South-east Asia. In China the hare in the moon is perceived carrying not an egg but a mortar and pestle, with which he mixes the elixir of life. This insight fits well with Pagan beliefs. The mortar and pestle, like the chalice or cauldron, is a woman's magical symbol and tool. In covens that use only Stone Age (i.e. nonmetal) tools, the mortar and pestle is used in place of the chalice and athame. The mortar and pestle also symbolizes herbology and alchemy, sciences that are influenced by the moon.

A Sri Lankan tale has the hare sacrificing himself by immolation for the Buddha, who then rescues him from the fire and gives him a home on the moon. The hare and fire association appears in many cultures. The hare's instinct to stay put when threatened works against her when the threat is fire, and hares often perish when farmers set fire to a field to remove scrub. This story is an example of how another late coming religion dealt with the issue of how to incorporate the hare into its theology.

With the solidification of Christian authority, many animals that had formerly been highly regarded by Pagans, such as the snake, bat, and pig, took on negative connotations. For these animals, positive symbolism can be found only from pre-Christian or early Christian sources, or from non-Western cultures. The hare is an exception. Because the hare continued to be viewed in a more or less positive light, hare symbolism has grown in richness and complexity over the millennia. Sometimes there is confusion regarding what the hare really is. Ted Hughes wrote, "The hare is the tiger is the woman is his blood is all kinds of things, I'm not quite sure."[11] What do we make of a creature that is spring and harvest, pugnacious and meek, masculine and feminine, sexual and chaste, rabbit and ram? Does the hare mean anything at this point or is she/he only an embodiment of contradiction?

In Western thinking there is an impulse to treat the hare as an archetype of whatever sentiment is exalted at the time. Thus when war is exalted the hare is fierce. When martyrdom is exalted the hare is victim. When sexuality is exalted the hare is promiscuous. This instinct only gets turned on its head when values are in flux, such as when Christianity as the new religion first confronted the hare's association with sexuality.

There are signs that the hare's position is again at a nadir, drawing connotations of powerlessness and ineffectiveness, the down side of martyrdom and self-sacrifice. The Christian image of the hare is simply not attractive at a time when people are searching for empowerment. The hare is resilient, however, and will no doubt be staging a comeback. The hare has always been here for humans, providing whatever is required, be it food, love, courage or inspiration. When needs and values change, a new hare emerges, one who continues to nourish and strengthen her tribe.

The Tortoise and the Hare

I debated including this story. Everyone has heard it, and I never much liked the "slow and steady wins the race" moral pegged onto the end.

A small amount of digging, however, revealed that the story has been slanted quite a few ways over the centuries, depending on the storyteller and the moral standard in vogue.

Any way you slice it, though, the hare loses this race.

Aesop, to whom this story is attributed, was a slave in Greece in the sixth century BCE. Older versions of Aesop fables have been found throughout the Middle East and India, with the oldest dating back to Sumer.

Hare and tortoise confer with fox in Francis Barlow's 1666 illustration.

The whole race in question would not have occurred if the hare had not decided to criticize the tortoise's feet. Why these feet were not perfectly acceptable for a tortoise is unclear, but when the hare laughed at his feet the tortoise smiled too and declared she could beat the hare in a race. This was even funnier.

The two went to the fox, known for her fair and trustworthy nature, and asked her to establish the boundaries of the race. With the fox as a judge, the tortoise started out immediately, without even waiting for a ready-set-go.

The hare could have bounded after the tortoise, making up the distance quickly, but the whole premise was absurd. She tarried at the starting line and even snoozed a bit. When she snapped out of it, she jolted forward, dashing as fast as her feet could carry her. The tortoise was already across the finish line, however, taking a little nap herself.

The hare then had to admit, the tortoise had won the race.

This is, technically, the end of the story, but it should be mentioned that an apocryphal version was asserted in 1915 by Lord Dunsany. He claimed that, though the tortoise did cross the finish line first, the story as it really happened was only passed on to a select few. He said this happened because:

... very few of those that witnessed [the race] survived the great forest-fire that happened shortly after. It came up over the weald by night with a great wind. The Hare and the Tortoise and a very few of the beasts saw it far off from a high bare hill that was at the edge of the trees, and they hurriedly called a meeting to decide which messenger they should send to warn the beasts in the forest.

They sent the Tortoise.[12]

The Cupid and the Hare

A recurring theme in leporid lore is the hare that eludes capture. This hare symbolizes things which we cannot obtain—or more precisely, things which we cannot and should not obtain.

There is an orchard in the land of the evening star belonging to nymphs most beloved of Aphrodite. The love-children of these nymphs are the Erotes—the Cupids—who pass their days in sheltered pleasure. Pelting each other with apples, wrestling on the ground, dancing like playful birds around the grove—there is nothing to disturb their mirth until the enchanted hare appears.

She slips cautiously in the orchard to browse the apples, but once discovered all commotion ensues. She is chased, shouted at, blocked and grabbed. She is faster than anything, and she must be captured alive.

The ancients inform us that the hare possesses the gifts of Aphrodite to a superlative degree. To these gifts the goddess added the gift of camouflage, the gift of wiliness and the gift of speed. She has instructed the hare to guard her possessions jealously, an edict which the hare obeys.

And so the hare cannot be caught. There is frustration, disappointment, groaning and tears across the enchanted orchard as she flees into the twilight.

The Cupids return to their games and soon there is laughter in the grove of the favored nymphs. The Cupids toss apples, flit above the garden, drop to the ground in peaceful slumber. There is nothing to mar their contentment, until the elusive hare appears, again.

Hare Review

Magical Qualities:
fast runner, stands upright on two legs, high reproductive rate, can store sperm while infertile (hares), raises young in ground nest (hares, Cottontails), burrows (European rabbits, Jackrabbits), aggressive (hares and wild rabbits), confuses predators, large ears, good hearing, good at camouflage, social (domestic and European rabbits)

Magical Applications:

Other Associations:

If it Looks Like a Duck, it Could Still be a Witch

Any three year old can tell you witches change into animals. Or they change other people into animals. Or they change animals into other animals. You'd think that's all we did with our time, when we weren't flying on broomsticks and making nasty tasting brew. But I have to admit, changing into animals is one of the coolest things we do.

Changing into animals is what shapeshifting is about. Shapeshifting doesn't mean to reincarnate as an animal—that's transmigration. It doesn't mean to invade the body of an animal—that's possession. It doesn't mean to become an animal in spirit while the human body remains behind—that's trance meditation. It doesn't mean to imagine yourself as an animal—that's imagination. It doesn't mean to put on an animal costume—that's pretending. Shapeshifting means to take the form of an animal. Literally. For a short space of time the shapeshifter's body turns into (or at least looks like) an animal body. Many people don't believe this is possible, and for this reason an important area of magic is misrepresented and poorly understood.

How is shapeshifting possible? The short answer is that no one knows. In the rationalistic mindset dominating the twenty-first century, we emphatically disbelieve what we don't understand. "I don't see how," is usually synonymous with saying, "I don't believe." Honestly, I don't see how either, but I will try to make some guesses.

I first experienced shapeshifting as an observer. Our group had defined a rather large ritual circle, and I noticed one of my companions had changed into a deer. When I looked away and back again, she had resumed her normal form. "My eyes were playing tricks on me," I told her. "For a moment, you looked like a deer." My companion had no sensation of changing form, but she told me this: "When I was a little girl I overheard my Cherokee grandmother and great-grandmother arguing about my 'Indian' name. My great-grandmother wanted to call me 'little spotted deer,' but my grandmother liked a different name, which I was later given." I got to know this spotted deer woman well, and I am sure she was telling me the truth. What I still find interesting is not that the woman changed form or that I noticed it or that someone else had noticed it before me, but that the woman herself had neither decided to change form nor noticed anything remarkable.

Years later I was to have a dramatic shift into animal form that I did not initiate. It happened in the daytime during sexual intercourse, another situation where minds are altered. I was facing away from my partner when suddenly I became aware that I had changed into a goat. I lost my forward, stereoscopic vision and my eyesight became directed to both sides. I was fascinated to find I had long, floppy goat ears. At this point I heard my partner mutter, "Pan ... Pan ... Pan ... " He was invoking the goat god Pan! Not only that, he was asking Pan to enter his body, and Pan, apparently not being into human/beast sexual interaction, had changed me into a nanny goat. I stayed in my goat body for some time, looking with my goat eyes at my lovely goat ears, until "Pan" had finished.

Most shapeshifting happens spontaneously in ritual space, usually in the context of "high magic," where formal boundaries define the place between worlds. Both the shapeshifter and the observers are in an altered frame of mind, so perhaps shifting is taking place on a different dimension than the physical. Shapeshifting is temporary and typically fleeting, although since timepieces are not allowed in ritual space, and perceptions of time in this space seldom correspond to sun measured time, the length of the transformation cannot really be known.

Shapeshifting can be observed by one person, by a few people or by everyone in the group. Those present who do not see the shifting cannot give useful feedback. They will say that they were looking the other way, not paying attention or otherwise not focused on the shapeshifter. It's considered bad form to interrupt the flow of the ritual by remarking, "Hey! Look at her! She's a dog!" and the outburst would probably startle the person back to human form anyway. Often shapeshifting occurs when there has been no pre-arranged decision to practice it, and the time it occurs cannot be predicted because time is not operating in a "normal" way within the ritual space. The unstable nature of shapeshifting leads me to suspect it is happening in a nonphysical dimension, even when there is collaboration by a number of people.

Yet since physical form is mutable in this altered, high energy space, perhaps the body really is changing. The circumstances that allow shapeshifting are also those which sometimes produce spontaneous physical healing. I once burned my fingers badly while putting out a fire during ritual. The skin on my fingers immediately blistered and tore. I grabbed my fingers with the other hand and held them a moment, channeling energy; when I let go, the skin was completely healed, like it had never been burned, though the carpet was still melted. The material world is much more plastic than we commonly recognize.

Spontaneous shapeshifting aside, why change—why consciously change—into animal form? Historically there have been many reasons why witches and others have taken animal form.

A pervasive belief through medieval times was that witches changed into animals to attend satanic rites with the Devil. The genesis of this Satan-based belief is well documented in Christian theology and developing legal theory. Though many clerics maintained that shapeshifting was an illusion planted in the minds of witches and witnesses, the idea explained away certain logistical problems, such as how satanic adherents were traversing wilderness areas after dark, how they could travel when old or infirm, and how they could travel without being noticed on the road or missed in the village.

The idea that a person could change into an animal as a form of disguise, however, was *not* new. The phenomenon was recorded in numerous classical writings. One of the most interesting examples, which greatly influenced medieval thinking on witches, was in a second century work of fiction called *The Golden Ass*, by Apuleius.

Apuleius was a lawyer of North African origin practicing in Rome. He was a priest of Isis and Osiris with a marked disdain for Christianity, so his view of shapeshifting, whether accurate or not, was not a Christian one at any rate. In *The Golden Ass* he presents a fictionalized version of the types of cases and criminals he encountered in the courts, and a significant portion of the book deals with witchcraft. Witchcraft, *per se*, was not illegal in the empire, but it was illegal to defraud through the use of magic, and the courts became involved in issues surrounding the sale of various ointments and potions, particularly love potions. Significantly, the ointments were not of concern because they didn't work—they were presumed effective—but because they were used to capture unwilling hearts or perpetrate other forms of fraud.

The sorceress in *The Golden Ass*, whose name is Pamphile, uses magic to coerce the affection of whatever young man she is currently enamored with. One of her methods is to change into animal form to gain admission to her loved one's chamber. The hero of the story, Lucius, peers through a chink in the wall and witnesses Pamphile applying an ointment to her skin, which transforms her into an owl. After Pamphile flies away, Lucius begs his girlfriend to swipe some of the ointment for him, as he is enthralled with the idea of becoming an owl. The girlfriend steals the wrong ointment, and Lucius is transformed into a donkey. The ensuing adventures follow the Ass née Lucius as he tries to obtain the antidote and escape animal slavery. Here, then, are two reasons presented by Apuleius for shapeshifting: to disguise oneself in order to commit some nefarious deed and to gain a novel experience. Apuleius is critical of both motives, arguing that a life lived for oneself, even if not at the expense of others, is fraught with bad luck and suffering. Only by dedicating oneself wholly to the Goddess, and doing solely her bidding, can one hope to escape life's inevitable miseries and misfortunes. This is, perhaps, a different point of view than many Pagans hold today (*Do as you will and harm none*), but it is typical of the time, particularly in the Egyptian priesthood.

Shapeshifting as a lover's deception is often mentioned in myth. Usually the sorcerer changes to an animal—a favorite cat or dog—to gain entrance to the loved one's bed. Sometimes the object of desire is changed to an animal. The temptation must have been strong to fraudulently invoke the concept to escape punishment for infidelity or other sexual transgressions. (*I didn't mean to sleep with her, honey; I thought she was Fido.*) There is little doubt that fabrications of shapeshifting were made to implicate enemies during the witch persecutions. For example, a Massachusetts woman was accused of changing into a cat by a man named Robert Downer, who later said he feared retribution from an earlier charge he had made against her.

A less sinister Christian use of shapeshifting was employed by early Irish converts, who had the task of reconciling the deluge recounted in the Bible with Irish oral history, which predates the Biblical flood by many centuries. Enter Tuan mac Cairill, who witnesses the annihilation of four populations of immigrants to Ireland. Tuan is born a man and survives for many years after the rest of his people succumb to plague. He gradually forgets what it is like to be human and pads through the forest like a cat and leaps over rocks like a goat. He is startled one day to see his reflection in a pool: part boar, part badger, part crow—naked as a fish, skinny as a stripped bush, wrinkled as an empty sack. On this same day a great storm batters the island,

and Tuan, sleeping in his cave, dreams he is a stag. Upon awakening, he discovers he has acquired a stag's body during the night. He notices that a few people were washed ashore in boats during the storm. Tuan observes the new people as they grow, multiply, decline and finally become bones glinting in the sun. By now an old stag, hounded by wolves who seek to eat him, Tuan goes back into his cave and dreams he is a boar. The story continues in this vein as Tuan becomes boar, hawk and salmon. After living an eon in the ocean, he is caught by fishermen and devoured by a descendant of Noah, who gives birth to him as a child. Tuan can thus report the histories of the peoples of Ireland to the scholar monk who baptizes him many years later. Elements of this story appear in other tales, so this is likely an old story adapted to a new use rather than a cynical fabrication for justifying scripture.

On the subject of Christian shapeshifting, mention should be made of St. Patrick's *fith-fath*. A *fith-fath* is a charm for changing into animal form. It comes from a Scottish word that translates as "deer likeness," although *fith-faths* can cause other transformations. Patrick invoked the *fith-fath* on himself and his comrades while fleeing the pursuing army of an Irish king. The endangered Christians escaped easily in the form of deer. Patrick's *fith-fath* involved appeals to Christian elements, but the *fith-fath* is a very Pagan concept.

In another *fith-fath*, the maiden Sadb, the beloved of the hero Fionn MacCumal, falls victim to a rival fairy who covets Fionn's affection. The young woman, now a deer, retires to the forest and gives birth to a son, the bard Oisin, who has human likeness except for a tuft of fawn hair on his forehead. The boy returns to live with his human family and Sadb lives out her days as a doe. She shapeshifts briefly back into human form when she encounters her son hunting in the forest to remind him that she is his mother. Oisin retains a fey quality even though he lives among humans and has human form. No doubt this imbues his poetry with a special magic.

Shapeshifting can involve any animal (and it doesn't have to be an animal), but there are some with stronger associations than others. Any animal associated with death, such as the owl, is a candidate. So is any animal that is all black or all white. Animals which change from dark to white with the seasons, such as the ermine, are strongly linked. Horses are common because they are used in travel. Amphibians are shapeshifters due to their developmental journey from water to land. Swans are very popular. They are white, and they live in water and air. Mute swans would be a logical choice for a *fith-fath*, since they presumably can't tattle on their enchanter.

In the story of Cerridwyn's Cauldron a young man gains poetic mastery through shapeshifting. This tale begins with the birth of Cerridwyn's twins, the beautiful Creirwy (meaning "light") and the ugly Afagddu (meaning "dark"). Cerridwyn seeks to compensate her son for his ugliness by making him extremely wise, and toward that end brews a collection of magic herbs in her cauldron. The first three drops of the brew will give the taster a vast degree of wisdom, but only after the concoction has boiled for a year and a day. During this time, the cauldron must be stirred frequently, and Cerridwyn enlists the help of a boy named Gwion. When the mixture is ripe, Gwion spills three drops of the burning liquid on his thumb, which he reflexively pops in his mouth. With his newfound enlightenment, Gwion recognizes that Cerridwyn will kill him for this transgression, so he lopes away quickly as a hare. Cerridwyn is right on his heels as a greyhound. Gwion becomes a salmon and leaps in the ocean; Cerridwyn chases him as an otter. Gwion flies away as a sparrow; Cerridwyn bears down on him as a hawk. Gwion changes to a grain of wheat and falls hidden on the ground. Cerridwyn as a hen easily discerns Gwion's seed and eats him. Notice there are four transformations here, one for each of the seasons. Each season has a predator, the goddess Cerridwyn hounding it to its next transformation.

In Cerridwyn's womb the seed of Gwion gestates. He is reborn as Taliesin (meaning "shining brow") and thrown into the ocean by his mother, who cannot bear to kill her offspring yet remains angry over the theft of magic. Taliesin is rescued by a fisherman and becomes the greatest of the Welsh poets. The ability to shapeshift is thus an enduring quality of the Celtic bard.

Pregnancy is a recurrent theme in shapeshifting mythology. When Gwydion and his brother Gilvaethwy rape a servant of King Math, the king in retaliation waves his wand and transforms the pair into deer. The next year the brothers return with their baby fawn, which Math names Hychdwn (stag-man) before transforming the pair into hogs. A year later the little hoglet is named Hychdwn (tall swine) by Math, and the two are changed into wolves. When the bad little wolves return with a wolf-pup, who is named Bleiddwn (wolfman), the brothers' punishment is determined complete and they are restored to their human forms.

The Norse god Loki changes himself into a mare to have sex with the giant horse of a giant in the epic *Gylfaginning*. Spurred on by Loki, the intrepid gamblers of Asgard have wagered that the giant cannot finish building a great wall by the first day of summer—and the sun, the moon and the goddess Freya are promised to the giant should he succeed. When the giant appears likely to win the prizes, Loki decides to sideline the giant's workhorse with a little hanky-panky. While in mare form he conceives the foal that becomes Odin's eight-legged horse Sleipnir. (All these shapeshifting animal pregnancies make me feel like I dodged a bullet in my tryst with Pan. I could have had a kid!)

Loki is an inveterate shapeshifter. He changes himself into a fly in an attempt to win a bet with a pair of dwarf magicians. He buzzes around irritating the craftsmen as they forge magical tools, hoping to distract them from their work and lessen the quality of the finished product. In this case, he succeeds only in being a nuisance. Loki also turns himself into a fly to enter Freya's house to steal the priceless Brisingamen necklace. Once inside, he changes into a flea and bites the cheek of the sleeping goddess until she shifts to a position where the necklace can be pulled over her head. Loki then switches to his own form and flees with the goods. This would be the end of the story, but Loki has to hide the necklace, for once it's missing he'll be prime suspect. He heads north, disguises himself as a seal and hides out with a bunch of other seals on one of those rocky seal islands, looking like any other plain ordinary seal except that he wears a piece of jewelry. The god Heimdall, who lives in the far north, sees through the ruse and also disguises himself as a seal. Since he is not wearing a necklace, Heimdall pounces on Loki unawares and the two seal-gods engage in combat until Heimdall has wrested the necklace away.

Loki is an irritant to the other gods even when he is not a flea or a fly. On the lam for some big time mischief, Loki tries to hide himself as a crow, a lizard and finally a salmon before he is caught and punished. While a salmon, he teaches humans about nets and fishing. The net turns out to be his undoing, because it helps the gods catch the salmon-Loki. They make Loki resume his normal form and tie him in a cave, where he remains.

Loki does not have a cult of worship, and he is acknowledged but not invoked. He is not just tricky: he is erratic, unpredictable and capricious, seeming to lack mastery even over himself. Nor is he equivalent to the Christian Devil. His actions can bring benefit as well as harm, and he is too disordered to represent a malignant force.

Most of the Norse gods shapeshift. Freya, for example, changes into a falcon, and she has been known to lend her plumage to other gods who desire the power of flight. The Norns sometimes shapeshift into swans in order to traverse water. The Old Norse word for Pagan is *eigi einhamr*, which means "not of one shape."

All this discussion about the reasons for shapeshifting makes it sound like it should make sense, but what do we make of Circe's shapeshifting of Odysseus' crew? The Greek heroes, on return from their victory in the Trojan War, run into quagmires everywhere, and none so dangerous as on the island of vowels, Aeaea, home of the sorceress Circe. The twenty-two from the ship sent to reconnoiter are met by wolves and lions, but not just any wolves and lions. These dangerous looking beasts behave in an exceedingly strange way, standing on hind legs and gently stroking the sailors like intimate friends. The men continue to the mansion of Circe, where they are warmly greeted and invited to supper—all but the leader, who falls back and hides, smelling a rat. He watches in horror as his fellow sailors devour a drugged meal, then lay about in a soporific state as Circe wields her wand above them, transforming them into hogs.

Odysseus, upon hearing the news, rushes out blindly without a plan. The god Hermes intercepts him and offers a sprig of moly as a charm against taking animal form. Odysseus meets the beautiful Circe and accepts her drugged meal, but smells the moly flower as she raises her wand, which gives him strength to raise his own sword.

Circe is immediately repentant, offering sex and companionship in exchange for her life. Here the story becomes truly odd, for Odysseus becomes coy, reluctant to embrace the increasingly ardent Circe. He exacts a promise for no enchantments of any variety before he will consent to have sex with her, then makes her promise to restore the "hogs," "lions" and "wolves" to their manly forms. Is Circe confused about the story line? Isn't she supposed to turn men into animals in retaliation for something, like sexual rejection? Her first choice is to make men beasts, then she makes the man a lover when that trick doesn't work.

Like Circe, the mind of the Russian Baba Yaga is hard to fathom. Baba Yaga appears in fairy tales as a bony old woman with a huge nose, though she can change herself into a snake, turtle, fox, crab or bee. Her most common animal form is some type of bird, especially a pelican. She lives deep in the forest in a small windowless house that stands on chicken legs. The house itself moves and sometimes spins in a circle. Baba Yaga is a woman of few words, for it is said that she ages a year for every question she answers. Sometimes she is helpful, sometimes diabolical, but in any event the hero or heroine who seeks her must summon strength and courage for the journey. When not flying as a bird, Baba Yaga flies in her mortar and pestle, using the pestle to steer. She can be secretive, erasing her path through the sky with a broom. Baba Yaga is often characterized as destructive, and it is said that she cuts the moon in half with her sickle, beats down crops in the field, and devours her human victims leaving their skulls on her fence posts. These are vivid metaphors for her rule of death, harvest and the cycles of light.

Baba Yaga, Cerridwyn and Cailleach Bhear are referred to as harvest, death, crone or battle goddesses, but they are more complex than any of these appellations; hence their need to assume many shapes in order to express their nature. Cultivating the favor of these goddesses brings greater insight and mastery in the art of shapeshifting.

When trying to shapeshift, you will find it easier at night in subdued lighting. The full moon aids tremendously. Though pretending to be a specific animal and acting as if you are that animal may help set the stage for shapeshifting, remember that shapeshifting is not the same as pretending. Try to let go of preconceived notions about what will happen while in animal form. Animals see the world differently than us, literally. This change in perception precipitates a change in view, bringing a deeper animal wisdom.

During the transformation, intellectual faculties and awareness remain intact. You might spontaneously shapeshift, but you cannot remain transformed against your will unless you are drugged. The cautions in the section on guided meditation remain relevant here. No drug or alcohol use and no camera flashes. Touching is discouraged. The shapeshifting goat episode I described earlier involved touching, but that was a special case, as the physical contact was not in any way startling.

It is best to shapeshift only within a well defined magic circle. The circle can be indoors or outside in a safe place, but do not allow pets in the vicinity as they may react in an unpredictable way. Be sure to ground and center when the shapeshifting ritual is over.

Expending the high levels of psychic energy needed for shapeshifting depletes electrolytes. This is one of the reasons we eat after ritual. Seaweed is a good food for replacing electrolytes. If you don't want to eat, at least have an electrolyte replacement drink. Alcohol taken directly after the ritual will further deplete your electrolytes. Rest is important following shapeshifting, both to restore electrolytes and to replenish energies. Plan to take it easy the rest of the evening, and possibly even to sleep a little later the next day.

In the long run, choosing to shapeshift and being able to shapeshift is less important than recognizing the phenomenon exists and could at some point happen to anyone. Who wants to live their life explaining away the things that happen because they "don't see how"?

The Little Red Cow

This Russian fairy tale begins, as many do, with a good princess, undeserving sisters and a wicked stepmother. The princess passes the test which makes her wife of the handsome prince, but does not live happily ever after, at least not at first.

After the young Princess Maria's mother died, a new queen married her father the king. The two daughters born soon after were treated well, but Princess Maria was given only crusts of bread to eat. Princess Maria did not starve, however, and daily brought the crusts back to her stepmother. "Find out why the naughty child is not starving to death," the queen commanded her eldest daughter.

The older half sister followed Princess Maria on her daily walk to the meadow. "Oh, my sweet sister," exclaimed Princess Maria when she spied her, "Come put your head on my lap, and I will pick the lice out of your hair." The sister put her head on Princess Maria's lap, and Princess Maria sang soft lullabies as she picked the lice. On her first song the sister's right eye shut; on the second song her left eye shut. The eldest half sister returned home that evening and did not know why Princess Maria was not starving.

The next day the queen sent her second daughter to follow Princess Maria. Again at the open meadow Princess Maria entreated, "Dear sister, place your head on my lap, and I will pick the lice out of your hair."

Princess Maria sang to her sister as she plucked the head lice. She sang a song that closed the sister's right eye, then she sang a song that closed the sister's left eye. But Princess Maria forgot that her youngest sister had three eyes. The sister came home and told her mother, "Princess Maria bows to the right leg of her little red cow, and the cow then gives her as much milk and cream as she wants. Princess Maria also has nice clothes that she wears in the meadow, but she takes them off before she comes home."

The wicked queen was incensed and demanded that the king slaughter the red cow, which he did. The rest of the family ate the cow, but Princess Maria begged a bit of the intestines, which she wrapped on the gatepost. From the entrails of the little red cow grew a tree with little red berries. The berries attracted legions of birds, who sang the most beautiful songs in exchange for their supper. From far away, Prince Ivan heard about the tree, the birds, the songs and the berries. He brought a large dish to Princess Maria's stepmother and said he would marry the sister who could fill the dish with red berries.

The younger sisters, each in turn, were given first chance to pluck the berries, but the birds would not allow this. The birds tried to peck all of the sisters' eyes out. Naturally, Princess Maria was allowed to fill the bowl unmolested, so she married the prince and left with him for far off lands.

In most fairy tales the story ends here, because the now favored princess has the sense to stay in the far away kingdom. Princess Maria's pride would not allow her to do that, however. She bore a child soon into her marriage, a strong healthy boy, and she felt compelled to go back and show him off to the family who had treated her so poorly. The wicked stepmother immediately turned her into a goose.

As the goose flew away, the stepmother enchanted Maria's oldest half sister, the one with only two eyes, to look like the Princess Maria. The imposter returned home with Prince Ivan, who was completely fooled.

There was an old man in Ivan's court, however, who saw through the ruse. This man was tutor to Ivan and Maria's precocious son, already studying though he was not yet weaned. The old man rose early the next morning, washed himself carefully, and brought the baby to an open field, where he waited until a flock of geese approached. "My geese, my gray geese!" he cried. "Where is the mother of this infant?" The geese replied, "You will find her in the next flock." The old man waited until another flock appeared and again asked, "My geese, my gray geese! Where is the child's mother?" At this, one gray goose dropped from the sky and discarded her goose feather skin. She took the boy and nursed him, but warned the tutor, "I will come here tomorrow to nurse him again, but the next day I must fly far away, beyond the dark forest and the high mountains."

Needless to say, the old tutor was scolded soundly by the imposter wife when he returned with the boy, but he rose early the next day to repeat the process just the same. Prince Ivan stalked the old tutor to the field and heard him cry "My geese, my gray geese! Where is the mother of this infant?" Again the geese replied, "You will find her in the next flock." When the gray goose who was Maria discarded her feathers to nurse, Prince Ivan burned the goose skin. As the mother returned the infant to the tutor, she smelled the burning feathers and saw her husband. As Prince Ivan grabbed her, she turned into a frog, then a lizard, then an insect, then a spindle that twirled furiously. Ivan broke the spindle in two and threw the top half behind him and the bottom half in front of him; Princess Maria returned in all her splendor.

As the two returned home the imposter sister declared that Maria was false, yelling "destroyer" and "murder" at her. But Prince Ivan recognized his true wife, and he killed the imposter sister. Maria now had her family back again.

Musings in a Different Form

1) What shapeshifting goddess do you most identify with?
2) Why would changing the brothers Gilvaethwy and Gwydion into animals be considered punishment for rape?
3) When we say the gods have tied Loki in a cave, what does that mean?
4) How is a spindle related to shapeshifting?
5) Finish the "Hare Review" by filling in the last two sections.
6) What does the "three hares" riddle say to you?
7) Here is another riddle to decipher: "A hopper of ditches, a cutter of corn, a brown little cow without any horns." How is the hare each of these things?
8) What are the gifts of Aphrodite which the hare possesses to a superlative degree?
9) What do you think of the bunny as an emblem of the girlie pinup? What leporid associations does this symbol draw on or distort?
10) Enough talking about it! Time to go to the rabbits, so to speak.

A full moon night is the best time for this ritual. Lighting should be subdued but it should not be completely dark.

For this first attempt, you will invoke the rabbit or hare. Think about the attributes you admire in the hare and write them here.

On the altar, place a hare picture, the moon card from the tarot, or the R (Rad) rune. Alternatively, you can inscribe R or the word hare on the candle that you light during the shapeshifting.

Cast a circle to raise energy. Light a candle and ask the hare goddess to join the circle. Praise her sterling qualities. Offer her a small food gift, such as alfalfa sprouts or a carrot.

Close your eyes and stand with your feet shoulder width apart and your arms over your head at approximately a 45 degree angle. Your palms should be flat, as if you were holding a large platter.

Now ask the spirit of the hare to come to you. Say something like "Hare Goddess, enter me now, and make me one with thee." She may respond quickly, or you may feel nothing at first. If your arms get tired, lower them and stand quietly. As soon as you feel the energy enter, follow it. You may feel compelled to move or dance, or you may just feel like standing there. Open your eyes and notice any change in your perception. You may hear or smell things in a new way. Pay attention to how you feel. Your next actions will be guided by instinct; again, you may just stand or sit quietly. This is what hares spend most of their time doing.

You may reluctantly regain your human form, or it may happen spontaneously. At any rate, this early exploration should be on the brief side. You must formally take steps to regain your human form, even if you think you're back or never changed. Stand and say, "I am ready to regain my womanly form. Hare, I thank you for your beautiful presence, and I ask your blessing as you depart. I am now a woman."

Now you can open the circle. Make sure you are well grounded before you leave the room or site. Have something to eat or drink.

For this ritual you need:

R rune, picture of hare, or moon tarot card

Candle

Carrot of other rabbit food offering

11) What if "nothing happened" in your shapeshifting ritual? Often shapeshifting experiences are transient and fleeting. Try several times until you are aware of the moment of change. Record your experiences even if you think nothing happened. Remember that other animals are not as different from us as we are conditioned to believe. You won't feel like a totally different person while in animal form, because you will still be the same person.

a. It's easier to shapeshift with other people. Members of your group may notice your change in form even though the experience completely misses you due to its subtlety. It's nice to get that validation.

b. Do an animal meditation with the hare or other animal and ask for guidance in your shapeshifting.
c. Try the ritual with your favorite animal, or try the raven, doe or bear.
d. "Fake it till you make it." After asking the animal to come into your body, begin vocalizing and dancing like that animal and see what happens.
e. Immerse yourself for a few weeks in thoughts, pictures and conversations about a particular animal. Pray to this animal daily. Then do the shapeshifting ritual again.
f. If the shapeshifting exercise becomes frustrating for you, put it aside for now and move on.

Chapter 9

Creatures of the Otherworld

Bow, Bow, wow, wow; the Moone's eclipsed,
Ile to the Church-yard and sup: Since I turn'd Wolfe,
I bark and howle, and digge vp graues, I will neuer haue
the Sunne shine againe, tis midnight, deepe darke midnight,
get a prey, and fall too, I haue catcht thee now.
Arrre.
—John Ford, *The Lover's Melancholy*

The Hounds of Hel

"Your grandfather wishes to speak to you," said my friend Rita. "He says to tell you Barney is with him." She giggled. "That's an odd name. Is that an American name?"

"Barney was my childhood dog," I replied. It is also the name of President George W. Bush's Scottish terrier and the name of a well-known children's character. It became a popular dog name, but few had heard of the purple dinosaur or Bush Jr. when Rita gave me this psychic reading. I was way ahead of the canine Barney craze.

"Did you really name your dog *Barnabas Collins*?" the kids at my school asked incredulously when I got my first puppy. It seemed over the top to everyone, but I was the #1 fan of the vampire soap opera, and I later mourned the demise of *Dark Shadows* almost as much as the death of Barney.

Rita was relaying messages from my grandfather, who had recently died. He was considered a difficult man by most, a curmudgeon even when young, but he had always been good to me. He related better to dogs than to people and formed a close attachment to the dogs of all his children and grandchildren. I had always felt uneasy about being away from home when

Barney died, and it relieved me greatly to know that my grandfather was watching over him in the spirit world.

When I gave Barney that unfortunate name, I did not understand just how much dogs and vampires have in common. Dogs, like vampires, belong to this world and to the land of the dead. They have a predatory aspect and are associated with blood. They incite fear. But unlike vampires, who operate as rogue agents, dogs are yoked to a greater authority. They are emissaries from the otherworld, sent to portend the end of life, protect us from untimely death, and guide us on the final passage.

The first dogs were domesticated to eat garbage as humans transitioned to a settled lifestyle 12,000 years ago. As carrion eaters, dogs assumed funerary functions formerly held by wolves. When dogs were later bred as sentinels, they logically began guarding the gates of death.

Mosaic from Pompeii, Italy. Inscription translates, "Beware of dog." CE 79 or earlier. Photo Eufrosine/Wikimedia Commons.

In Greek mythology, the many headed dog Cerberus guards the portal. It is said that one head watches the dead to keep them from escaping while another warns the living not to enter. Each head is maned with serpents and the tail is barbed. When Psyche goes to the underworld to ask a favor of Persephone, she gets around Cerberus by throwing a single piece of bread to the beast and slipping past as the three heads fight over it.

Herakles in lion skin bowing before Cerberus, who has snakes on her heads. Cerberus is often pictured with two heads, not three. Greece, Sixth century, BCE. Photo Bibi Saint-Pol/Wikimedia Commons.

The Norse hound Garm guards the gate of Helheim, which is where the dead belonging to the goddess Hel reside. Garm has four eyes and a bloody chest and, when not challenging newcomers, crouches in a hole called the Gnipa Cave, which is like a doghouse for death hounds. The dead were once buried or cremated with a piece of food called a Hel-cake, which they gave to Garm as they passed through the gate. Garm is noisy, fierce and vigilant. The god Odin can get past Garm on his mission to Helheim only because he rides the magic horse Sleipnir.

In the Welsh fairyland of Annwn, white hounds with red ears

hunt with the ageless kings. They are called the Cwn Annwn, the Hounds of the Abyss, or Cwn Mamau, the Hounds of the Mothers. The entries to Annwn can be accessed through ancient burial mounds or caves, but these are portals to a parallel world, not roads to an underground realm. On Beltane and at other unpredictable times, the Cwn Mamau leave their home in the company of the god Gwynn ap Nudd to recruit living souls. They howl loudly racing over the land and across the sky. It has been said that they sound deafening in the distance and grow softer as they approach.

Similar to the flight of the Cwn Mamau is the Wild Hunt of Germanic lore. A noisy cavalcade of dogs, goats and horses thunders across the sky accompanied by high winds, led by various deities, such as Odin, Perchta or Holda. The Wild Hunt can happen at any time, but is especially linked with Winter Solstice.

Another related event is *La Santa Compaña,* The Holy Company, a pilgrimage of figures garbed in white robes (or black), accompanied by a black dog. *La Santa Compaña* occurs in the Celtic province of Galicia, in the northwest corner of Spain, and portends death in the vicinity. Unlike the cacophony of the Wild Hunt, *La Compaña* is silent, and only those gifted with second sight can see the figures. They are perceived by others by the smell of candle wax and the restive behavior of domestic animals, particularly dogs. Mortals used to be commandeered to lead the procession, and there are magical techniques for avoiding participation, but in recent years the holy ones seem to have abandoned this aspect of the rite.

The Black Dog in *La Santa Compaña* appears as a solitary phantom throughout Western Europe and the Americas. The Black Dog haunts gates, crossroads, trails, wells, ponds, streams, churchyard cemeteries, gallows' sites, ancient burial places and prehistoric worship sites. She is often large—the size of a calf—and has large round piercing eyes, usually blood red but occasionally green or yellow. She leaves no footprints or huge footprints or webbed footprints. She has an eerie howl but may be preternaturally silent. In one Irish legend she sings a dirge. The black dog usually appears to warn of an impending death, but she may also offer protection or guard treasure. She is associated with violent weather and may be spotted by those witnessing cloud-to-ground lightning. The black dog that appears during lightning strikes may be a source of the "raining cats and dogs" saying. She is common on the British Isles, with specific locales all boasting their peculiar Black Dog legends.

A panel on the Gundestrup Cauldron shows the death goddess with a dog at her right hand and a fallen man at her left breast. Denmark, third century BCE. Photo Kim Bach/Nationalmuseet.

The Black Dog followed the Spanish to the Americas, blending with indigenous beliefs. In keeping with the Devil theme, the Central American *Cadejo* looks like a dog but has goat feet and smells of sulfur (and urine). Phantom dogs haunting Argentina are the poorly controlled familiars of unscrupulous sorcerers.

The Black Dog has many hangouts in North America. Again

because of the Devil connection, there are people who believe the Black Dog haunts former U.S. Route 666 (since renumbered 491, in fulfillment of a campaign pledge by former Governor Bill Richardson). This notoriously twisted stretch of highway has elevated fatalities, so the Black Dog might be expected to haunt this road even without the suggestive name. The most famous death canine in America is the Black Dog of Hanging Hills, Connecticut. This little dog haunts a rocky mountain range with unique geology from volcanic activity. The mountain's reddish face and striking crevasses make it attractive to bushwhackers despite its dangerous topography. The legend was first recorded in the late nineteenth century by W.H.C. Pynchon, after the Black Dog got a hold of his friend, the geologist Herbert Marshall. According to Pynchon, the first sighting of the Black Dog is pleasant, the second foretells calamity and the third means sudden death. The Black Dog is reported to be a friendly attractive dog with a silent bark. The Black Dog of Hanging Hills does not leave footprints.

Phantom dogs like to pester isolated rural communities. Riding home late one night in the Ozarks, a country doctor came upon a huge shadowy dog as his horse waded across a stream beside a cemetery. The dog was walking on top of the water, without causing a ripple. The doctor knew this was a "booger dog," a dog that was really a ghost. The doctor saw the dog often after this, on dark nights and in bright moonlight, crossing beside him or ahead in the distance, always padding on top of the water. Once, as the doctor crossed the stream, the booger dog jumped on the saddle behind him, making the horse panic. The doctor fired his pistol to no avail, and when he tried to push the dog away his hand passed through air. Whether you believe the brave doctor repeatedly crossed a stream guarded by a booger dog or not, the story has many elements of the earlier underworld myths: the burial ground, the river, the huge scary dog, the shaman (in this incarnation, a medical man) who travels past the dog on his horse and survives the encounter.

Sometimes the Black Dog isn't black. The Cù Sìth of Scotland is a dark shaggy green with huge footprints and a long tail braided over her back. The name is pronounced "coo shee" and means "fairy dog." Green is an unusual color for a phantom dog, but it is a color worn by the fairies. Like most phantom dogs, the Cù Sìth is unnaturally large, and she always moves in a straight line. She has a far ranging yelp that warns everyone to hide, because she either warns of death or kills you herself—no one is quite sure. It is believed some women aren't actually killed, but abducted to bring milk for the fairy children. So many problems in Celtic lands could be solved by convincing fairies and witches to go nondairy.

Phantom white dogs, while not as common as the black, are also found in graveyards, especially adjacent churches. They leave the cemetery to forewarn death. The appearance of the white Mexican *cadejo,* however, is benign; only the black *cadejo* means death. Armenian folklore also has a killer black dog and a protective white dog. These are innovations based on Christian concepts of white/good and black/bad. Originally both white and black dogs were associated with death.

In Middle Eastern folklore the sometimes evil, sometimes benign spirits known as *jinn* will take the form of dogs to snoop around cemeteries. A black dog *jinn* is said to be the Devil. Phantom hyenas or jackals take over many functions of the European Black Dog, molesting travelers, portending death, digging up graves, drinking blood, et cetera. Muslim scholars view these beliefs, which are not in the *Qur'an,* as remnants of pre-Islamic superstition.

A dog does not have to be a phantom to be a messenger for the dead. Live dogs barking at "nothing," according to folklore, are reacting to spirits that humans cannot see. Dogs howl plaintively when a family death is imminent, with a howl at the moon particularly inauspicious, since the full moon channels the souls of the dead. While the phantom Black Dog is associated with lightning strikes in Britain, in the Ozarks the belief is that the tail of a live dog will draw lightning.

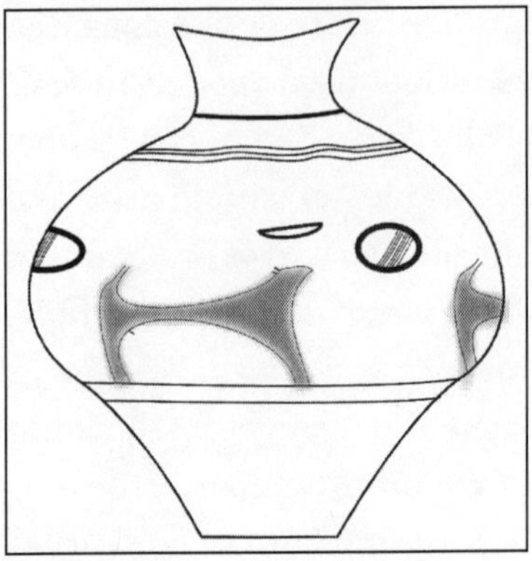

Dogs howl at crescent and full moon. Romania, 3500 BCE.

Dogs accompany Artemis in her death aspect as The Huntress. The Greek scholar Arrian, in his second century hunting treatise, describes a curious hunting-dog festival observed by the Celts, dedicated to a goddess he identifies with Artemis. During the course of the year, hunters would contribute payment to a kitty for each piece of wild game bagged, with larger payments going to more valuable animals. When the day of the festival arrived, the kitty was used to purchase a domestic animal which was sacrificed to the goddess. Dogs were the guests of honor at the feast, garlanded with flowers and given generous portions of meat.

An animal associated with death usually has a birth aspect as well. Dogs were sacrificed to

Two dogs (or dog and wolf) lap up the moon's essence in Tarot of Marseilles card. France, circa 1700.

the birth goddess Eileithyia, worshiped in Mycenaean Crete and later throughout the classical world. Eileithyia could obstruct a birth by crossing her legs and clasping her hands on her knees, so a dog, one of her sacred animals, would be sacrificed to coax Eileithyia into spreading her legs.

Because the dog aids in birth, she protects children, sometimes even fostering them. The golden hound Laelaps was sent by Rhea to guard the infant Zeus. Poor Laelaps was the most passed around doggy in history, going from Zeus to Europa to Artemis to Minos to Prokris to Kephalos to Pandareos. He was a coveted hound because he always caught his prey. Laelaps is called the Hurricane Dog and his name means "storm wind." Laelaps met his last human master when Amphitryon borrowed him to hunt the savage Teumessian Fox, who was ravaging the community to the point where she had to be appeased by human sacrifice. This fox was fated never be caught, so her pursuit by the hound fated never to be defeated created an uncomfortable stalemate. Eventually Zeus moved the pair to the sky as the constellations Canis Major and Minor.

The dog was a sacrificial victim throughout Europe. Dogs were sacrificed during the holy days, at funerary rites, when events called for propitiation to the gods and at the dedication of temples. Many believe the early churches in France, Germany, Scandinavia and the British Isles have a dog buried at the entranceway. In many pre-Christian sites dog remains have been recovered, such as the carefully arranged dog skeletons at the Mesolithic burial site of Lenpenski Vir in Serbia or the dog skeletons in Romano-British wells.

While the Celts buried the remains of actual dogs at entranceways, Mesopotamians placed dog figurines of clay, bronze, silver or gold at the gates of the temples. Inscriptions identify the dogs as having protective power. Other dog effigies were dedicated to the healing goddess Gula, usually depicted with a canine companion.

Votive offering to Gula. Sumer, early second millennium BCE. Photo Marie-Lan Nguyen/Wikimedia Commons.

The healing Greek god Asclepius, mentioned earlier with snakes, has a canine association, having been nursed by a dog (and a goat) as an infant after being abandoned on a mountain by his mother. In the hospitals of Asclepius, dogs appeared in dream incubations as messengers, with prescriptions for healing. Cures also occurred through ritual offerings to the temple dogs. Sometimes the dogs healed the patients directly by licking them.

The idea that dog saliva cures open sores, a logical result of seeing dogs lick their own wounds, was a part of healing folklore throughout Western Europe. The fourteenth century French Saint Roch, the patron saint of dogs, was cured of a disease involving bodily sores by a dog that befriended the festering saint when he was cast out of town. The dog licked the man's sores and brought him bread. Much has been made of the selective breeding of dogs for hunting, herding, guarding and sledding, but given the role of dog licking in traditional healing, it is likely that dogs have also been selectively bred to slobber on people.

Dogs are used today in hospital settings with the aim of attending to the emotional side of healing. Patient morale noticeably improves with regular doggy visits, even when patients have frequent human visitors. It would be dangerous, however, to allow these dogs to lick patient sores, because the medical staff would go into cardiac arrest.

A pair of dogs guard Lyfjaberg, the Hill of Healing, where the Nordic goddess Mengloth lives with her nine maidens. One of the dogs guards by day, the other by night, so the hill is always fortified. Lyfjaberg is surrounded by a wall of fire, a wall of clay and an iron gate fashioned by dwarves and guarded by a giant. The world tree, Yggdrasil, grows on this hill. Women can pluck the fruit of the tree to aid childbirth, and they can climb the hill to regain good health, but the only man granted admission is the one fated to be Mengloth's husband. Even so, Mengloth's consort must receive a spell from his dead mother before he can safely begin the journey. Mengloth is able to recognize her future husband because the dogs fawn on him instead of killing him. Such signs are unmistakable.

The goddess Nehalennia is almost invariably depicted with a single canine companion. Inscriptions on her many altars express gratitude from supplicants for a safe passage, and she appears to have been wildly popular with sailors, merchants and other travelers. Nehalennia's cult was centered in the Netherlands, where she was worshiped by Germans, Romans and Celts.

The most well-known deity of travelers is the goddess Hecate. Before embarking on a voyage, Greek travelers of means would sacrifice a dog to this powerful goddess. Hecate's emblems of horse and dog signify that she holds possession of the open road. Where Hecate's cult arose is contentious, with everyone agreeing only that it did not originate in Greece. Perhaps this mystery of origin is appropriate, since who can say where the proverbial road begins or ends?

Hecate has strong underworld associations, as her fondness

for hounds implies. She has therefore been a favored patron of fortune tellers and spellcasters, who tap into that otherworld energy to work magic or divine the future. Her followers worship her at the dark moon, which is identified in modern witchcraft as the "crone" phase. Hecate is not, however, a crone goddess. She is portrayed as a lovely young woman in Greco-Roman art, as Mediterranean goddesses almost invariably are. Hecate's reputation as an old woman was started in late classical times when Roman officials, uncomfortable with their inability to regulate a cult dominated by women from the lower classes, began depicting Hecate's priestesses as unsavory hags. Of course, early Christians pounced on this view of Hecate, especially when the old bitches proved hard to convert. Ironically, the characterization of Hecate as crone guaranteed that she would be regarded favorably by northern Pagans, who recognized a grandmother goddess and accorded her more power. But Hecate cannot be cast simply as a beautiful goddess ruling "crone" territory. Hecate is a healer, a protector, a purifier, an ally in fertility and birth, and a foster mother for those who feel abandoned. She is embodied in the three roads that meet in a Y, the pivotal place in the path of the spiritual seeker.

The dog's link with Hecate, her healing powers, her historic use in Pagan sacrifice, her presence in frightening weather and above all her guardianship at the gates of hell made her a familiar suspect during the Witch Craze. We think of cats, toads and owls as familiars in witch trials, but dogs were also common. Alice Kyteler, the alleged Irish witch famous for having escaped the gallows through political connections, was accused of having a dog familiar. The fate of Englishman John Walsh, who confessed to summoning a dog from a spell in a book, is unknown. Franconian Junius Johannes invented a flying black dog to satisfy torturers, a confession he later renounced. Having two black dogs did not help Marco Antonio Bragadino in his trial for alchemy in Munich—or maybe it should be said that the association did not help the dogs, who were also executed. Three dogs (two in Salem and one in Andover) were condemned and hanged in Massachusetts during the New England Witch Craze.

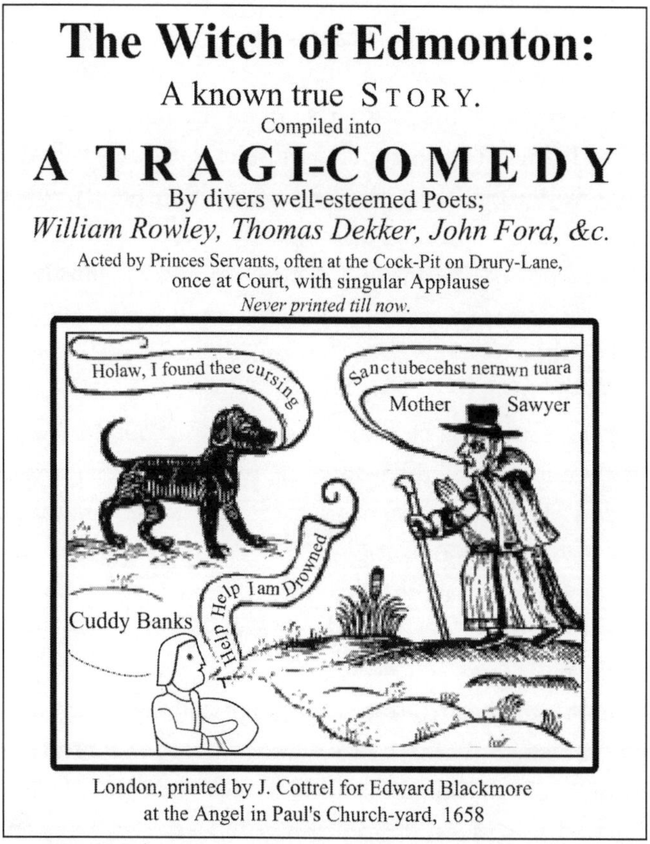

The Witch of Edmonton:

A known true STORY.

Compiled into

A TRAGI-COMEDY

By divers well-esteemed Poets;

William Rowley, Thomas Dekker, John Ford, &c.

Acted by Princes Servants, often at the Cock-Pit on Drury-Lane,
once at Court, with singular Applause

Never printed till now.

London, printed by J. Cottrel for Edward Blackmore
at the Angel in Paul's Church-yard, 1658

Title page (restored in Serif font) from a play about an old woman enticed into witchcraft by the Devil posing as a Black Dog.

Medieval Christian attitudes about dogs mirrored conflicted opinions toward animals in general. The official view was that nature worship, including animal worship, was incompatible with Christianity, yet in many cases Christians continued to worship animals, sometimes with the tolerance of local clerics, who either agreed with the practice or understood what they were up against in trying to eradicate it. The twelfth century English abbot Aelred of Rievaulx denounced the profusion of animal imagery in monastic settings. A century later near Lyon, France, the Inquisition brought attention to an even more shocking animal incursion: a canine saint.

The greyhound Guinefort, whose date of birth and death is unknown, was worshiped as a saint by country women at an outdoor shrine. The legend was that Guinefort had been martyred while guarding the heir of a noble family when the adults were called away. The vigilant greyhound tussled with and killed a poisonous snake. Upon returning, the family, seeing the room in disarray and the baby on the floor, jumped to the conclusion that the dog had attacked the child. Guinefort was slain without hesitation, but the error was soon discovered. In remorse for treating such a loyal servant so shabbily, the family dropped Guinefort's body down a well, covered the well in stones, and planted a grove of trees around the site. Local people referred to the martyred dog as "Saint Guinefort," and women brought sick infants to the grove for healing.

At the time the Inquisition took notice of St. Guinefort, the area surrounding the shrine was wild and uninhabited. Similar tales about other martyred dogs have circulated throughout Europe, but we know there was a dog interred at this site, as the Inquisitor wrote that he dug up the bones and burned them. He also claimed to have destroyed the grove, scolded the populace and persuaded the governing body to enact heavy fines for further devotion to the sainted dog. Still, women continued to visit St. Guinefort's shrine into the twentieth century.

While on the subject of dog saints, St. Christopher should get a mention. St. Christopher was born in the third century in a North African tribe on the fringes of the settled Mediterranean. He was not, originally, a dog. The Greeks believed people outside the wealthy city-states of the Mediterranean were not only barbaric, but distinctly odd looking—giants or dwarves, with one eye or a dog's head. Even when they found out the foreigners didn't actually have canine craniums, they still called them dogheads. St. Christopher the doghead came to be pictured with a dog's head in Christian art, and he assumed patronage of two areas traditionally associated with dogs: protection during travel and protection from storms. The honchos in Rome were somewhat successful in squelching the canine depiction of the saint, but it continued through medieval times in the Orthodox Church and in Ireland, where there were still a few scholars who read Greek. The meteoric acceptance of this saint, who was never really liked by Christian authorities, makes sense in the context of cultures accustomed to worshipping canine deities.

Speaking of dogheads, the Aztec god Xolotl is also pictured with a dog's head. Xolotl sacrificed other gods and himself to make the first humans. Xolotl has feet going backwards, and he is another deity of lightning. In Aztec cosmology dogs guide souls of the dead across water to the underworld. Skeletons of sacrificed dogs have been found near Aztec waterways and inside tombs.

The Egyptian god Anubis, technically, is a jackal head, but that's close enough, since dogs and jackals are similar in behavior and genetic makeup. More to the point, ancient Egyptians viewed them as related, and Anubis is sometimes depicted as a dog or a dog/jackal hybrid. Anubis is the lord of mummification, which he invented, and the overseer of a wealth of other funerary rites the Egyptians considered essential. He is the controller and mediator of malevolent forces. When shown as a jackal-headed man, he holds the scepter named "power." Anubis is always painted jet black, since this is the color of skin treated with embalming powder. In the hall of the goddess Maat, Anubis weighs the heart of the deceased against a feather on the scale of truth. If the heart is lighter than the feather, the spirit can move on to the happy place. Anubis guides and protects the dead on every step of their transformation, physical and spiritual, and he watches over their earthly resting place. His cult was centered in Cynopolis (Greek for "dog city"), but he had other city centers identified by large numbers of mummified dogs.

Respectful burial of dogs in the ancient world was common, but the reasons varied. In Celtic Europe, the burial concluded a sacrificial rite. The dogs buried outside the temple of the goddess Gula died of natural causes and were probably divine dogs who resided there. Epitaphs of pet dogs given special burials by their loving owners survive in classical Greek literature. In the South American Chiribaya culture, which preceded the Inca, a cemetery has been discovered with dogs buried beside people. The dog would have either guided the deceased to the next world or served as a worker and companion. The story behind the huge dog cemetery at the Ashkelon archeological site in Israel remains a mystery.

The dog deity Kimat, of the Tinguian people of the Philippines, may provide a clue about the Black Dog and lightning. Kimat is the pet dog and messenger of the thunder god Tadaklan, and this divine pooch does his master's "biting" with the lightning strike.

North American Indians tend to emphasize loyalty rather than death in canine myth. A Lenape legend relates how dogs and wolves once lived together as one family, until a dog was sent on a raid to steal fire. Instead of returning with the fire stick as promised, the dog decided to remain with the humans. When the pack realized the dog was not coming back, the wolves declared war on the dogs and the two groups split. The wolves remained angry and attacked the dogs at every opportunity. Dogs and wolves now had to hold separate council meetings, and the dogs were careful to assert their purity and sanctity when they went into council. Each dog would leave his genitals in a basket at the door to show how holy he was. One day a wolf entered the meeting and all the dogs fled in terror. They each took a set of genitals as they ran, but of course most of them grabbed the wrong one. This is why dogs sniff each other's crotch when they meet: they're still trying to locate their original equipment.

The long and close history between dogs and people means the priestess can draw on a wealth of tradition surrounding dogs, but associations in the present are also important. Today dogs are considered companions, close friends and even part of the family. Like other household members, they often have their own little jobs, like licking plates for the dishwasher or cleaning up messes on the floor. Dogs are enthusiastic workers, and as civilization has grown more complex, dogs have become increasingly diversified in the jobs they perform.

Being useful to humans is a trait that invites animal worship, but perhaps the main reason people worship dogs is that dogs worship us. The love, respect and friendship offered by these intelligent animals has fostered an implicit trust in the dog-god. The dog deity is always there to lead us where we need to go.

A Girl and Her Dog-Groom

This tale is based on the one collected by Francis Hindes Groome in the late nineteenth century, which he attributed to Romani living in the area that is now Romania. It is similar to the Irish legend of the Black Woolley Dog.

There was once a girl, a beautiful girl, who had lost her mother but still had a possessive father. Her father hoped to marry her to some man of high status, and toward that end he guarded his daughter's virginity ferociously, to the point of forbidding the girl to play and dance with people her own age. The girl grew up sad and lonely, until a white dog mysteriously appeared and befriended her. Soon the pair were inseparable, and the girl forgot her unhappiness until her father announced one day that he was leaving for the city to sell some things. The girl would be left for several days in the care of some women she did not like and who did not like her. The girl moped when her father left, until the dog said to her, "Let's sneak out of this place and go walking in the countryside, where no one can hear us talk."

The girl had never heard a dog speak, so she was surprised and a little afraid, but she eluded her captors and went with the white dog. Once out of sight and earshot of the enclave, the dog pleaded with the girl to kiss him. She finally complied, and the dog immediately became a handsome well-dressed young man. He confided this secret to her:

"Though I am from a good family, I once disobeyed my parents and did something I should not have done. I slipped into the garden of an evil sorceress and stole some of her golden apples. She cursed me, and I became a dog. There are only two ways that I can regain my manly form. One is to be kissed by a girl on a certain day of the year; then I become a man for that night only."

The girl stayed that night with the handsome youth and they

slept together in the tall grass. At dawn the man was transformed into a dog once again, and the two slipped back into the camp. The dog remained close to the girl, but did not speak to her again.

The mistrustful father returned never the wiser, and life went on as before. Many months later, he again left for business in a distant city, but events unfolded for the girl in a different way. Instead of whiling her time away with her talking, transformative dog, the girl gave birth to a white puppy. She was horrified, and she drowned herself in the nearby river.

The father returned to a distraught community desperately trying to retrieve the corpse of the girl. No one knew why she had jumped in the river, because no one realized the white puppy was her child. The father decided to go into the river himself and either recover the girl's body or drown and be released from his suffering. But a handsome man unknown to him appeared and said, "I will bring your daughter's body back."

The man threw a chunk of bread into the water, and the bread floated to where the corpse was, then floated with the body back to shore. The girl was pulled onto dry land, and the man put the puppy at her breast to suck. When the puppy was sated, the girl opened her eyes to much rejoicing.

The girl and the handsome youth were married immediately. Their son transformed himself from a puppy to a baby, and he was soon baptized. Everyone lived happily ever after.

Cuchulainn, the Tempered Hound

This excerpt is from a long and bloody tale called the Ulster Cycle. I lost track of all the severed heads on the pikes. I've used Irish name spellings for consistency. Often there is disagreement on how a name should be pronounced. English speakers generally pronounce Cuchulainn's name coo-CULL-inn. Medb is mave. Morrigan is more-again. Badb is baav. Just don't call them late for dinner—or for the battle.

The hero would say of himself, "I have the sickness that comes on dogs, that fierceness that causes a provoked hound to attack blindly and persevere until the enemy falls."

He was called hound, specifically hound of the smith Chulainn; Cuchulainn. He received his name as a young boy by killing Chulainn's favorite dog. The smith was angry with him for doing this, and he himself was saddened by the event, but this is how it happened: His uncle King Concobar was enjoying a feast with Chulainn, and he forgot to tell his host that the boy would be joining them later. The smith put out his watchdog to roam the grounds for the night, and the child, who was following the king's wagon tracks, encountered the dog as he approached the house. There was a bedlam of howling and yelling as the dog attacked, and the boy threw his ball into the dog's mouth, temporarily choking him. The boy then picked up the incapacitated hound and dashed the body against a rock. Concobar was relieved that his nephew had survived, but Chulainn was devastated by the loss of his best watchdog. "I will lose everything," he wailed. "My herds, my foundry, my food stores—all will be stolen from me when I am asleep or away." The boy reassured him, "I will find a puppy and raise him to be as good a watchdog as the one you have lost. Until that dog is ready, I will be your hound. I will guard your stores and your lands." From that day on, he was Cuchulainn.

Cuchulainn had the blood of the women but not the men of Ulster. Cuchulainn's mother Dechtire conceived her little hound on her wedding day by drinking a cup of wine that contained a worm. The draught made her fall into deep sleep, and the god Lugh of the Long Hand appeared in a dream, telling her that he was the father of her child, and that she must fly away to a fairy place. Dechtire and her fifty maidens then transformed into birds and flew away, staying in the fairy place until the child was past infancy.

Cuchulainn was a beautiful child who grew into a strong and handsome youth, loved by many a fair maiden. But he thought too highly of himself to take a wife who was merely beautiful. He scoured the whole of Ireland to find the young woman most skilled in embroidery, who could thereby complement his prowess in warfare. He found that extraordinary needle worker in a place named Lugh's Garden. She was the lovely yellow-haired Emer, who could match Cuchulainn in every way, including riddle. She said of herself, "I am the hill of Tara, a watcher who sees no me, an eel hidden in the water, a rush out of reach." This meant that though she loved him, he would have to fight to win her.

Emer's father did not wish her to marry Cuchulainn, but he did not want to say this, so he put a condition on their union. Cuchulainn was to prove his mettle by accepting tutelage in warfare from the greatest teacher. In those days the most powerful warrior trainers were women, and they lived in northern Scotland. The journey to the war school was a dangerous one, strewn with many monsters, but Cuchulainn accepted the challenge, confident that he could meet any obstacle so long as he did not break his *geis*.

Every warrior holds a sacred vow, a *geis*, that cannot be broken without great cost. Cuchulainn's *geis* was this: that he would never eat the flesh of dogs.

With the warrior women, Cuchulainn learned the subtle arts of warfare, those that went beyond strength and speed. He obtained more than enough skill to free Emer from the grasp of her reluctant father. He also was given the prophesy that he would scatter his enemies, that he would fight great armies and that his name would be spoken long and far, but that life for him would be cut short.

This is how Cuchulainn was vanquished: he provoked the wrath of the warrior queen Medb; he provoked the wrath of the warrior goddess Morrigan; and he provoked the wrath of the warrior witch Badb.

The conflict that was to turn so many fortunes began innocuously enough. Queen Medb of Connacht was indulging in some pillow talk with her husband Ailil, and the two began reviewing their individual wealth—their lands, their armies, their jewelry, their kitchen utensils, et cetera, et cetera. In the course of the comparison, the queen made a terrible discovery: her husband had one more head of cattle than she did. This she could not allow. She sought to borrow a magic brown bull from a cattleman in Ulster, offering to pay handsomely for the loan, so that the bull could sire some magic calves. When the cattleman refused, she marshaled her troops.

Naturally, Cuchulainn came to the aid of his countrymen, but he ended up fighting alone against Medb's army for weeks, as the men of Ulster were laboring under the curse of a fairy. Literally, they were in labor. Generations ago, the fairy woman Macha had imposed the curse that the men of Ulster and their progeny would experience labor pains when they most needed their strength. While his comrades moaned and held their bellies, Cuchulainn faced Medb's forces on his own.

This is how Cuchulainn earned the enduring resentment of Medb: 1) He killed her best warriors; 2) he killed the little dog that sat at her feet; 3) he killed the marten and the tame bird that sat on her shoulders; 4) he killed her serving woman, thinking it was her; 5) he refused three offers of bribes to switch to her side; 6) he staved off the warriors of Connacht until the men of Ulster had finished their labor pangs; and 7) he fought so fiercely that

Medb had to plead protection for her forces as they retreated in defeat.

One night while Cuchulainn was sleeping, during the time when he was still fighting the men of Connacht, during the time when the men of Ulster were still fighting their labor pangs, he was awoken by a piercing cry from the north. He scrambled from his tent to find his chariot driver yoking the horses, and the two drove out on the plain to investigate the sound. There they met a woman in a chariot pulled by a red mare. The woman had red eyebrows and red hair, a red dress and a red cloak. Tied to her back was a gray spear. "I hear you have performed heroic and wonderful deeds," she told Cuchulainn, "and I have come to offer you my love." "I have no time for lovemaking," Cuchulainn replied emphatically, "for I am completely worn out. I have been fighting all day and must prepare for battle tomorrow. Your visit could not come at a more importunate time." "I will help you in your struggle," the woman countered. "I have already helped you greatly, Cuchulainn, and you have benefitted from my protection." "It is not a lady's help I need in this fight!" Cuchulainn argued hotly, "and I will not trust your protection." "Very well," she answered, "prepare to do battle with me as well as the others." With that the lady in red, her mare and her chariot disappeared, and he and his driver were left completely alone, except for a crow sitting in the high branch of a tree. Cuchulainn felt his own pang of sickness then, because he realized he had been speaking to the warrior goddess Morrigan.

If Morrigan had chosen an importunate time to share her love, her chosen time for battle was hellacious. Cuchulainn was confronting the worthy combatant Loch Mor, who heretofore had not deigned to battle with a beardless youth, whatever his reputation. Cuchulainn had slaughtered Loch's brother only the day before, however, so Loch was ripe for the fight. As the warriors engaged at the ford, the goddess rushed Cuchulainn in the form of a white heifer with red ears, with fifty more heifers reinforcing her. He wounded one eye on the white heifer with his slingshot, but she immediately changed into a black eel and entangled his feet in the water. Sensing an advantage, Loch wounded Cuchulainn in the chest as Cuchulainn disentangled from the eel by smashing half her brains on a stone. Morrigan shifted to the form of a gray wolf, biting Cuchulainn's arm as Loch wounded him in the crotch. With a small javelin, he wounded the other eye of Morrigan before giving Loch a fatal blow with his spear.

It was after conquering Loch Mor that Cuchulainn made enemies with the enchantress Badb, who was not yet born. On a single day Cuchulainn slaughtered Badb's father, her twenty-seven brothers and her cousin, then dismembered them in numerous places. Badb's mother was pregnant at the time, and when she gave birth to Badb and her two sisters, each had only one eye. When the war was finished, Medb took the girls under her wing, instilling in them a desire to avenge their father. She taught them all the forms of enchantment she knew and sent them to Scotland to learn more. Badb was the most powerful of the three, and her sole mission was to destroy Cuchulainn.

Meanwhile Morrigan with half a brain was down but not out. She took the form of an old hag milking a three-teated cow, and placed herself in Cuchulainn's path one morning when she knew he would be thirsty. Sure enough, he asked for a drink. As she shot a stream from the first teat into his mouth, he blessed her, and her left eye was cured. She shot a stream from the second teat into his mouth, and as he blessed her the right eye was cured. She shot a stream from the third teat and his blessing cured her brain. Thus, Cuchulainn was tricked into healing Morrigan of the wounds he had perpetrated, and they were squared on that account. The original score remained to be settled.

Does it matter who ended up with the brown bull? From the fighting hound's point of view, what remained important after the fighting had concluded was that he had earned the glorious reputation he craved, and that the most powerful women in Ireland were determined to kill him. Medb bided her time, waiting until King Concobar and Cuchulainn were temporarily separated to strike. With Concobar's army several days' march from the star warrior, she began border raids calculated to tempt Cuchulainn to fight her. Badb and her sisters cooperated by raising high pitched noises that sounded like a fierce battle with great slaughter. The druids warned Cuchulainn that this was all a trick, but in the end he could not resist.

As he bridled his gray mare and prepared for battle, his gold broach fell off his coat and pierced his foot, telling Cuchulainn not to leave. The mare cried tears of blood. As he said goodbye to his mother Dechtire, he refused three times the wine she poured for him, because it turned to blood. His wife Emer said, "Little Hound, I have never protested any battle or adventure you chose to undertake, but I beg you now to reconsider." He stopped and weighed his life and his wife's happiness against his courage and his good name and continued on.

Leaving the compound, at the first ford there was a thin girl with pale white skin and yellow hair. She was wailing. She washed and wrung and washed again a bright red shirt that stained the water. Cuchulainn crossed the ford and continued on.

Further down the road he encountered three one-eyed women camped in the middle of the path. They were roasting dog meat on rowan sticks. "Come and have some supper with us," they yelled. "No, I cannot," Cuchulainn replied. "That's right, you are too mighty and we are too poor," they complained. "If we had something better than dog to offer you, then you would stop." Cuchulainn protested, "No, I would love to dine with you, but I have a pressing engagement." The sisters rejoined, "You refuse our hospitality because the fare is simple, and we are cripples." The conversation continued in this vein until Cuchulainn believed he had no choice other than to accept. To refuse their hospitality would mean violating a social law.

As soon as he tasted the shoulder blade of the dog, the hand that held the meat weakened. As he dropped the morsel on his thigh, the thigh weakened. As he continued to the border to confront Medb's men, his strength had left him in his whole left side.

During the ensuing battle, Cuchulainn took many lives. There were more tricks, but the hound held his own for much of the day, even though he could not fight indefinitely with only half his strength. When he received his mortal wound, he went to the lake to drink and wash himself, then he belted his body to a stone pillar, so that he would die standing up. His combatants, still leery of him, did not approach his body for some time.

When a bird flew down and rested on his shoulder, they knew the warrior hound was dead.

Dog Review

Magical Qualities:

Magical Applications:

Other Associations:

Wolf Bane, Wolf Brew

In this section we will explore the scarier side of shapeshifting, exemplified by the werewolf. The werewolf is a complex creature that is part science, part magic, part tradition, part superstition. She embodies a concept that has become confused over the centuries as Christianity and science have attempted to understand the phenomenon in their own terms. Fears and misconceptions about shapeshifting have been projected mainly onto wolves, which makes the werewolf a good study on the crazier side of shapeshifting.

Let's recap the traits that make an animal significant in Euro-shamanism. An animal becomes prominent if she has economic value, for instance as food (hare), medicine (toad) or work (dog). An animal also stands out if she has a feature that appears human, such as the bipedal stance of the bear or the close set eyes of the owl. If an animal exemplifies family and community values, such as the bat or bee, this is very important. Animals with an androgynous aspect, such as snakes, have a special place in magic. The animals which represent danger, such as mice with their destruction of grain, are often worshiped, and the animals which prey on these species, such as cats, are also elevated. Since magic involves traveling to the worlds between life and death, any animal associated with death, such as the raven, will be called upon frequently. Within these areas, the wolf has death, danger and family to her credit.

The wolf's dedication to family is her most salient magical quality. Wolves live in large family groups, with litters from previous years hanging on to help raise the next set of pups. As the little ones develop, older brothers and sisters bring meat, which they chew and regurgitate for the voracious puppies. When the pups are mostly weaned, a sibling will babysit while the rest of the pack is out hunting. Although food resources are constrained by months of living at the pup-rearing sites, the young adults stick around camp until the current litter is old enough to travel. The pack concentrates in autumn and winter on large prey, which they hunt in a coordinated fashion. Younger wolves respect and obey their parents, who actively guide the pack but do not lead in all situations. Pack members protect each other, and the father is particularly fierce in guarding the mother and cubs when they are still in the den.

Legend arose that the wolf goddess Spako nursed Cyrus the Great, ruler of the first Persian Empire. The founder-raised-by-wolf-mother was a method of legitimizing a dynasty, but legends about children raised by wolves persisted well into the twentieth century. There have only been two documented cases of children even partially raised by animals—a three year old girl from Ukraine who lived with dogs and an older boy from tropical Africa who lived with apes. Child development professionals have a hard time accepting the child-raised-by-beasts idea, since successfully raising the slow developing and vulnerable infant is so difficult even for a human mother. Psychologist Bruno Bettelheim proposed that the root of the wolf-child theme lies in parental guilt about infanticide. A mother forced in difficult times to allow her newborn to be exposed to the elements could console herself with the possibility that a wolf mother rescued her infant. Wolves would be the preferred rescuers because they live in families analogous to our own.

Some say "suckled by a wolf" refers to a family clan named for the wolf. This would mean that when legend gives the hero a wolf, bear or deer foster mother, it reflects the hero's human family ties. Since the wolf is a popular clan totem, this would also explain why wolves do the most work in the field of infant adoption.

Be that as it may, Cyrus was not the only ruler reputedly raised by wolves. Cormac mac Airt, whose visit to the Land of Promise was described in the last section, was fostered by a wolf. King Miletus, who founded the eponymous city where Arachne lived, was exposed on Crete and rescued by wolves, possibly with the intervention of his father, the god Apollo. The founder of Rome, Romulus, and his twin brother, Remus, were nursed by a wolf-mother after they were abandoned in the wilds for the crime of being born to a Vestal Virgin. The god Mars, who was the father, helped with the rescue efforts by appearing in woodpecker form to drop food. The brothers were later discovered by a shepherd and fostered by the shepherd's wife, Acca Larentia. The mother of household gods, Acca Larentia, whose symbol is the wolf, was honored on the December 23rd Roman holiday of Larentalia. Larentia's origin is Etruscan, and as the dead were buried under houses in Etruria and elsewhere, this wolf mother may have been an ancestor as well.

Wolf mother nursing Remus and Romulus. Rome. Date is disputed but similar images date from the first century. Photo Xuan Che.

Julius Caesar reported that the Continental Celts considered themselves descended from wolves. Caesar is known for getting the story line confused when reporting on the Celtic tribes, so perhaps this is another case of an ancestral hero fostered by wolves. The Greek historian Herodotus, who wrote in the fifth century BCE, records (with skepticism) that the Neuri people, who lived in the far north, changed into wolves for a few days every year. The entire tribe took part in the transformation.

When only one person changes into a wolf, the werewolf still maintains family ties. In Russian belief a werewolf comes back to beg among kin, visiting cordially and licking hands, while the Scottish *wulver* shies away from human habitation but occasionally leaves food at her family's doorstep.

Closely allied with the wolf's dedication to family is her link with love, sex and marriage. Wolves are monogamous and typically mate for life. The parental pair breed once a year, the time varying with climate and latitude but usually occurring in February. They will mate repeatedly during the female's two-week fertile period. As mating time approaches, the pair become affectionate, sleeping together and spending most of their time with one another.

Dogs are descendents of the Gray Wolf.

Polish folk tales have witches transforming wedding parties into wolves, while the Lithuanian Ragana likes to turn the groom into a wolf on his wedding day. Perhaps these transformations are related to older ceremonies involving animal clan alliances in marriage. The classical Greek interpretation of wolf-love is somewhat predatory, an autumn-spring romance being described as wolflike. Wolflike is an epithet of Aphrodite, and people with large sexual appetites were deprecatingly compared to wolves.

The Romans associated wolves with sexual desire and fertility, and a Roman bride would anoint her new husband's doorpost with wolf fat. Romans used hair from a wolf's tail in love charms. Acca Larentia, in addition to being the goddess of the household, was goddess of prostitutes, who were called she-wolves. Christian leaders had a particularly hard time suppressing courtship rituals that arose around the wolf-centered fertility rites of Lupercalia.

During Lupercalia (February 15th) a dog and a goat, two vexing targets of wolf predation, were sacrificed to the wolf goddess. Two priests of the death god Soranus, called Wolf-Brothers, were anointed with the bloody knife from the sacrifice. The blood was washed from their foreheads with wool dipped in milk as the Brothers laughed. Then they took thongs cut from the sacrificed skins and ran naked around the city walls. Women would reach into their path to be struck by the thongs in order to become fertile or obtain an easy delivery. Another ceremony on this day took place at the cave where the wolf-mother nursed Remus and Romulus. Lupercalia rites were part of a nine day ceremony called Parentalia, honoring ancestors. Rituals for Parentalia were centered in the home and cemetery.

The wolf habit of caching dead animals—burying them in pieces to eat later—plays a role in this animal's reputation as a courier from the land of death. The wolf's greater profile in winter, the time of year dominated by death goddesses, strengthens the death association. Wolves begin coordinating pack hunts in late autumn and winter, and this involves traversing a bigger territory. Vocalization becomes stronger at this time. This is why wolf ceremonies occurred in late autumn and winter. It was recorded in CE 1600 that the Livonians, of the modern Baltic region, changed into wolves in the thousands during the twelve days of Christmas. On the old Anglo-Saxon calendar, January was the wolf-moon or month.

A wolf, or sometimes a dog, sits at Odin's feet in the hero's death world of Valhalla, and wolves accompany Odin on the Wild Hunt. The heroine Gudrun, mourning the loss of her lover, hears death calling her in the howling of wolves. Perchta, who is honored at the winter solstice, has a wolf companion, as does the Swedish winter goddess Skadi. The fierce goddess Hyrrokin rides a wolf through the sky. During the Witch Craze, women in the southern German provinces were sometimes accused of riding wolves.

An animal linked with the death realm is not necessarily dangerous to the living, but wolves have under certain conditions been quite troublesome. The most important concern in early historical times was predation on domestic animals. The flock played a large role in community prosperity, and the loss of a good herding dog would be felt acutely. Wolf predation of humans did not become a huge concern until medieval times, although it was not unknown.

Humans are the melba toast of the animal world, appetizing only under select circumstances. Nonetheless at least 278 people died of wolf attacks in India in the last half of the twentieth century, only five of them from rabies. Some would dismiss these statistics by pointing out that the deaths happened in areas where natural prey is scarce, garbage is unsecured, domestic animals are well guarded and children are allowed to wander unattended—but these are precisely the conditions that were operant five centuries ago when Europeans were developing their hysteria around wolves. In order to understand this hysteria we have to recognize that yes, Virginia, wolves can be dangerous (so lock yer trash afore you set them down that holler).

An animal that is dangerous can be invoked for protection. Germans often carried a wolf's tooth for protection, as did Irish travelers. In Naples a wolf head might be nailed above the door to ward off evil.

The Arcadians had an important yearly rite designed to discourage wolf predation. Recall that the Arcadians lived in a mountainous region geographically isolated from other Greeks, called themselves the bear people, and mainly worshiped Artemis and Pan. Other Greeks considered them only slightly more civilized than the barbarous tribes to the north. Classical sources say the Arcadians worshiped a form of Zeus they called wolf-Zeus, that they sacrificed many men, including the king's own son, to this false idea of Zeus, and that the real Zeus punished them by sending the great flood we know from the Bible. The Greek travel writer Pausanias wandered through Arcadia in the second century and described a ceremony where shepherds killed a man and made him into soup, which everyone partook of. The entrails were given to a shepherd boy who ate them. He then walked over to a lake, disrobed, and swam across the lake. When he reached the other side, he became a wolf, and he stayed a wolf for a full eight years. In the ninth year, provided he had not eaten any more people, he swam back across the lake and picked up the clothes he had worn many years ago, becoming human once again. One former werewolf went on to win the boxing medal in the Olympics.

Assertions of human sacrifice are difficult to evaluate. On the one hand, many European tribes did sacrifice humans, at least occasionally, probably in situations where survival of the tribe was in jeopardy. Ritual cannibalism played a part in some sacrifices.

On the other hand, accusations of human sacrifice were a preferred way for Mediterranean people to slander those they considered less civilized. Athenians, especially, enjoyed feeling superior to their neighbors by leveling charges of human sacrifice—which is particularly rich when you consider how much evidence there is that the Athenians themselves practiced human sacrifice in the early years.

The place Pausanias wrote about was excavated in the twentieth century and discovered to indeed be the site of a sacrificial shrine. The problem is that the site was abandoned several centuries before Pausanias, indicating that he was recording folklore and not a witness to the events themselves. Domestic animal sacrifices were found in abundance at the shrine, but no human remains. Even without a human blood sacrifice, the story does have a sacrificial element: a young man is loaned to the wolf god and gives up his youth so the community's livestock can be secure.

A story about an Irish werewolf couple recorded in the twelfth century also has a sacrificial theme. A traveling priest is accosted by a wolf, who begs him in human words to aid his dying wolf-wife. The priest is reluctant to give last rites to a wolf, since this is not allowed for some reason. Finally the wolf-wife opens her wolf skin, allowing the priest to view the human face underneath. The wolf-husband tells the priest that he and his wife are obliged to live as wolves for seven years, until another werewolf couple takes their place. This arrangement is attributed to a curse from St. Natalis, imposed on the district for unexplained reasons. Stories of werewolf curses from saints abound in early Celtic literature.

In early medieval lore the werewolf is obeying God or his emissary by taking wolf form. There is nothing evil about this form per se, although some prior misdeed may be implied. The wolf became the ally of early Celtic saints when they took over functions and symbols of druids. St. Ailbe, a disciple of St. Patrick who miraculously preached the gospel long before Patrick was born, was nursed by a wolf after being abandoned in the forest. Ailbe remained grateful to his foster mother and regularly fed her and her pups at the monastery. At his death he became the patron saint of wolves.

There is no explanation for the good baron Bisclaveret's thrice weekly transformation in Marie de France's twelfth century tale, but the change becomes permanent when he ill-advisedly confides to his wife where he hides his clothes. She prevails on her lover to snatch his everyday attire while the baron is in wolf form. This being a folk tale, the two miscreants hide the garments instead of doing the logical thing and destroying them. Bisclaveret remains in the woods until he is hounded by the king's hounds. Although he looks completely like a wolf, Bisclaveret does not act like one, beseeching his majesty for mercy with paws raised in prayer. The king keeps the mute and docile wolf as a pet until the cruel baroness comes to visit and truth emerges. She is forced to produce the garments, Bisclaveret changes back to a man, and the faithless wife is banished with her lover.

Germanic wolf lore emphasizes the ferocious aspect of the wolf. The wolf-monster Fenrir is one example. Fenrir is the child of Loki and the giantess Angurboda and is a wolf of gigantic proportion. He is not actually accused of doing any harm, but the gods were concerned about his potential for destruction. They sought to chain Fenrir, and the wolf playfully allowed this, confident that he could free himself. The first chain was easily broken, and then the wolf-giant snapped a much larger one as if it were nothing. The gods saw that magic was the only way to keep Fenrir fettered and enlisted the aid of the dwarves. The dwarves fashioned a slim thread from the sound of a cat's footstep, a woman's beard, the roots of a mountain, the pining of a bear, the voices of fish and the saliva of birds. Fenrir was suspicious of such a slender chain and refused to let himself be bound.

There was much cajoling and negotiating, and finally Fenrir allowed the thread to be tied, provided that the warrior god Tiwaz would place his hand inside Fenrir's jaw. When Fenrir could not break the magic bonds, he naturally bit away the right hand of Tiwaz. Fenrir is still tied safely, but now he is very angry and has vowed to destroy the gods who participated in his capture, especially Odin.

The fierce danger of the wolf was demonstrated by a segment of the berserker ranks known as Wolf-Coats, who considered themselves warriors of Odin. The Wolf-Coats were said to achieve their transformation by donning wolf pelts or a special girdle. Distrusted even within their regiments, they fought with an irrational fury and could not be depended upon to obey an order for retreat. Like the god Tiwaz, who could hold a spear but not a shield, they had no sense of self-protection. Fierce as they were, even they were unable to manage the wolf steed of the goddess Hyrrokin mentioned earlier.

The Wolf-Coats deliberately took on wolf form in special ceremonies preceding battles, but the change could possess some of them unbidden. A man named *Ulf*, "wolf," developed the nickname Evening Wolf, for the violent manias that seized him. His story is recorded in the Icelandic *Eglis Saga*, attributed to the ninth century.

Evening Wolf and his cohorts were ambushing a rival vessel when the berserker rage came upon them. Before seizing the ship and cargo, they slaughtered many of the crew members and forced the rest to jump overboard in a display of carnage excessive even in the context of the saga. The text does not make clear whether the band literally took wolf form, and possibly this distinction is unimportant to the tale. Evening Wolf was left so exhausted by his berserker frenzy that he soon died.

Even when not berserkers, werewolves in Norse tales are often predatory and lethal. In the *Volsunga Saga*, the nine brothers of the hero Sigmund are eaten by an enemy queen while she is in wolf form. Sigmund himself tricks the werewolf queen with honey and slays her.

Later Sigmund is marauding with his son-and-nephew (that's right) Sinfjotli, when the two discover magic wolf pelts in a forest cabin. The owners of the pelts have sloughed off their wolf skins for a half-day of manly slumber, which they partake every tenth day. Sigmund and Sinfjotli don the pelts and become werewolves themselves. They then separate and resume their pillage with greater ferocity. Sinfjotli evokes Sigmund's ire when he kills eleven men in battle, despite his promise to howl for Sigmund if he is fighting more than seven. Sigmund attacks his son's throat with his wolf fangs and severs his windpipe, then in remorse drags the body back to the cabin and watches over it. During his vigil, Sigmund observes a fight between weasels which results in a severed windpipe. The surviving weasel forages into the bush and returns with a herb that heals the injury. As the weasels scamper off, a raven appears carrying the same healing herb. Sigmund hastily applies it, and Sinfjotli springs back unharmed. The two return home and remain in self-imposed seclusion until the tenth day, when they resume their human form and burn the wolf skins.

Though werewolves in the sagas are devastatingly fierce, the assumption of wolf form does not precipitate a change in character. The evil queen is bent on murder to begin with and takes wolf form to further her goal. The men accompanying Evening Wolf are on a planned raid, prepared to inflict at least a few casualties, when the berserker rage overtakes them. Sigmund and Sinfjötli have already embarked on a violent journey when they discover the wolf skins, and becoming werewolves only exacerbates their ferocity. Sigmund's response to the youth's disobedience would presumably have been less lethal if he had remained in human form, but the attack is in character nonetheless. These two werewolves retain their faculties and eventually abandon their pastimes until the charm wears off, recognizing that assault and plunder under wolf guise gets out of hand.

Christianity profoundly transformed the way werewolves were perceived. The werewolf became a tool of the Devil, bent on mayhem for its own sake, no longer the fearless warrior, the ardent lover, the dedicated mother, the self-sacrificing son, the magician penetrating the death realms or the leader favored by the goddess. The werewolf was either a witch causing willful destruction or, more commonly, a victim cursed not just with involuntary animal form but with an uncontrollable appetite for evil. Part of this change came from the Christian view that shapeshifting was intrinsically wrong; part came from Christian beliefs about the wolf.

In Judeo-Christian belief, the godly man is superior to all animals, but the Old Testament wolf is specifically compared to immoral men. In the New Testament, the wolf is the enemy of Christ and Christians, who are described as lambs and sheep. These lines appear to be metaphorically describing predatory men, but then as now many people took their scripture literally. Some clerics went further and identified "the Beast" of The Revelation as a wolf. As theology around Satan developed, this deity was typically drawn with wolf features.

Church leaders encouraged the faithful to hunt and kill every wolf possible. A synod in Spain ordered all priests, knights and peasants to spend Saturdays hunting wolves or risk a fine. The target in the early days was the wolf animal, not a shapeshifting human. In the eleventh century, the Bishop of Worms addressed the belief in shapeshifting in general, and werewolfery in particular, by prescribing penitence for those who believed such things possible. The consensus of theologians in the ensuing centuries would gradually shift to the belief that shapeshifting—or the appearance of shapeshifting—did occur at the behest of Satan. Detractors maintained that Satan only caused a person to *think* they had taken animal form. This interpretation, especially as it pertained to werewolves, was favored by physicians and intellectuals of the time.

Those who believed werewolfery a delusion were drawing on a fair amount of Roman scholarship on the subject of lycanthropy, a disease first documented by the Greeks and noted (in some permutation) in cultures around the world. A lycanthrope is a person who believes she changes into the form of an animal, as opposed to those of us who really do. Lycanthropes in classical times loitered in cemeteries, cried pathetically, dug up graves and shunned human contact. Though they believed they had taken wolf form, others could see no change. The wolf was the most common form of this delusion, but sometimes the transformation was to another animal, in which case they would behave like that animal—or like that animal was conventionally expected to behave.

In medieval legend, the Irish king Suibhne of Ulster believes himself transformed to a small bird and flees human contact, hopping among the trees. His madness begins on the battlefield, perhaps as a result of a saint's curse, and various friends, supporters and clerics attempt to help him without success. During brief periods of lucidity, he resumes rulership. During periods of extended, involuntary transformation, others note his strange behavior but cannot see the bird form. Suibhne clearly exemplifies lycanthropy, as opposed to genuine shapeshifting.

In psychiatry today, lycanthropy is understood as a form of psychosis, a severe mental disorder characterized by confused thinking. The afflicted person has trouble organizing thoughts in a coherent manner, and this gives rise to delusions and hallucinations as well as problems with communication. The hallmark of a psychotic disorder is a difficulty distinguishing inner and outer reality.

Psychosis can manifest in some people during periods of severe depression, which is interesting in light of the onetime classification of lycanthropy as a type of melancholy. Psychosis can be induced (occasionally) by extreme trauma. Remember that Suibhne's lycanthropy first manifests during battle. The berserkers known to suffer from permanent or intermittent insanity could also have been reacting to battle trauma, although drug use would explain this as well. Psychosis caused by chemical hallucinogens can be permanent if the dosage is high enough.

It is believed that the incidence of psychotic disorders increased in the twentieth century, even accounting for better diagnosis, but the reasons for this are poorly understood. The incidence of lycanthropic delusions of all kinds, on the other hand, decreased substantially. Common psychotic delusions today involve alien encounters and intrusions by government intelligence agencies. The reasons for this are not a mystery. While we tend to label people with new and revolutionary ideas as "crazy," originality is actually a luxury reserved for those who can take normalcy for granted. Individuals plagued by psychotic thinking try to put their irrational thoughts and perceptions in the most conventional framework at their disposal. Alien delusions have developed because a majority of non-psychotic people believe that contact with other intelligent life forms has already happened or is at least possible. On the other hand, the idea of a person changing into an animal, a phenomenon that was widely credible a few hundred years ago, has become fantastic.

As Christianity advanced and ideas about Satan solidified, the manifestation of lycanthropes who believed themselves wolves (by far the majority) changed significantly. Lycanthropes now snarled and attacked their physicians, spoke about pacts with the Devil, and readily confessed to abduction, murder and cannibalism of children. Usually no crime was evident.

When charged with werewolfery, it did not bode well for the accused to appear sane. Those ensnared by circumstantial evidence who appeared to have control of their faculties were destined for torture and execution. How many were charged and how many executed? We don't even know how many were arrested for witchcraft, let alone werewolfery, so it's impossible to tell. The cases involving werewolves appear to have been a significant minority, although shapeshifting in general was involved in many accusations and confessions under torture. Female witches were more likely to be charged with shapeshifting into cats or hares, while most of the alleged werewolves were men. Although prosecuted under the same laws as witches, werewolves tended to be viewed as victimized rather than depraved, transformed by Satan or by witches. Recall that the Celtic werewolves of legend were usually cursed by saints.

The scarcity of female werewolves in the witch persecutions can lead to the assumption that werewolfery is a male phenomenon; however, evidence of female werewolves can be found. One tidbit from the Netherlands says that when seven sisters are born in a row, one will be a werewolf. Male werewolves are still more prevalent, but men are always more prevalent in surviving folklore, as they are in recorded history. The dearth of female werewolves at a time when persecutions under the anti-witchcraft laws were mostly directed at women probably reflects a dissonance between medieval conceptions of women and wolves.

Most werewolf persecutions occurred in France, which boasted the only jurist of the Witch Craze to specialize in werewolves. France may have had more wolves with a predatory bent toward humans. In 1573 one district even requested and received a special dispensation for killing werewolves until mayhem was successfully halted. The dispensation was necessary because it was believed werewolves could revert back to human form once they were dispatched, and no one wanted to be charged with homicide.

It was once common for animals which killed humans to be tried in local courts under formal murder charges. The animal was assigned a representative to speak for them, since they could hardly be expected to arrange counsel on their own. Wolves were dressed in clothes for their day in court, since they could be werewolves rather than ordinary wolves. The guilty animal was usually hanged.

In the Baltic region in 1692, a trial occurred that is much more interesting than the usual stereotyped scenarios. An eighty year old man named Theiss was arrested on charges of "idolatry" and pressured to admit to diabolical sorcery, which he consistently denied. This in itself is not remarkable, nor is it strange that the old man acknowledged deeds that were considered heretical by his accusers, such as shapeshifting into a wolf. Interrogators armed with the same witch hunt manuals used in Western Europe tried to guide his statements, but Theiss, though ready to confess, refused to follow the script. He maintained that he and other werewolves, male and female, were the "dogs of god" who visited hell three times a year, one of these times being Christmas eve. Hell was located "at the end of the sea" and there he and his cohorts battled witches who had stolen sheaves of grain. The god-dogs carried iron whips and the evil sorcerers had broomsticks wrapped with horse tails. If the werewolves were successful in their mission, there would be plenty of barley, rye and fish; otherwise, famine would result. Accounts of Theiss' confession do not mention the use of hallucinogenic ointments.

A lynchpin of witchcraft theology was the magic ointment used for shapeshifting, documented in Roman classics such as *The Golden Ass*. Interrogators tried to make accused witches confess that they had used a special ointment to change shape or to fly through the air, perhaps on an animal's back or a broom. But by the sixteenth century, physicians and even some witch hunters were questioning this tenet, which was a basic one since it explained how witches were getting to their meetings undetected. The ointment recipes recounted by victims, probably under torture, included the predictable ingredients that caused witch hunters to salivate, such as baby's fat and bat's blood, but also included recognized hallucinogens such as belladonna, mandrake, wolfsbane and henbane. Physicians with a background in herbology began openly speculating that accused witches had dreamed the scenarios of their confessions while under the influence of hallucinogenic herbs. This line of reasoning became solidified during the Enlightenment and remains the predominant theory for accounts of shapeshifting that cannot be explained by torture or psychosis.

The possibility of hallucinogenic involvement allows shapeshifting and other "paranormal" experiences to be placed in terms that can be better understood by the modern mind. Adding to a compulsion to "make sense" of things within frameworks that are not developed to understand them is the natural appeal hallucinogens hold for many people. Those who are enthusiastic about their own drug use often promote ointment theories to explain werewolves, or the Witch Craze, or the medieval dancing manias or just about anything else.

Ergot is a ubiquitous hallucinogenic theory in a class by itself. Ergot is a fungus that grows on cereals, especially rye, replacing the ripe grain with a hard, black, slightly larger capsule. It is a toxic substance with uncomfortable side effects that does not bring a big "bang for the buck," until its psychedelic components are isolated in a laboratory. What makes the ergot theory attractive is that it is possible to ingest ergot unintentionally, if those harvesting and processing the grain are careless. If the ingestion is accidental, there does not need to be evidence of

Ergot. Photo Dominique Jacquin/Wikimedia Commons.

magic ointments, mushrooms or other deliberate drug use. For those addicted to pharmacological theories of the occult, ergot is the drug of choice.

Yet the possibility of accidental ingestion of ergot going undetected is problematic, since ergot was commonly used in small doses to induce abortion, promote labor and alleviate migraine headaches. In slightly larger doses ergot restricts circulation, making it useful in stanching blood. In still larger doses ergot causes muscle spasms, severe pain and even convulsions along with the psychoactive qualities. Midwives and other herbalists who used ergot therapeutically would have been aware of the symptoms of ergot poisoning.

Widespread ingestion of ergot in rye flour is another matter. Since ergot has a foul taste, some effort was probably made to reduce the quantity of spurs processed with the grain, but even small amounts of ergot in flour can cause grave illness. The milling, kneading, fermentation and cooking of grain mixed with ergot causes dangerous mutations in the ergot alkaloids, thereby poisoning those who eat the bread with the dreaded St. Anthony's Fire. Yet the symptoms of St. Anthony's Fire were well known in medieval times, even if the cause was not, and this type of poisoning is epidemic in nature, affecting the whole community.

In German the ergot capsule is sometimes called a *wolfzhan*, a "wolf's tooth," perhaps partly because it resembles a canine incisor, and there are fairy tales about a *Roggenmutter*, a "rye mother," who lives in the grain with her *Roggenwulf* or *Roggenhund*. The *Roggenmutter* is a crone reminiscent of the Celtic Cailleach. Recall that the Cailleach lives in the ripe grain in the form of a hare. Crone goddesses are usually involved with the harvest and the death of the grain spirit. In Russia the last stalk of wheat is called the *Baba,* the Grandmother. Hares would naturally inhabit fields for camouflage or food, and wolves living close to farms might be found hunting in the grain fields.

Stalking amongst the ripe grain, the hare and the wolf, like the crones associated with them, would signify death. Black is a color linked with death, so the black spikes poking out of the grain would be named for the wolf as death creature. Perhaps the *Roggenmutter* shapeshifts into a wolf like the Cailleach shapeshifts into a hare. Either way she brings with her the ultimate transformation.

Sometimes in folklore werewolves stalk the fields attacking domestic animals, still retaining human faculties. They might howl as a wolf or speak as a human, although sometimes they lose their voice altogether. Their eyes may have a human glint. They do not wear clothes, but sometimes they enjoy tearing up clothes. They drink large quantities of beer or wine, sharing the legendary thirst attributed to spirits of the dead.

While in human form, werewolves usually have no wolf attributes at all. Sometimes there is unusual hairiness, especially about the hands, or there might be a uni-brow. They are exhausted after they leave their wolf shape. Sometimes they have indigestion from eating things humans wouldn't touch, and they may vomit the paws of dogs.

There are numerous explanations for how a person becomes a werewolf. The tendency toward werewolfery is believed to run in certain families. A baby conceived at the new moon is supposed to become a werewolf. (Since menstruation formerly was linked to the new moon, this could be another way of saying a werewolf is conceived during menstruation.) Being born on Christmas is often a sign. Being born with the caul, a portion of the amniotic sac covering the face is mentioned as a sign, although it is more common for this to mean the child has psychic powers or a propensity for sorcery in general.

A person does not have to be born a werewolf. The most common way of changing is with a magic girdle or a charmed wolf skin. Water is a strong theme in werewolf spells—drinking water from a wolf footprint or out of a certain stream. Ointment is sometimes mentioned, although it is relatively uncommon outside of trial records. The old saw about being bitten by a wolf is also less common, but it does have precedents before the gothic romances.

Smelling wolfsbane flowers can reportedly cause shapeshifting, although wolfsbane is more often a prophylactic against shapeshifting. It is believed that wolfsbane got its name as a poison used to tip arrows when hunting wolves. The poison was only used in wolf hunting, since unlike most other game the wolf would not be eaten. (That would cause werewolfery.) Greek myth says wolfsbane grew from the foaming spittle of Cerberus when Heracles dragged her from the underworld during one of his labors. Another name for wolfsbane is hecateis, after Hecate.

A belief from Eastern Europe says that a werewolf is a bad person who refuses to go to hell. Instead, they claw their way out of the grave and take the form of a wolf. Hollywood is not the only place werewolves and vampires meet; the two are often found together in the Balkan region. Vampires can shapeshift into wolves, and they become werewolves after death.

Folklore emphasizes certain times as significant for transformation. It almost goes without saying that a werewolf transforms at night. Moonlight is integral to many werewolf spells. A man sleeping with the moon on his face on certain days, for example, is believed to become a werewolf. One account of the werewolf transformation (from France) describes young men jumping into a fountain on the full moon and donning wolf skins after they emerge. They then roam the countryside causing werewolf mischief (unspecified) and later return to the fountain to repeat the sequence in reverse.

The time of year also stands out. By far the most common time for a werewolf to emerge is Christmas. The second most common time is mid-February, followed by January dates, especially Epiphany (January 6th). Other folk belief simply states that any time after Halloween is ripe for werewolfery. All of these werewolf times correspond to significant wolf dates on Pagan calendars.

We know all about the silver bullet, but back in the day there were many ways to confront a werewolf. A method for at least temporarily restoring the human form was simply telling the werewolf they were in wolf form. (*Wolfgang, thou art wolf now.*) Saying the person's baptismal name three times was another strategy. (*Wolfgang! Wolfgang! Wolfgang! Why dost thou not return a man as I call thee Wolfgang?*) If that still didn't work, the werewolf would be scolded harshly until he was shamed into resuming human form. (*Wolfgang, think of thy mother, that she be not called a bitch.*) A werewolf could voluntarily change back to a human by rolling in dew or washing with water, and some werewolves would resume their human form by latching their belt in the ninth notch. (*Wolfgang, thou deceivest me not. I know by thy leather belt about thy naked fur that thou art no true beast.*) A stubborn werewolf could be transformed by silver or other metal touching the forehead. Drawing small amounts of blood was a trick that worked well, especially if it came from the paws. (*Wolfgang! Stand still and do not bite me while I prick thy paws.*) Some swore by a bloody rusted key pressed to the forehead. Burning the wolf skin while the werewolf was in human form would effect a permanent cure, but how to force the werewolf to change back remained the issue.

In situations where the werewolf was a former vampire, drastic measures were required. The only sure way to stop the werewolf from wreaking havoc was to burn the vampire corpse, but this posed problems since the Orthodox Church frowned on cremation. A variety of magical solutions would be tried first, but if, in the end, the body had to be burned, at least the werewolf/vampire was already going to hell.

Gypsies are linked in popular imagination with werewolf lore, but there is little specifically linking the Romani people with werewolf beliefs. Charles Leland, who knew more about

Romani folklore than any other nineteenth century scholar, does not mention werewolves in his treatise, nor is there anything significant in *Buckland's Book of Gypsy Magic*. This does not mean the Romani did not believe in werewolves—they did—but up to the twentieth century most rural Europeans believed in werewolves, so this was in no way remarkable.

Gypsies apparently got their reputation as werewolf experts from the 1941 film *The Wolf Man*. The protagonist, Larry Talbot, is bitten by a traveling gypsy fortuneteller, and the fortuneteller's mother is the repository for the werewolf "folklore" brought to the story. As a plot device the presence of the gypsies works well, allowing Larry to be a werewolf in an area where few understand his condition without introducing some contrived element into the script, like the trip to Tibet in the earlier *Werewolf of London*. Maria Ouspenskaya's inspired performance as the old gypsy woman solidified the gypsy association with werewolf lore.

The werewolf as an abstract concept was developed by Sabine Baring-Gould in *The Book of Werewolves* (1865) which laid the foundation for study of the subject. Some complain that this book dwells too much on serial killers and not enough on werewolves, but Baring-Gould actually defines the werewolf in terms of killing, the salient feature of the werewolf for him being an uncontrollable thirst for violence, with or without delusions of wolf form.

To Baring-Gould, the werewolf is aberrant, but followers of Sigmund Freud would later characterize the werewolf as an antisocial aspect lurking within civilized man. Freud lays the foundation for his theory of the unconscious in his study of a patient he calls The Wolf-Man. The Wolf-Man speaks to Freud in the course of treatment about a troublesome wolf dream he experienced as a child. Freud interprets The Wolf-Man's dream as an expression of unresolved sexual trauma coming from the unconscious. There is nothing in Freud's analysis about werewolves or even about the nature of the wolf: what is significant to Freud, and indicative of a restive unconscious, is the disturbance the dream brings to the patient. Nonetheless it is a short step, even without the provocative alias, to equate the bestial wolf with Freudian understanding of the unconscious, which is characterized as a part of man that is primitive and irrational, untamed and unclaimed, unrecognized and often frightening. This conception of the werewolf as a horrifying bestial force hiding in a subterranean vault of the mind has been very persistent. Stephen Sommers, writer/director of the 2004 monster film Van Helsing, said in a trailer for that movie, "The werewolf is more like a drug addict or an alcoholic ... He's really a good guy, but at night his demons come out."[13]

A feminist variant of this theory views the werewolf as the unconscious feminine self within the girl or woman, an instinctual self that has been denied and repressed by patriarchal dominance. The werewolf is the good, authentic self of the woman emerging first into the cold light of the moon and eventually into the warm light of day.

This feminist reinterpretation of the werewolf has paralleled and fueled a changing concept of the wolf herself. The wolf has become the embodiment of wilderness, with all the purity, sustainability and natural beauty that implies. She exists in opposition to the degradation, pollution and artificiality of civilization. She pursues her virtuous life in a world far removed from our own in distance, geography and perspective. We may never see her, but we need to know she is out there because she has come to represent a core wild part of ourselves.

Yet for all the attractiveness of this idealized concept of wolf and werewolf, it is still a Christian model with the polarities reversed. Now the civilized self is the self that is the problem, its character disfigured by pollution and patriarchal stereotypes. Even if we decide to accept the tension inherent in the idea of good and bad struggling for control within us, we need to ask ourselves if the wolf belongs in this paradigm. Must the wolf be cast as an oppositional force?

In the Pagan view the wolf is simply another creature with whom we share the world—not a separate world, but the same world. She has at times been a poor neighbor, but then again, so have we. She shares our devotion to family and our ability to survive in challenging environments. She is a part of our history and, for better or worse, we are a part of hers. The wolf mother says to us, stop trying to make me what you fear me to be, what you want me to be or what you need me to be. Become like me, temporarily, and let me show you who I am.

An Early Horror Classic

The following story is a bit of an anomaly among the others related here. It is not a true story, nor is it a myth, nor is it myth disguised as romance, nor is it a fictionalized collection of beliefs and experiences à la The Golden Ass. *This is a werewolf story composed for entertainment, which makes it similar to werewolf films and novels of today. It could almost be called a prototype of the genre. It is attributed to Petronius, a first century Roman style consultant and man of leisure. Notice the elements of the Arcadian werewolf ritual woven into the story.*

After we had finished our meal, and made a toast to good health and sound mind, our host, Trimalchio chided, "You have been so quiet, Niceros, and you are usually such an entertaining guest. Tell us a story—tell us that story about the wolf soldier, and I will forgive you for your reticence."

I am nothing but loquacious, whatever Trimalchio says, so I told the story with little prodding. "Gentlemen, I would tell you this story gladly, but I'm afraid you'll laugh at me ... No ... No ... You say that now, but wait 'til you hear the story. I'll have to pretend to be laughing with you, when in reality I was scared to death. I've never been more frightened."

"This happened back when I was still a slave, when I lived on the narrow street in that old house Gavilla has now. I was in love with Melissa—you remember Melissa of Tarentum—such a lovely woman! Small, fat cheeks, so pretty—but I wasn't in love with her looks, so help me Hercules! I loved her for her kindness. Whenever I asked for money, she was generous. She'd give me half of what she had. Then, when her husband died, I used to spend even more time up at her place. She liked having a man about, and I thought it only right to help her out."

"Well, my master, the old Gaul, was called away to Capua on business, and I made plans to slip out and see Melissa as soon as I could. I persuaded a lodger at my master's house, a soldier brave as they come, to escort me half way, because I didn't want to wait for morning."

"The moon was rising as we set out, and when we got to the stretch of road with the grave stones, you could see the shadows clearly in the night. My companion ducked behind the stones when we got to that part, and I sat down and waited, thinking he had left to take a whiz. I sang to keep the shudders away, then counted all the stones, but he never appeared. Finally I went looking for him."

"He was standing naked in the moonlight, his clothes in a pile by his feet. He did the most curious thing—he peed in a circle around his clothing, and when he finished the circle, he howled and turned into a wolf! No, don't laugh at me. My heart is in my mouth just thinking about it! I ran into the woods until the wolf scampered off, then I crept over to where his clothes were. They had turned to stone."

"I ran the rest of the way to my mistress's house. My heart was pounding, my breath came in gasps, sweat poured down my back and legs. I collapsed at her door, and she was surprised to see me, but she said, 'Oh, if only you had come a few minutes sooner. Something terrible has happened! My sheep were attacked by a wolf—he broke into the pen and left them bleeding all over the ground. One of the slaves speared him in the neck, but he ran off. Oh, I wish you had been here.'"

"I was terrified when I heard this, and I didn't sleep at all that night. At first cockcrow I was on the road home. I stopped at the place where my companion had stripped, and there were neither rocks nor clothes there, but a pool of blood. I continued home and found the soldier in bed, with a physician attending to a gash in his neck. He recovered, but I never did. I could never eat with him, or sit beside him or even look at him for long. He was a werewolf, I tell the truth. No, don't ask me if that really happened. It did, and you gentlemen can think what you like."

Musings on Canine Shapeshifting

1) One werewolf spoof film from the eighties (*Curse of the Queerwolf*) has the bitten one becoming effeminate under the full moon instead of a raging beast. Can you think of a reason why, on some levels, this makes more sense?
2) In the 1940s the werewolf experienced a revival in both America and Germany, but with sharply divergent interpretations. A right-wing underground group calling themselves Werewolves was established by Nazi propagandist Joseph Goebbels. This group idealized remorselessness in battle and operated as a covert terrorist organization. Hitler himself had a wolf fetish, referring to himself as Wolf and calling his secret police his pack of wolves. To what extent, if any, was the Nazi werewolf drawing on genuine werewolf tradition? To what extent, if any, was this version contradicting tradition?
3) Folklore about the causes of werewolfery suggests you might be able to deliberately conceive a werewolf child. Would you do this?
4) Here is a werewolf movie synopsis to test your understanding about werewolves. Highlight the aspects of the werewolf that have some basis in science, superstition and legend in one colored pen, then highlight Hollywood innovations with a different color. This scenario was inspired by the films *The Werewolf of London, The Wolf Man, Frankenstein Meets the Wolfman* and *House of Dracula.*

Our story begins in the Welsh countryside. A botanist whose name rhymes with hairy—we'll call him "Barry"—arrives for a working holiday, spending his days and nights scouring the hillsides for plant specimens. The villagers recite poems warning Barry he must desist from collecting when the wolfsbane blooms and the moon shines strong, or he could become a werewolf. Barry only laughs, especially when an old gypsy woman offers him a pentagram necklace for protection.

Barry begins flirting with the village beauty, suggesting they visit the nearby gypsy camp and have their fortunes read. Barry is hoping the gypsy will see a tall, handsome man in the pretty girl's palm, but instead the gypsy sees a pentagram. For some reason this alarms the fortuneteller and he screams at the girl to run away. She flees in hysterics with Barry following, but up ahead a wolf is closing in on the beauty. Barry tackles the wolf just in time, beating it with his silver cane, gradually discovering to his horror that he is bashing the head of the fortuneteller. Funny, he could have sworn he was beating a wolf. The police are sympathetic, this time. Obviously, from the bites on Barry's arm, he was tussling with a wolf and accidently killed a gypsy in the process.

Barry returns to London to find his scientific schedule annoyingly disrupted by a series of brutal attacks on local women. The police track the footprints of a large predatory beast to Barry's laboratory, but Barry tells them, truthfully, that he knows nothing about this.

Meanwhile, the grave of the gypsy werewolf is exhumed under a full moon by a grave robber, looking for a valuable ring. As the coffin is opened, the wolfsbane is pushed to the side and the moonlight strikes the werewolf on the face. The werewolf immediately kills the robber and runs away.

Barry is in his laboratory the next evening, pursuing his scientific studies, when the fortuneteller believed to have died in the wolf attack appears. The gypsy man tells Barry about the curse of the werewolf and recites a poem about it. He says he has come for a flower specimen Barry took back with him from Wales. It is the only plant of its kind in all of Britain, and it is the only cure. Barry is incredulous regarding all aspects of the story and refuses to surrender the plant. The older werewolf overpowers the good botanist and absconds with the flower.

That night the moon is still full. Barry begins to feel his feet swell and takes off his shoes. He notices that his feet have gotten hairier. Suddenly his hands become hairy, his nails grow long and he develops fangs. When the transformation is complete he looks like a stooped

Sasquatch with yak hair and a pronounced underbite. Barry puts on his coat and hat, then goes outside and kills another innocent young woman. He has amnesia for the episode, but when he reads about the event in the newspaper he realizes what has happened.

Barry shows up in the local emergency room, demanding treatment. He tells the doctors and nurses that he has killed a woman, and they call in Scotland Yard. The detectives refuse to take Barry's confession, saying that the recent death was caused by a large animal, possibly a wolf. An enterprising young doctor looks up Barry's symptoms in a book and discovers the strange patient has lycanthropy. *The doctor attempts to reassure Barry that he has a mental illness and only* thinks *he is a werewolf. But that night, Barry tears off his straitjacket with superhuman strength and breaks out of the hospital for another killing rampage.*

Meanwhile the body of the grave robber has been discovered by local police. There is a huge gash in the throat of the victim and a corpse is missing. The village authorities are determined to get to the bottom of this.

Barry returns to the village seeking the old gypsy woman who tried to give him the pentagram. He must find another flower-antidote before he kills again. The gypsy woman tells him, sorrowfully, that she cannot help him, then recites a poem about how the whole predicament is not his fault. As Barry continues to plead, the old woman relents and says she knows a man who may be able to help. The two set out for a hamlet on the continent.

The London doctor is soon in close pursuit, along with various policemen. The fair villager is also in tow, deeply concerned about Barry's welfare. The crew closes in on Barry as he approaches the estate of the presumed werewolf doctor. Valuable time is lost as the experts and authorities heatedly debate the course of action. The doctor wants Barry to return to the hospital. The policeman from the village wants to arrest him. Barry readily admits to being a murdering werewolf, which makes the representative from Scotland Yard favor the doctor's point of view. At this point the man in the castle, who turns out to be another research scientist, joins the huddle. The scientist explains that the physical and personality changes Barry undergoes in his "wolf" phase are caused by swelling of the brain, which puts pressure on his pituitary gland. The scientist will apply his patented chemical formula, developed to cure hunchbacks, to Barry's head, softening the skull and allowing his brain to expand.

Suddenly the gypsy woman looks to the sky and cries out that the moon is full. She has only just now realized this, despite the fact that she spends most of her time outside and superstitious people generally know what phase the moon is in.

Barry quickly runs away to avoid killing anyone, with the young woman pursuing him for reasons that are unclear. This can only end one way. The onlookers see a strange beast appear through the billowing fog, and they rally to save the damsel who is now pursued by the savage animal. Shots are fired into the fog, and as they approach the wounded beast they discover that Barry has been hit by mistake and is dying.

The good doctor comforts Barry's onetime love interest as the troop encircles the dead botanist. A country policeman—not the one from Scotland Yard—recites a poem about werewolves, and the movie ends.

5) Fill out the "Dog Review" page based on your knowledge and the information in this section.
6) What type of bird would you guess landed on Cuchulainn's shoulder in the end?
7) Why would a skilled needle worker complement a great warrior?
8) It is said the Cwn Mamau can shapeshift into geese as they run across the sky, their barking sounds belying their feathery forms. Many mammals (and some reptiles) have an alternate bird form. What bird would you associate with the following land animals?
   a. Cat
   b. Snake
   c. Fox

d.Toad

e. Hare

f. Mouse

9) Why does the phantom dog sometimes have webbed feet?

10) What type of bird did Cuchulainn's mother Dechtire and her maidens change into during their flight to the fairy land?

11) Why are the death hounds loud in the distance and soft as they approach?

12) What magical quality would you assign to the dog's keen sense of smell?

13) In the year 1880, in Peach Tree, West Virginia, a large brindled dog appeared that frightened even the meanest dogs. The mean dogs would hide under their houses with their tails between their legs. The brindled dog only appeared at night, never in the daytime. People did not like the dog and began throwing stones to discourage the dog from hanging around. The stones would pass completely through the body. The intervention of the preacher was sought, and he shot the dog five times from five feet away—but each bullet passed through the dog's body as if it were air. Finally, after three weeks of harassment, the brindled dog went away, never to return.

    Why was the preacher elected to shoot the dog, and why five bullets from five feet away?

14) The Lenape tale about dogs and wolves is more than a funny story. It has some interesting insights. What would have happened if the dogs had brought fire to the wolves? Why were the dogs so anxious to proclaim their sanctity at council meetings?

15) People used to leave a plate of food at the crossroads for Hecate, which would later be eaten by stray dogs. Today this is not practical. You can, however, go to a deserted crossroad at night when you need to make a decision and pray to Hecate there. A three-formed crossroad, where three paths

meet in a Y, is the best. Leave a coin as an offering, go home using a different path, and don't look back.

For this ritual you need:
Coin

16) The Portuguese werewolf differed from the rest of medieval Europe by acting more like you would expect a real wolf to behave: photophobic, shy of people, most comfortable in a forested area. This Portuguese werewolf spell was outlined in 1933 by Christian scholar Montague Summers, who is surely turning over in his grave. I have fleshed it out a bit.

During a full moon, go to a deserted four-way dirt crossroad. It doesn't have to be a road that cars can drive; a trail is fine. If you can cross water by foot on the way to your destination, so much the better.

With your flashlight, reconnoiter the spot carefully, removing any prickles, sharp stones or glass. Sweep the area if you can. A scorpion or snake in your chosen spot is an auspicious sign, generally meaning that a needed transformation is coming. However, it is also a sign that this is not a good time for the werewolf ritual.

Do not cast a circle. You will be working where the roads meet, which at night in a deserted place is already between the worlds. Ask a guardian angel to guard each of the four entryways.

Take off a piece of clothing and put it aside where you can find it again. Removing your shoes may not be practical; remember that a prick to the paws is one way of bringing a werewolf back to human form.

Invoke the wolf goddess. Turn around clockwise five times quickly, then roll over five times in the dirt. Get on all fours and howl loudly. You are now a wolf, at least for a short while.

When you are ready to return to human form, stand on two legs and thank the goddess for being with you. Put your discarded clothing back on and say, "I am now a woman." Release the guardians from their posts and ask them to protect you on your journey home. A snack back at the car will be welcome. Make sure you're grounded enough to drive.

I recommend you consider bringing a friend or two with you for the ritual. Even if the possibility of encountering threatening wildlife is low (and it's always higher at night), you may find yourself jumpy in the darkness, and this is not conducive to ritual. When entertaining thoughts of ritual outdoors, the big bugaboos that come to mind are wild animals and violent men, but a more common and benign mishap like a twisted ankle can become a frightening ordeal if you're alone in the darkness some distance from the car. I admit that I have gone to all kinds of wild places alone at night, but I have also collected some interesting stories along the way. It's safer, more effective and more fun to have women with you.

I do not lead werewolf rituals in suburban areas anymore, because I've found that neighbors become alarmed by the howling. Apparently the unease stems from confusion over what is making the noise, which sounds uncanny to the uninitiated.

Final Words

Our animal friends have been generous. They have kindly offered insight and assistance with our magic, helping us to learn, find happiness and get the things we want. What have your animal friends given you in this journey? What have you learned? How have you changed? The last words in this book belong to you.

Appendix I Heroes and Deities

Acca Larentia Roman and Etruscan wolf goddess.

Achilles Greek hero of the Trojan War.

Agamemnon Father of Iphigenia, who played a pivotal role in the Trojan War.

Anagtia Goddess of a lake in southern Italy, associated with witchcraft, fortunetelling and curing snakebite.

Anansi West African (Ashanti) spider god.

Andraste Celtic warrior goddess associated with the hare.

Andre Mari Basque fire goddess of caves and subterranean caverns.

Anubis Jackal-headed Egyptian psychopomp and supervisor of embalming processes.

Aphrodite Greek goddess of romantic love.

Apollo Greek god of light and harmony. Also a mouse-god.

Arachne Greek spider goddess of weaving.

Artemis Greek goddess of wilderness, animals, birth and death.

Artio Celtic bear goddess. Also called Andarte.

Asclepius Greek god of healing. His symbol is the snake.

Aspelenie Lithuanian household goddess who lives behind the stove. She takes the form of a little ringed snake.

Athena Greek goddess of agriculture, science and government, usually pictured with an owl or a snake.

Attis Bee god and consort of Cybele.

Avanyu Hopi snake and rain deity.

Baba Yaga Complex Russian crone goddess.

Badb Celtic goddess of war and death.

Badurn An Irish king. His wife brings the vessel of truth from the fairy world.

Bast Egyptian cat goddess.

Blodeuwedd Welsh flower and owl goddess.

Brigid Celtic sun goddess, also associated with wells, healing, poetry, textile arts and smithery.

Cailleach, Cailleach Bhear Celtic crone goddess.

Cerberus Greek dog-headed guardian to the entrance of Hades.

Cernunnos Celtic forest god depicted with stag horns, one of the "horned gods" of the witches.

Cerridwyn, Caridwen, Cerridwin Welsh shapeshifting goddess and goddess of the cauldron.

Circe Sorceress who rules an island in the Aegean. She turns men into animals.

Clytemnestra Mother of Iphigenia and murderer of Agamemnon.

Coatlicue Aztec mother and death goddess. She wears a snake-fringed skirt and has two snakes growing out of her neck.

Cormac mac Airt The hero who brought the cup of truth from the Land of Promise.

Cu Sith Phantom dog of Scotland.

Cuchulainn Celtic warrior associated with dogs.

Cupid Roman name for the Greek god Eros, the son of Aphrodite. Can also mean any cherubic offspring of Aphrodite or her nymphs.

Cwn Mamau, Cwn Annwn The hounds of the mothers from the underworld, white with red ears.

Cybele Anatolian animal mother and mountain goddess.

Demeter Greek goddess of the grain, mother of Persephone.

Diana Sky goddess equated with Artemis by the Romans.

Dionysus Greek fertility god who had an ecstatic cult involving wine and other intoxicants.

Dumuzi Sumerian consort of Inanna. Bull god and god of vegetation.

Dylan Celtic fish god of the sea.

Eileithyia Greek birth goddess, represented as a snake or a dog.

Ereshkigal Sumerian and Akkadian goddess of the Underworld.

Eros Greek god of love, son of Aphrodite.

Enki Sumerian god associated with fresh water. Generous and capricious.

Enlil Sumerian father god. He exerts influence over the earth and other gods, but is more distant from humans.

Eostre Saxon goddess of spring.

Epona Celtic horse goddess.

Fionn MacCumal Irish hero beloved of Sadb.

Fenrir The giant wolf-child of Loki and a horse.

Freya Germanic fertility goddess and warrior maiden.

Furies Roman name for sister Greek goddesses (Erinyes) who stand for conscience.

Gaia Greek goddess of the earth.

Garm The dog that guards the portal to the Germanic land of the dead.

Geshtinana Dumuzi's loyal sister, who volunteers to take his place in the underworld for half the year. Sumerian.

Gilgamesh Sumerian hero. Listed as an actual king in Sumerian historical documents.

Gula Sumerian healing goddess, usually portrayed with dogs.

Gwion Entrusted with Cerridwyn's cauldron, which he pilfers. An incarnation of Taliesin.

Gwydion Celtic magician. He is turned into various animals in retribution for serious crimes by his uncle, King Math.

Gwynn ap Nudd Welsh fairy king who leads the Hounds of the Mothers.

Hades Greek lord of the underworld death realm that bears his name. Consort of Persephone.

Hecate Greek goddess of witches and travelers.

Heimdall Germanic god of the far north, who returns Freya's Brisingamen necklace.

Hel Germanic goddess of the underworld and the frozen lands of the North.

Hera Greek goddess of marriage and wife of Zeus.

Hermes Greek god of communication, medicine and magic.

Herophile Priestess of Apollo. One of the most celebrated prophets of antiquity.

Hittavainen Finnish/Karelian hare god.

Holda, Holle Goddess of the Wild Hunt who appears as a witch in German fairy tales. Twin sister of Perchta.

Hygeia Greek goddess of healing, especially preventative medicine. Associated with snakes.

Hyrrokin German crone heroine who rides a wolf.

Idunn Germanic goddess of spring.

Inanna Sumerian equivalent of Ishtar.

Iphigenia Priestess of Artemis, probably an honorary title.

Ishtar Akkadian sky and fertility goddess. Source of civilization.

Jormungand Norse sea serpent who encircles the world.

Jupiter Roman equivalent of Zeus.

Kimat Philippine (Tinguian) lightening dog and companion of thunder god Tadaklan.

Laelaps Hurricane dog who became Canis Major.

Laima, Laime Lithuanian/Latvian sun and weaving goddess.

Lakshmi Hindu goddess of wealth.

Lamia Greek fairy creature, half woman/half snake. Appears in scary stories about baby snatching.

Leda Mother of Helen of Troy, raped by Zeus in the form of a swan.

Leto Mother of Artemis and Apollo.

Lilith Hebrew and Akkadian goddess of uninhabited places.

Llew Llaw Gyffes Welsh name for Lugh.

Loki Germanic trickster god/goddess.

Lucifer Roman god of light later cast as the Christian devil.

Lugh Celtic sun and vegetation god.

Maat Egyptian goddess of justice, associated with the vulture.

Macha Celtic warrior goddess.

Maenads Priestesses of Dionysus who worshiped in all-female ecstatic covens.

Manasa Hindu snake goddess.

Mars Roman woodpecker god, associated with spring. Later identified with Greek war god Ares.

Marsyas Anatolian master of the flute and priest of Cybele.

Math fab Mathonwy, King Math Welsh magician who transforms Gwydion and Blodeuwedd.

Maya Hindu and Buddhist goddess who creates the physical manifestation of the world.

Medb, Maeve Celtic goddess of wealth whose name is derived from mead.

Mengloth Beautiful Germanic goddess of the underworld, probably another name or aspect for Hel.

Mertseger Egyptian cobra goddess.

Mielikki Finnish forest goddess and mistress of animals.

Minerva, Menrva Etruscan/Roman goddess of wisdom and weaving.

Minyades Three sisters who decline to attend the celebrations of Dionysus. Changed into bats.

Moirae Three sisters known as "The Fates." Clotho weaves the thread of life, Lachesis measures it and Atropos cuts it at the place of death.

Morrigan Irish triple warrior and death goddess.

Muses Nine goddesses of various artistic and scholarly disciplines.

Nanna Sumerian moon god.

Nehalennia Sea goddess of the Netherlands, usually portrayed with dog companion.

Nimue Maiden Welsh goddess. Name spellling is French.

Ninhursaga Sumerian mother of gods, humans and animals.

Ninshubur Steadfast priestess of Inanna.

Norns Sisters who sit at the bottom of the world tree, Yggdrasil, and water its roots. They tell the future and assign fate.

Nydhogg Serpent who nibbles at the roots of Yggdrasil.

Odin Germanic father-god and warrior. Quintessential shamanic deity, traveling to the lands of the dead to receive wisdom.

Odysseus Greek hero whose long journey after the Trojan War is chronicled in *The Odyssey*.

Oisin Irish bard. Son of Sadb.

Osiris Greek name for Egyptian vegetation god.

Pan Arcadian goat god. One of the "horned gods" worshiped by witches.

Perchta Germanic goddess of winter. Associated with death and the Wild Hunt.

Persephone Greek goddess of death and rebirth.

Poseidon Greek sea god.

Proserpina Roman snake and death goddess.

Quetzalcoatl Aztec feathered serpent god.

Ragana Lithuanian/Latvian death goddess. A shapeshifter especially associated with the toad.

Rama. Consort of Lakshmi.

Ran Swedish sea goddess.

Renutet Egyptian cobra goddess.

Rhea Greek mother goddess.

Roggenmutter "Rye Mother." German crone goddess who waits in the ripened grain with her Roggenwulf or Roggenhund.

Romulus and Remus Twin offspring of a Vestal Virgin and the god Mars, rescued from exposure by a wolf.

Sadb Maiden beloved of Irish hero Fionn MacCumal and mother of bard Oisin. She is transformed to a doe by a rival.

Sebek Egyptian crocodile god.

Sheela Na Gig Name given to carvings of unclothed women that adorn church entrances and other structures in Western Europe.

Sigmund and Sinfjotli Norse warriors who become werewolves during one of their adventures.

Sirona Celtic healing goddess. Depicted with snakes, eggs and occasionally dogs.

Skadi Swedish goddess of winter. She has a wolf companion.

Soranus Sabine wolf god.

Spako Persian king allegedly adopted by a mother wolf.

Spider Woman, Spider Grandmother Heroine in southwest Native American creation myths.

St. Christopher Patron saint of travelers. Often depicted with a dog head.

St. Melangell Welsh patron saint of hares.

St. Patrick British saint who reputedly Christianized Ireland.

St. Roch French healing saint who was himself healed by a dog.

Suibhne of Ulster Irish king who suffered from lycanthropy.

Taliesin Welsh bard and magician.

Teumessian Fox Rampaging Greek fox monster who became Canis Minor.

Theseus Greek hero and monster slayer.

Thiassi Nordic eagle giant.

Tiresias Renowned Greek psychic who began life as a man, but was changed into a woman for seven years.

Tiwaz Germanic god of the spear, who has one disfigured hand.

Ukko Finnish god of thunder.

Uttu Sumerian weaving, marriage and household goddess. A spider goddess.

Utu Sumerian sun god.

Vestal Virgins Unmarried priestesses who served the Roman fire goddess Vesta.

Wadjet Egyptian cobra goddess, symbol of royalty.

Wagyal Australian snake goddess.

Xolotl Dog-headed Aztec lightening deity.

Zeus Sky and thunder god, head of the Greek pantheon.

Appendix II Ancient People and Places

Akkadians

See Mesopotamians.

Anatolia

Asia Minor, the western protrusion of Turkey, bounded by the Mediterranean and Black Sea.

Anglo-Saxons

Germanic tribes that ruled much of Britain from the sixth to eleventh centuries.

Arcadians

Inhabitants of a mountainous region in the center of the Peloponnese peninsula, at the southern tip of Greece. The modern Arcadian province is larger, with a coastal area. See Greece.

Catal Huyuk

Archeological site in south central Turkey, location of one of the world's first permanent settlements. Pronounced chattel-who-YOOK.

Caria

Kingdom along the western Anatolian coast.

Celts

Early Celts were Indo-European peoples arriving in Europe by the fourth millennium. They adopted many cultural practices of existing inhabitants. By the sixth century BCE the Celts dominated central Europe, and in the ensuing centuries they could be found in significant numbers in central Anatolia, the upper Balkan region, parts of northern Italy, France, the northern

Iberian Peninsula and the British Isles. The Celtic tribes were related by similar language, art and burial practices but did not form alliances until they began resisting Roman conquest in the first century BCE. The area they dominated did not represent a monolithic culture and included non-Celtic tribes. Today the "Celtic countries" are the regions where Celtic languages are still spoken, specifically Ireland, Isle of Man, Scotland, Wales, Cornwall and Brittany, although vestiges of Celtic culture continue elsewhere. Especially when discussing the British Isles, the term "Celtic" usually refers to the Celtic tribes *and* the pre-existing cultures they assimilated.

Cretans

See Minoans.

Egyptians

The ancient inhabitants of the Nile valley are mentioned frequently here, as they had a highly developed system of animal worship that has influenced traditional and modern Paganism. Yet Egyptian religion retained a complex cosmology that differed from the rest of the Mediterranean, even as it evolved and absorbed outside influences.

Etruscans, Etruria

Etruria was an ancient kingdom in the northwest Italian peninsula, roughly corresponding to modern Tuscany. The Etruscan civilization flourished from the eighth century BCE until Etruria was absorbed into the Roman Empire in the second century BCE. At its zenith Etruscan influence extended to the southern peninsula and to the Adriatic Sea. We know tantalizingly little about this influential civilization, considering its possession of written language and its persistence almost to the Common Era. Part of this has to do with Etruscan being another "language isolate," difficult to decipher because it is unrelated to any known language group. Another factor is the early Church's decision to destroy all Etruscan literature it could find.

Flemish
Belonging to the medieval country of Flanders, now part of France, Belgium and the Netherlands.

Germanic Peoples
The Germanic tribes which dominated Europe in the hole left by the collapsing Roman Empire spoke a similar Indo-European language and had parallel religious beliefs. Most of what we know about these beliefs comes from archeology and from the Norse Sagas, historical legends penned by later generations of Scandinavian Christians.

Greco-Roman
See Romans.

Greece, Greeks
Ancient Greece encompassed a wide range of people and geography, not to mention a long timeframe. The first agrarian peoples of the Greek peninsula, often called the Pelasgians, settled there by the seventh millennium and eventually developed or imported animal husbandry, pottery, weaving and bronze metallurgy. Culturally, they had much in common with other peoples in the Aegean islands, Anatolia and the rest of the Balkan region. The invasion of an Indo-European tribe known as the Mycenaeans around 1600 BCE had a profound impact, especially on the status of women. The Mycenaeans, who were patriarchal, warlike and socially stratified, superimposed their own pantheon, headed by the god Zeus, onto the indigenous ones. Yet while the myths changed, they did not disappear, and worship of many old deities continued under new names. The Mycenaeans built the first Greek city-states and continued to develop culture in the region. This is

the Greek era immortalized by Homer's *Iliad* and *Odyssey*. Around 1100 BCE, a precipitous drop in population meant Greece could no longer support the large urban centers necessary for continuation of what had become a complex culture. The reasons for the decimation are unclear (perhaps plague, internecine war or another invasion), and little is known about life in Greece for the next five hundred years, except that it continued. By the seventh century BCE. the population had recovered, and a few centuries later "classical" Greek civilization was in full flower. Greek colonies proliferated during this time, as they had in the Mycenaean era, and many of the "Greek" cities of the ancient world were not actually in Greece.

Jews, Judaism

Judaism is the religion originally practiced by Hebrew-speaking Semitic people living along the eastern Mediterranean coast. Jews spread throughout the Mediterranean during the Roman Empire, as did many other people. When Rome became Christianized, Jews fled Rome and Greece for Central and Eastern Europe, and migrations continued spurred by religious persecution.

Livonians

Members of an ethnic group from the former Baltic state of Livonia, which is now Estonia and Latvia.

Lydians

Inhabitants of an inland Anatolian city-state southeast of Troy, who apparently spoke an Indo-European language. Early Greek writers were imprecise with their geography, so a "Lydian" could refer to any resident of a non-Greek section of Anatolia.

Mesopotamia

Mesopotamia was a region of intensely cultivated land with a large settled population, running south and west of Anatolia to the Persian Gulf. It was dominated by two rivers, the Tigris and Euphrates, and included present day Iraq and parts of Iran, Syria and Turkey. The first cities arose in the southern section, known as Sumer. Mesopotamian cities really were cities, with the larger ones having diverse ethnic groups and populations of 50,000 to 200,000. Sumerian was the language used in serious writing and religious functions, while the language of the prevailing king or emperor was official, and a variety of languages were presumably spoken on the street. Sumerian is considered a "language isolate," unrelated to other known languages, while Akkadian, the language of the region's first empire, is a Semitic language. Later empires in the region included the Assyrian, Hittite and Babylonian. Throughout the 3500 years that Sumerian was used in religious contexts, the pantheon remained stable despite frequent changes in government, with a few deities added, many conflated and some rising to higher prominence for political reasons.

Miletus

A coastal city in the state of Caria, Anatolia.

Minoans

We call the early inhabitants of the island of Crete Minoans. They arrived in the seventh millennium, and their Bronze Age culture flourished by 2000 BCE. They are believed to have been related to the Pelasgian civilization, perhaps coming from Greece or Anatolia, but they had extensive contact with Egyptian and other Near Eastern cultures. The Minoans were conquered by the Mycenaeans around 1350 BCE. Mycenaean Crete flourished for over a century, then abruptly deteriorated along with Greece.

Mycenaeans

See Greeks.

Neuri

Described in Greek literature as inhabitants of what is now Belarus and eastern Poland. They are speculated to have eventually settled in the Baltic region.

Norse, Norsemen

See Germanic Peoples.

Pelasgians

See Greeks.

Phoenicians

Phoenicia was a collection of city-states along the eastern Mediterranean coast, south of Anatolia. The Phoenicians were accomplished seafarers and traders, voyaging as far as the Atlantic coast. They were integral to the diffusion of Mediterranean culture, especially during the years 1000–300 BCE.

Romani, Romany, Roma

Called "Gypsies" because other Europeans thought they originated in Egypt, the Romani actually came from India and spoke languages related to Sanskrit. The Romani entered Eastern Europe by the thirteenth century and were present in Western Europe by the fifteenth. In Medieval and Renaissance times the religion of most Romani, like that of most other Europeans, was Christian with ethnic Pagan elements.

Romans

The Romans were the Latin tribe which founded the city-state of Rome around 1000 BCE. Rome from its inception was strongly influenced by the Etruscans and by Greek traders and colonists. More conscious adoption of Greek mythology and culture occurred as the Roman Empire expanded, especially near the start of the Common Era and during its first few centuries.

Sabines

One of the non-Latin tribes of central Italy, displaced and eventually absorbed by the Romans.

Sumerians, Sumer

See Mesopotamians

Taurians, Tauri

A tribe that lived in the southern portion of the Crimean Peninsula, along the Black Sea. Not to be confused with a resident of the Taurus mountain range in southern Turkey, a person born under the sign of Taurus or the alien orange characters in Marvel Comics. Little is known about the Taurians, since Greek accounts of this tribe describe human sacrificial practices in gory detail but don't tell us much of anything we want to know.

Notes

1 Apollodorus, *The Library of Greek Mythology*, trans. Keith Aldrich (Lawrence, KS: Coronado Press, 1975), 46.

2 *The Iliad of Homer; and the Odyssey*, trans. Samuel Butler (Chicago: Encyclopaedia Britannica, 1987), 293.

3 Charles G. Leland, *Aradia or the Gospel of the Witches* (Custer, Washington: Phoenix Publishing, 1990), 18.

4 John Abercromby, *The Pre- and Proto-historic Finns Both Eastern and Western with the Magic Songs of the West Finns, vol. 2* (London: David Nutt, 1898), 157.

5 Charles Godfrey Leland, Etruscan Roman Remains in Popular Tradition (London: T. Fisher Unwin, 1892), 262.

6 Cat Yronwode. "The 'Lucky W' Amulet Archive." http://www.luckymojo.com/spider.html. Accessed 10/2/2012.

7 Caesarius of Arles, "Sermon 54," in *Witchcraft in Europe 400-1700: A Documentary History*, 2nd edition, ed. Alan Charles Kors and Edward Peters (Philadelphia: University of Pennsylvania Press, 2001), 49.

8 Anonymous, "Les Nouns de un Levre en Englais," trans. HMR. Original at http://www.forgottenworks.org/poem_les_nouns_de_un_levre.html. Accessed 10/2/2012.

9 Lady Wilde, *Ancient Legends, Mystic Charms, and Superstitions of Ireland, vol. 2* (London: Ward and Downey, 1887), 61.

10 Jamie Sams and David Carson, *Medicine Cards* (New York: St. Martin's Press, 1999), 158.

11 *Letters of Ted Hughes*, ed. Christopher Reid (London: Faber & Faber, 2007), 213.

12 Lord Dunsany [Edward J.M.D. Plunkett], *Fifty-One Tales* (Project Gutenberg, 2005), http://www.gutenberg.org/ebooks/7838, 24. Accessed 10/2/2012.

13 Stephen Sommers film interview for *Van Helsing* trailer, *The Wolf Man* – The Legacy Collection, 2004.

Selected Bibliography

Abercromby, John. *The Pre- and Proto-historic Finns Both Eastern and Western with the Magic Songs of the West Finns, vol. 2.* London: David Nutt, 1898.

Aero, Rita. *Things Chinese*. Garden City, NY: Doubleday & Co., 1980.

Afanas'ev, Aleksandr, *Russian Fairy Tales*. 1867. Norbert Guterman, trans. 1945. Reprint. New York: Pantheon, 1973.

Apollodorus. *The Library of Greek Mythology*, trans. Keith Aldrich. Lawrence, KS: Coronado Press, 1975.

Apuleius, *The Transformations of Lucius Otherwise Known as the Golden Ass*. Robert Graves, trans. New York: Farrar, Straus and Giroux, 1951.

Bahn, Paul G. and Jean Vertut. *Journey Through the Ice Age*. London: Seven Dials, 1997.

Baring-Gould, Sabine. *The Book of Werewolves*. 1865. Reprint. London: Smith, Elder & Co., 1995.

Barrett, Clive. *The Egyptian Gods and Goddesses: The Mythology and Beliefs of Ancient Egypt*. London: Diamond Books, 1992.

Bellows, Henry Adams, trans. *The Poetic Edda*. Princeton, NJ: Princeton University Press, 1936. Archived at http://www.sacred-texts.com/neu/poe/poe00.htm. Accessed 9/30/2012.

Bierhorst, John. *Mythology of the Lenape: Guide and Texts*. Tucson, AZ: University of Arizona Press, 1995.

Black, Jeremy and Anthony Green. *Gods, Demons and Symbols of Ancient Mesopotamia: An Illustrated Dictionary*. Austin, TX: University of Texas Press, 1992.

Bottero, Jean. *Religion in Ancient Mesopotamia*. Teresa Lavender Fagan, trans. Chicago: The University of Chicago Press, 2001.

Bourgault Du Coudray, Chantal. *The Curse of the Werewolf: Fantasy, Horror and the Beast Within*. London: I.B. Tauris & Co., 2006.

Brodeur, Arthur Gilchrist, trans. *The Prose Edda of Snorri Sturlson*. New York: American-Scandinavian Foundation, 1916. Archived at http://www.sacred-texts.com/neu/pre/pre00.htm. Accessed 9/30/2012.

Buckland, Raymond. *Buckland's Book of Gypsy Magic*. San Francisco: Weiser, 2010.

Butler, Samuel, trans. *The Iliad of Homer; and the Odyssey*. 1901. Reprint. Chicago: Encyclopaedia Brittanica, 1987.

Camille, Michael. *Image on the Edge: The Margins in Medieval Art*. Cambridge, MA: Harvard University Press, 1992.

Carnell, Simon. *Hare*. London: Reaktion Books, 2010.

Ceanadach, Siusaidh. *A Ceremony for Every Occasion: The Pagan Wheel of the Year and Rites of Passage*. Alresford, UK: Moon Books, 2012.

Cooper, D. Jason. *Using the Runes: A Comprehensive Introduction to the Art of Runecraft*. Wellingborough, UK: The Aquarian Press, 1986.

Cooper, J.C. *An Illustrated Encyclopedia of Traditional Symbols*. London: Thames and Hudson, 1978.

Crawford, Henry S. *Irish Carved Ornament*. 1926. Reprint. Dublin: The Mercier Press, 1980.

Curran, Bob. *Dark Fairies*. Pompton Plains, NJ: New Page Books, 2010.

Curtin, Jeremiah. *Myths and Folk Tales of the Russians, Western Slavs, and Magyars*. 1890. Reprint. Mineola, New York: Dover, 1999.

DeGaris, Marie. *Folklore of Guernsey*. Channel Islands, Britain: The Guernsey Press, 1975.

Douglas, Adam. *The Beast Within: A History of the Werewolf*. New York: Avon Books, 1992.

Durdin-Robertson, Lawrence. *The Year of the Goddess: A Perpetual Calender of Festivals*. Wellingborough, UK: The Aquarian Press, 1990.

Ellis, Bill. *Lucifer Ascending: The Occult in Folklore and Popular*

Culture. Lexington, KY: The University Press of Kentucky, 2004.

Elworthy, Frederick Thomas. 1895. *The Evil Eye: The Classic Account of an Ancient Superstition.* 1895. Reprint. Mineola, NY: Dover, 2004.

Fairbanks, Arthur, trans. *Elder Philostratus, Younger Philostratus, Callistratus.* London: William Heinemann, 1931.

Friedlander, Gerald. *Jewish Fairy Tales.* 1920. Reprint. Mineola, NY: Dover, 2001.

Gainer, Patrick W. *Witches, Ghosts and Signs: Folklore of the Southern Appalachians.* Morgantown, WV: Seneca Books, 1975.

George, Andrew, ed. *The Epic of Gilgamesh: The Babylonian Epic Poem and Other Texts in Akkadian and Sumerian.* London: Penguin Books, 1999.

Gimbutas, Marija. *The Language of the Goddess.* San Francisco: Harper & Row, 1989.

—*The Living Goddesses,* Berkeley, CA: University of California Press, 1999.

Ginzburg, Carlo. *Ecstasies: Deciphering the Witches' Sabbath.* Raymond Rosenthal, trans. New York: Pantheon Books, 1991.

Graves, Robert. *The White Goddess: A Historical Grammar of Poetic Myth,* 2nd edition. New York: Farrar, Straus and Giroux, 1966.

—*The Greek Myths,* Complete edition. 1960. Reprint. London: Penguin Books, 1992.

Gregory, Lady Augusta, trans. *Cuchulain of Muirthemne: The Story of the Red Branch of Ulster.* London: John Murray, 1902. Archived at http://www.sacred-texts.com/neu/celt/cuch/lgc00.htm. Accessed 9/30/2012.

Grimassi, Raven. *The Witch's Familiar: Spiritual Partnerships for Successful Magic.* St. Paul, MN: Llewellyn, 2003.

—*The Witches' Craft: The Roots of Witchcraft and Magical Transformation.* St. Paul, MN: Llewellyn, 2002.

Grimm, Jakob and Wilhelm Grimm. *Household Tales,* Margaret Hunt, trans. 1812. Archived at http://www.sacred-texts.

com/neu/grimm/index.htm. Accessed 9/30/2012.

Guerber, H.A. *The Norsemen*. 1909. Reprint. London: Senate, 1994.

Johns, Andreas. *Baba Yaga: The Ambiguous Mother and Witch of the Russian Folklore*. New York: Peter Lang, 2004.

Johnson, Buffie. *Lady of the Beasts: The Goddess and Her Sacred Animals*. Rochester, VT: Inner Traditions, 1994.

Jordan, Michael. *Encyclopedia of Gods: Over 2,500 Deities of the World*. New York: Facts on File, 1993.

Keeler, Clyde. *The Laboratory Mouse: Its Origin, Heredity and Culture*. Cambridge, MA: Harvard University Press, 1931.

Kors, Alan Charles and Edward Peters, eds. *Witchcraft in Europe 400-1700: A Documentary History*, 2nd edition. Philadelphia: University of Pennsylvania Press, 2001.

Lang, Andrew. *Custom and Myth*. 1884. Reprint. Project Gutenberg eBook, 2004. Archived at http://www.gutenberg.org/ebooks/14080. Accessed 9/30/2012.

—*The Violet Fairy Book*. London: Longmans Green, 1901. Archived at http://www.sacred-texts.com/neu/lfb/vi/index.htm. Accessed 9/30/2012.

Leland, Charles Godfrey. *Aradia: Gospel of the Witches*. 1890. Reprint. Custer, WA: Phoenix, 1990.

—Etruscan Roman Remains in Popular Tradition. 1892. Archived at http://archive.org/details/etruscanromanre00lelagoog. Accessed 9/30/2012.

—Gypsy Sorcery and Fortune Telling. London: T. Fisher Unwin, 1891. Archived at http://www.sacred-texts.com/pag/gsft/gsft00.htm. Accessed 9/30/2012.

Littleton, Scott C., ed. *Mythology: The Illustrated Anthology of World Myth and Storytellling*. London: Duncan Baird, 2002.

Lombardo, Stanley and Diane Rayor, trans. *Callimachus: Hymns, Epigrams, Select Fragments*. Baltimore: Johns Hopkins University Press, 1988.

Lonnrot, Elias. *The Kalevala*. 1849. John Martin Crawford, trans. 1888. Reprint. Cincinnati: The Robert Blake Company, 1910.

Archived at http://www.sacred-texts.com/neu/kveng/. Accessed 9/30/2012.

MacMullen, Ramsay. *Christianity and Paganism in the Fourth to Eighth Centuries.* New Haven, CT: Yale University Press, 1997.

Matthews, Caitlin and John Matthews. *Encyclopedia of Celtic Wisdom: A Celtic Shaman's Sourcebook.* Shaftsbury, UK: Element Books, 1994.

—*Ladies of the Lake.* London: Thorsons, 1992.

Miles, Clement A. *Christmas Customs and Traditions: Their History and Significance.* 1912. Reprint. New York: Dover, 1976.

Milnes, Gerald C. *Signs, Cures and Witchery: German Appalachian Folklore.* Knoxville, TN: The University of Tennessee Press, 2007.

Monaghan, Patricia. *The Book of Goddesses and Heroines,* rev. edition. St. Paul, MN: Llewellyn, 1990.

—*The Encyclopedia of Celtic Mythology and Folklore.* New York: Checkmark Books, 2008.

Morgan, Adrian. *Toads and Toadstools: The Natural History, Folklore and Cultural Oddities of a Strange Association.* Berkeley, CA: Celestial Arts, 1995.

O'Sullivan, Patrick V. *Irish Superstitions and Legends of Animals and Birds.* Dublin: Mercier Press, 1991.

Patai, Raphael, *The Hebrew Goddess,* 3rd edition. Detroit: Wayne State University Press, 1990.

Peterson, M. Flora. *The Simple Sabbat: A Family Friendly Approach to the Eight Pagan Holidays.* M. Flora Peterson, 2011.

Petronius, Gaius. *The Satyricon.* Alfred R. Allinson, trans. 1930. Archived at http://www.sacred-texts.com/cla/petro/satyr/. Accessed 9/30/2012.

Plunkett, Edward, *Fifty-One Tales by Lord Dunsany,* 1915. Archived at http://www.sacred-texts.com/neu/dun/fotd/index.htm. Accessed 9/30/2012.

Randolph, Vance. *Ozark Magic and Folklore.* 1947. Reprint. New York: Dover, 1964.

Ristic, Radomir. *Balkan Traditional Witchcraft*. Michael C. Carter, Jr., trans. Los Angeles: Pendraig, 2009.

Sams, Jamie and David Carson. *Medicine Cards*. New York: St. Martin's Press, 1988.

Scudder, Vida Dunn. *Le Morte d'Arthur of Sir Thomas Malory and Its Sources*. New York: E.P. Dutton, 1921.

Spence, Lewis. *Legends and Romances of Brittany*. 1917. Reprint. Mineola, New York: Dover, 1997.

Stone, Alby. "Hellhounds, Werewolves and the Germanic Underworld" in *Mercian Mysteries* vol. 20. 1994. Archived at http://www.indigogroup.co.uk/edge/hellhnds.htm. Accessed 9/30/2012.

Stone, Merlin. *Ancient Mirrors of Womanhood: A Treasury of Goddess and Heroine Lore from Around the World*. Boston: Beacon Press, 1979.

Storm, Hyemeyohsts. *Seven Arrows*. New York: Harper & Row, 1972.

Summers, Montague. *The Werewolf in Lore and Legend*. 1933. Reprint. Mineola, NY: Dover, 2003.

Teish, Luisah. *Jambalaya: The Natural Woman's Book of Personal Charms and Practical Rituals*. San Francisco: Harper & Row, 1985.

Valiente, Doreen. *The Rebirth of Witchcraft*. Custer, WA: Phoenix, 1989.

—*Natural Magic*. Custer, WA: Phoenix, 1975.

Weinstein, Krystyna. *The Owl in Art, Myth, and Legend*. 1985. Reprint. London: Grange Books, 1990.

Whitmore, Ben. *Trials of the Moon: Reopening the Case for Historical Witchcraft*. Auckland: Briar Books, 2010.

Wilde, Lady Jane. *Ancient Legends, Mystic Charms, and Superstitions of Ireland, vol. 2*. London: Ward and Downey, 1887. Archived at http://www.sacred-texts.com/neu/celt/ali/index.htm. Accessed 9/30/12.

Wolkstein, Diane and Samuel Noah Kramer. *Inanna Queen of*

Heaven and Earth: Her Stories and Hymns from Sumer. New York: Harper & Row, 1983.

Filmography

Bewitched Bunny. Dir. Chuck Jones, 1954, USA.

Born Free. Dir. James Hill, 1966, UK.

Curse of the Queerwolf. Dir. Mark Pirro, 1988, USA.

Elsa's Legacy: The Born Free Story. PBS Nature Episode 29:7, 2011, USA.

Frankenstein Meets the Wolfman. Dir. Roy William Neill, 1943, USA.

House of Dracula. Dir. Erle C. Kenton, 1945, USA.

Monty Python and the Holy Grail. Dir. Terry Gilliam and Terry Jones, 1974, UK.

Sorceress, Dir. Suzanne Schiffman, 1987, USA.

The Werewolf of London. Dir. Stuart Walker, 1935, USA.

The Wolf Man. Dir. George Waggner, 1941, USA.

True Adventures of the Ultimate Spider Hunter. PBS Nature Episode 24:8, 2006, USA.

The Yogi Bear Show. "A Bear Living," Episode 18. Dir. William Hanna, Joseph Barbera, 1961, USA

Index